PLÉIADE POETICS

PLÉIADE POETICS

❄

*A Study in Sixteenth–Century
Thought and Terminology*

BY

GRAHAME CASTOR

Lecturer in French in the University of Cambridge

CAMBRIDGE
AT THE UNIVERSITY PRESS
1964

PUBLISHED BY
THE SYNDICS OF THE CAMBRIDGE UNIVERSITY PRESS
Bentley House, 200 Euston Road, London, N.W. 1
American Branch: 32 East 57th Street, New York 22, N.Y.
West African Office: P.O. Box 33, Ibadan, Nigeria

©

CAMBRIDGE UNIVERSITY PRESS
1964

Printed in Great Britain at the University Printing House, Cambridge
(Brooke Crutchley, University Printer)

CONTENTS

PREFACE

The work on which this study is based was originally undertaken for a doctoral thesis in the University of Cambridge, and I would like to thank the Board of Research Studies for the generosity with which they have subsidised the present publication. In the writing of the book I have profited more than I can adequately acknowledge from the kind help of many friends and mentors. My greatest debt is to Dr Odette de Mourgues, who was a constant source of inspiration and guidance at all stages of the work. I am particularly grateful to Professor Ian McFarlane and Professor Alan Boase for their most helpful and stimulating criticism of the preliminary draft. I am also much indebted to Dr Dorothy Coleman, with whom I first discussed many of the points raised in the following pages. Finally, I wish to thank my wife for her patient and unfailing encouragement.

G.C.

May 1963

[1]

INTRODUCTION

The most obvious problem confronting the commentator of the Pléiade's theory of poetry is that no one member of the group produced a full and coherent theory of poetry as such.[1] In order to obtain a complete account of their ideas about poetry it is necessary to synthesise the various treatises and the poems which deal, directly or indirectly, with theoretical questions into a single composite *art poétique*. This has been very efficiently done by W. F. Patterson, for instance.[2] Once this task has been performed, however, we can find remarkably little commentary of a truly critical or evaluative nature. Patterson himself is concerned above all to emphasise the continuity between the Greek philosophy of poetry and the theoretical activity of the French Renaissance, and he therefore sets out to demonstrate that 'the greatest dynamic force in the deepening French Philosophy of aesthetic values, which is a progressive *eclecticism*, made up of many elements, derives *ultimately* from the Hellenic philosophers and critics of literature, across whatever devious paths their thought may have descended'.[3] Patterson sees the Pléiade theorists in terms of their Greek mentors, and while this undoubtedly gives a valuable insight into their work, it leads him to regard them only as in-betweens, preparing the ground in a rather muddle-headed way for the Golden Age of French literature, 'le siècle de Louis XIV'.[4] He neglects to consider them, as they have surely every right to be considered, in the light of what they themselves were trying to do, as theorists

---

[1] The one possible exception to this generalisation is Pontus de Tyard. But in the divine fury passages of the *Solitaire Premier*, where his theory of poetry is to be found, Pontus is interested primarily in the reunion of the human soul with its source in the divine being; poetry is taken to be merely a means to that end, and not an end in itself (see pp. 195–6).

[2] W. F. Patterson, *Three Centuries of French Poetic Theory* (1935), I, 835–65.

[3] Patterson, *op. cit.* I, 948, his italics.

[4] *Ibid.*

1

attempting to solve the problems posed by their own historical and literary situation.[1]

The link with the Greeks which Patterson stresses is not entirely helpful, but it is at least an attempt to provide some considerable background for the poetic theory of the Pléiade. Most writers in the past have contented themselves with a simple repetition of the points made by the theorists in the form of a more or less straightforward catalogue. Such is the thesis of A. Rosenbauer, *Die poetischen Theorien der Plejade nach Ronsard und Du Bellay* (1895), which, however, acknowledges itself to be a piece of literary history and not of evaluation: 'ein Beitrag zur Geschichte der Renaissancepoetik in Frankreich'. Henri Chamard's chapter on the conception of poetry in his *Histoire de la Pléiade* is also a straightforward exposition of the various items in the Pléiade's poetic credo, with sections devoted to 'Le culte de l'art', 'L'inspiration ou "fureur" poétique', 'L'union de la nature et de l'art, dons communs de Dieu', and 'Le sacerdoce du poète'.[2] Again, Henri Franchet is concerned with setting out Ronsard's views on 'le poète et son œuvre' and with investigating their literary antecedents, rather than with discussing the significance of these ideas in terms of a full-scale theory of poetry.[3] Finally, R. J. Clements in his *Critical Theory and Practice of the Pléiade* (1942) limits himself to the study of the criteria adopted by the Pléiade in their judgements of other writers. This work also tends to be mainly a catalogue, with exhaustive illustrations but comparatively little critical examination of the concepts involved.

A much more interesting treatment of the poetic theories of the Pléiade is given by Henri Weber in his book *La Création Poétique au XVIe Siècle en France* (1956). He sees in the sixteenth-century poetic theories two main sets of contradictions, each characteristic of the period. First there is the contra-

---

[1] Another striking instance of the tendency to consider the Pléiade theorists only in relationship to seventeenth-century French classicism is to be found in R. Morçay & A. Müller, *La Renaissance* (1960), 270: 'avant même d'aborder leurs œuvres, il convient...de nous demander ce que vaut leur doctrine, ce qu'elle apporte de nouveau, ce qui lui manque pour être vraiment la doctrine classique.'

[2] H. Chamard, *Histoire de la Pléiade* (1939–40), IV, 146–56.

[3] H. Franchet, *Le Poète et son Œuvre d'après Ronsard* (1923).

diction between the mutually opposed dogmas of 'imitation', that is, imitation of the ancient writers, and 'inspiration'. Weber takes the doctrine of imitation to be part of the 'retour passionné vers la civilisation antique' which was operated by the early humanists. The theory of the divine inspiration of poets he links with another mark of the humanists, namely their 'orgueilleuse confiance dans les forces de l'individu'. Weber then goes on to explain the reasons for the great attraction which this idea of divine inspiration seems to have held for the Pléiade poets: 'le caractère sacré reconnu à l'inspiration est une défense de la liberté du poète contre l'esclavage de la vie de cour et la poésie officielle, à laquelle il se trouve contraint par les exigences de sa situation matérielle.'[1]

This interpretation is very much in accordance with the sociological preoccupations which dominate the early chapters of Weber's book. I am fully in agreement with him in considering this emphasis upon divine inspiration to be highly significant in the Pléiade's theory of poetry. My own inclination, however, is to link it with the wider literary and indeed philosophical issue of the defence of poetry. The poet had not merely to defend himself against the pressures imposed by his own financial and social situation; he had above all to defend, or rather to convince people of, the status of poetry as something special and supremely valuable in its own right, which does not have to be pre-judged by reference to standards outside itself, be they moral, metaphysical, or religious. I would further argue that this struggle of the poet to achieve some measure of self-justification was also carried on in terms of Weber's second set of contradictions, that between *vérité* (i.e. imitation of 'reality') and *fiction*, which Weber construes as the use in poetry of 'les fables antiques'.[2] It seems to me that this is to give too narrow an interpretation to the concept of fiction, which, like inspiration, was of crucial importance in the defence of poetry. In fact the term may be said to contain within itself precisely that problem to which Renaissance theorists of poetry were seeking a solution, namely the problem of the nature of poetry.

I have found fault with some who have written accounts of the

---

[1] Weber, *op. cit.* I, 108.   [2] Weber, *op. cit.* I, 127.

poetic theory of the Pléiade for failing to provide much in the way of critical discussion. Yet we should recognise that sixteenth-century theories of poetry do constitute a considerable puzzle for the modern reader. The common reader's reaction to the theoretical work of the Pléiade is often to feel that it is almost trivial, and certainly rather disappointing, compared with the practical achievement measured in terms of excellent poems written. For one thing, a great deal of time was spent on technical matters, on stanza-forms and rhymes, line-lengths, elisions, mute -e's, and so on, but comparatively little attention seems, at first sight at least, to have been given to any general ideas about what poetry is, or should be. Nowadays the position is normally reversed. Technicalities of that sort tend to be either ignored or taken for granted, which simply reflects the interest of modern critics in the problems of imagery and metaphor rather than in those of harmony and rhythm. Then again we find in the sixteenth century no recommendations to the poet to distil into his work the quintessence of his experience, or to endeavour to extend the frontiers of human sensibility. Nor do we meet the suggestion that in writing poetry one is performing an act of creation; rather is the poet held to be the imitator of a world already created. We may readily feel that we have little in common with the sixteenth-century theorists, and be tempted to dismiss what they have written with the easy argument that in those days they did not know any better and that we have made a lot of progress since then. This quasi-evolutionary view of literature can be a very misleading one, and the attitude it seems to encourage towards the poetic theory of the Pléiade is to my mind a case in point. It is not to be a question here of whether we in the twentieth century have arrived at a more nearly perfect theory of poetry than the Pléiade had done four hundred years ago, nor of whether modern theorists are more able than were the theorists of the Pléiade. I leave that for others to decide. I wish merely to make the point that the kinds of poetic theory produced in the two ages are necessarily very different, since they are built up out of very different conceptual materials.

To a large extent our difficulty in dealing with the poetic

theory of the sixteenth century is a terminological one. It is not
at all unusual to find modern commentators using terms in this
connection which are completely anachronistic. I will take two
fairly obvious examples. One of the sections in Weber's
chapter on 'Les Théories poétiques' is headed 'Imitation et
Originalité'.[1] Then Patterson, summarising the sixteenth-
century doctrine of artistic imitation, claims that poetry was at
that time held to be 'freely creative'.[2] In the sixteenth century
itself it would not in fact have been possible to use either of these
expressions. Originality did not become the antonym of imitation until the seventeenth century at the earliest,[3] and creativity
was not regularly attributed to poets or to poetry until the
eighteenth century.[4] I feel that it is most unwise to super-
impose the terminology of post-sixteenth-century theories of
poetry upon sixteenth-century concepts, for this inevitably
causes some distortion in our view of those concepts. Ways of
thought have changed radically in the four centuries that separate us from Ronsard and his school, and the meanings of words
have also changed in order to accommodate themselves to the
new thoughts. It is impossible to translate earlier terminology
into modern terminology without altering its significance, either
by adding something which was not previously there or by
ignoring certain important areas of reference. Conversely, we
also should not take the words used by an earlier age than our
own and assume, without calling further evidence, that they
carried the same meaning then as they do now. It is for this
reason that I make so much effort in this study to pass beyond
the limited sphere of purely literary theory and to explore the
general semantic and conceptual fields in which the terms of
sixteenth-century poetic theory operated.

The second major source of difficulty in any treatment of the
poetic theories of the Pléiade is closely related to the first.
Most commentators have simply followed, with slight modifications, the divisions of the subject as laid down by the theorists
themselves. They have thus accurately mirrored the Pléiade's
own treatment of poetry, where the bulk of space is taken up by

[1] Weber, *op. cit.* I, 120. [2] Patterson, *op. cit.* I, 838.
[3] See p. 78, n. 1. [4] See pp. 90 ff.

questions of versification and so on, without producing an adequate account of their general theory of poetry. This, in my view, is due to the fact that they do not investigate what is going on beneath the surface of the Pléiade's discussions. It is my contention that the basic problems of sixteenth-century poetic theory were not being tackled on the surface level of the various *arts poétiques* at all, but rather within the actual terminological and conceptual systems which those treatises employed. In order to understand what the sixteenth-century theorists were about, therefore, we should not merely cover the same ground with them, paraphrasing as we go, but we should also carefully examine the connotations and implications of the individual terms which they use. This method, it seems to me, offers a more satisfactory insight into the nature of the problems with which the sixteenth-century theorists of poetry were dealing.

In the sixteenth century there was a great resurgence of poetry in France. The school of the so-called *grands rhétoriqueurs* —Chastellain, Molinet, Cretin, Jean Marot, and the rest—had produced at the end of the fifteenth century poetry which Chamard divides into three main categories: 'sujets amoureux ou galants...sujets historiques ou politiques...sujets religieux ou moraux'. And, again in the words of Chamard, 'tous ces ouvrages...sont d'une monotonie désolante, d'une fastidieuse banalité.'[1] In mitigation of this damning judgement one should make it clear that these men took a very serious view of their task as poets, even if very little of the poetry they actually produced repays the trouble of salvaging it from its present near-oblivion. They demanded that poets should be well-read, erudite with the *science* of their time, and they made something of a cult of the mythology of Latin antiquity. In these two respects we may perhaps regard the *grands rhétoriqueurs* as genuine forerunners of the Pléiade. A more noteworthy point may be that the *grands rhétoriqueurs* laid great stress upon the importance of form and technique, so much so in fact that their poetry is characterised by highly fantastic feats of verbal acrobatics which are most disturbing, to say the least, to the modern taste. But all their technical extravagances were merely a

[1] H. Chamard, *Les Origines de la Poésie française de la Renaissance* (1920), 131-4.

INTRODUCTION

reflection of the belief that not only what the poet said was important, but also how he said it. They were bringing right into the foreground the question of the high aesthetic value of form, which after all is a very reputable thing for poets to do: witness Mallarmé and Valéry, to mention only two among the moderns.[1] To be sure, it seems that the *grands rhétoriqueurs* considered aesthetic merit to reside only in what was *rarissimum* and excessively complex; but in their concern with aesthetic values we may again see some foreshadowing of the Pléiade's attempt to justify poetry in terms of itself rather than in terms of ethics and theology—which had been the standard medieval practice.

It must be acknowledged, however, that in their dealings with antiquity the *grands rhétoriqueurs* were more concerned with the surface trappings than with the underlying substance of its beliefs and ideals. But gradually, and then more rapidly, French poets became aware of the high ideals of art which were embodied in the literature of classical antiquity. Eventually, with the Pléiade, this growing awareness resulted in the (theoretical) rejection of the national poetic tradition as they conceived it,[2] and a concerted attempt to follow the lessons of the ancients in a more fundamental manner than by simply cannibalising the latter's works in order to produce ornamentation for their own. All this, of course, would have been quite impossible had not the printing-presses of the Renaissance unlocked the literary treasure-chest of the past by giving the classical texts an unprecedentedly wide circulation. A large amount of fine poetry had suddenly been made readily available to interested readers. The main Greek and Roman poets, Homer, Hesiod, Pindar, Aeschylus, Sophocles, Euripides, Aristophanes,

[1] A most convincing account of the genuine value of *rhétoriqueur* poetry is given by Raymond Picard in the article he contributes to the Gallimard *Tableau de la Littérature française* (1962), I, 186–95.
[2] We should remember that the Pléiade had rather a limited view of medieval French literature, since they ignored everything which we now think of as most characteristic of that period: *contes pieux, chansons de geste, romans d'aventure, chansons de toile, fabliaux gaulois.* For Ronsard and his friends pre-sixteenth-century French literature consisted of the *Roman de la Rose* (which they admired with reservations) and the *grands rhétoriqueurs.* Villon was *trop peuple* for them to consider him seriously as a poet, and the work of the one aristocratic writer of real merit whom the fifteenth century produced—Charles d'Orléans—was to remain in manuscript until the eighteenth century.

7

Callimachus, Virgil and Ovid (already twin pillars of medieval culture in Western Europe), Catullus, Propertius, Tibullus, Lucretius, Martial, Juvenal, together with many others of lesser note, could soon all be read in more or less scholarly editions, and they served to inspire the new generation of French poets to deeds of imitation and emulation. Poetry, it was decided, should henceforth be written by scholars (they declined to acknowledge that this had already been the view of the *grands rhétoriqueurs*, and paid really no more than passing tribute to Maurice Scève), by men who through long study were steeped in the wisdom of 'les anciens Grecs et Romains', and who had formally dedicated themselves to the service of knowledge and virtue, thus making themselves worthy to receive the precious gift of divine inspiration.

This lofty conception of poetry as a sort of *sacerdoce* and of the poet as a man of the greatest virtue and learning was coupled with the determination, widespread in Western Europe in the sixteenth century, to 'illustrer la langue'. Throughout the Middle Ages Latin had been the universal means of communication between learned men, and the vernaculars were regarded as uncouth, barbarous tongues, in which it was impossible to compose works of any real value or merit. At the time of the Renaissance there was a sudden increase in self-awareness on the part of the major 'powers' which were finally emerging as political entities from the hurly-burly of the Middle Ages. It was slowly being realised, mainly through the influence and example of the Italians, that one's language and the literature written in it could be a valuable source of national pride. The masterpieces of Dante and Petrarch, both written in the 'vulgar tongue', encouraged some Frenchmen to attempt the substitution of their native language for Latin in all branches of learning and literature. Geofroy Tory's *Champ Fleury*, which appeared in 1529, is usually regarded as the first manifesto to set out the claims to excellence of the French language. The campaign was already at its height when Du Bellay published his *Deffence et Illustration de la Langue françoyse* in 1549. Those who defended the vernacular claimed that potentially it was just as capable of copious, apt, and elegant expression as were Greek and Latin.

In the past the vernacular had been neglected in favour of Latin, with the result that it still had only limited powers of expression and little elegance. But now it was up to Frenchmen to enrich their language and to exploit its own individual qualities, until it should become at least the equal of the languages of the ancients. An early result of this linguistic patriotism was the spate of translations from Latin and Greek which poured from the presses in the 1530's and 1540's. Translation, however, only demonstrated that any material which had already been treated in another language could be rendered into French. There still remained the individual character of the French language, which could only be expressed in an independent body of literature.[1]

Mere translations were not enough, for it was felt that the vernacular, and the poets who wrote in it, should not be content with derivative and reflected glory, but should strive to achieve immortality on their own account. It would not do merely to translate the work of a Latin poet into French, no matter how skilfully the exercise were performed. But the ancients could not be discarded entirely. Theirs was quite obviously very great poetry, and it would have been foolish to ignore the practical lessons in the art of poetry which it offered. Thus intensive study of the ancients was held to be an essential part of the young poet's training. In familiarising himself with the work of these model authors, the would-be poet should concern himself not simply with its outward appearance, but more with the inner principles which had guided its composition. What was advocated was not a slavish copying, but an intelligent imitation. And so the first problem which faced poets and theorists of poetry was 'What is right imitation?' How can we

---

[1] While it is proper to dwell upon sixteenth-century French ambitions to produce a great literature in the vernacular, we should not ignore the contribution to the poetic revival made by the neo-latins. They too were concerned to break with the immediate literary past, and to renew poetry by emulating the ancients. As Paul van Tieghem has written: 'la poésie latine...joue un grand rôle dans la création de l'atmosphère littéraire de la Pléiade; celle-ci compte parmi ses membres de bons poètes latins; même goût, dans l'une et l'autre langue, pour un art savant et nourri de l'antiquité' ('La littérature latine de la Renaissance', in *Bibliothèque d'Humanisme et Renaissance*, IV (1944), 215. See also the study by D. Murarasu, *La Poésie néo-latine et la Renaissance des Lettres antiques en France (1500–1549)*, 1928, and P. de Nolhac, *Ronsard et l'Humanisme*, 1921, viii–ix).

learn from the ancients and profit from the example of their work, so that our own poetry achieves an equal degree of excellence with theirs? How does imitation differ from straight-forward translation, or from paraphrasing? What precisely is it that ought to be imitated: words, metaphors, metres, stanza-forms, diction, subject-matter—all or only some of these? At what point should imitation cease and 'invention' begin? What are the relative values of these two elements in a poem? These and similar questions were always in the forefront of the Pléiade's discussions of poetry.

Behind this first problem of imitation, however, there lurked the more fundamental difficulty of finding out what was the nature of poetic activity. It was obvious enough that poetry could be distinguished from prose by the simple fact that it was written in verse, that it was 'numbered', whereas prose was not. However, when one came to consider the subject-matter of poetry, the relationship of that subject-matter to the truth of things, or reality, and the relationship of the poet to both, the question became rather more complicated. Poets and theorists of poetry felt that it was not proper to judge poetry by the same standards of factual accuracy and exact conformity with the 'truth' which could justifiably be applied to, say, history. Poetry was 'fable', or 'fiction', but it was not easy to decide upon the criteria which should be used to determine the proper relationship of fiction with truth. As C. S. Lewis has written, 'The defence of poetry...is a defence not of poetry as against prose but of fiction as against fact.... What is in question is not man's right to sing but his right to feign, to make things up.'[1]

For a long time poetry had been on the defensive. The medieval Church, despite its attempts to render imaginative literature harmless by reading into everything an allegorised sermon, had on the whole been antagonistic to poetry. This purely religious antagonism was reinforced on the philo-sophical level by Plato's banishment of poets from his ideal republic on the grounds first that they represent the appearances of things and not their true natures (and are therefore liars), and secondly that they appeal to the passions of their hearers (the

[1] *English Literature in the 16th Century* (1954), 318.

baser part of their beings) rather than to their reason. In the sixteenth century, however, apologists of poetry began to use the arguments contained in Aristotle's *Poetics*; previously his theories had been generally known only in the watered-down versions presented by Horace and other late popularisers. In Aristotle was to be found a full-scale metaphysical justification of poetry as an 'imitation of reality' which portrayed not the actual but the possible, not *le vrai* but *le vraisemblable*. We may question whether Aristotle's doctrine of imitation was fully understood by sixteenth-century theorists,[1] but its great merit from their point of view was that it treated the arts as a unique kind of human activity, which was not to be judged in the light of criteria borrowed from other kinds of human activity. Thus poets could now hope to establish for themselves some independent position which did not condemn them to the alternative of being either historians on the one hand, or liars on the other.

In this attempt on the part of poetry to achieve complete autonomy two of what I consider to be the more difficult concepts of sixteenth-century poetics were very closely involved. These are the concepts of 'invention' and 'imagination'. Invention was the name used to designate the element of originality, as we would nowadays call it, in a work of art; in this sense it was the opposite of imitation (of other authors). But the word was also used to refer to the relationship of the poet with his subject-matter, which he was said to 'invent', or find (invent comes from the Latin *invenire*, meaning to find) in reality. Invention was thus the first step in the Aristotelian process of imitation. Once the objects of imitation had been found, then they could be represented in the form of an artifact. This was effected by means of the imagination, whose function it was to make copies or images of things outside the mind, thus enabling the mind to apprehend non-mental material. In addition it pictured forth the pure ideas of the mind, so that they could eventually take on material shape. To write poetry was not simply to record facts and events passively, adhering strictly to the details and sequence of what had actually happened; that, so

[1] See pp. 54 ff.

the sixteenth century believed, was what the historian did. Rather was poetry in some way a making, a fashioning of one's material.[1] Invention and imagination are thus likely to be important concepts for the theory of poetry, since they embody, in part at least, sixteenth-century views on the active functions of the mind in relation to reality. In both processes the mind is at grips with things outside itself, using them for its own purposes, which in our context are the production of poetry.

The significance of these two terms for the poetic theories of the sixteenth century has not hitherto been examined in any great detail. Yet they represent the reverse side of the coin whose face is labelled 'imitation'; and that is generally acknowledged to be a major issue in sixteenth-century poetics. Certainly imitation, together with the allied concept of verisimilitude, was to be the chief tool of the literary theorists of the next century, both in France and elsewhere. But in the sixteenth century other possibilities were being explored simultaneously with imitation, and invention and imagination were not the least important among them. Despite this fact, invention is perhaps too readily assumed by modern commentators to be merely the sixteenth-century equivalent of our 'creative imagination',[2] and its implications tend for that reason to be left unexamined. Similarly imagination is thought to present no difficulty, since we still use the term in the context of literary theory. But the sixteenth-century concept of invention is by no means equivalent to the modern concept of creative imagination, nor are our ideas and attitudes concerning imagination *tout court* the same as those of Ronsard and his contemporaries. In the sixteenth century the concepts of invention and imagination were embedded in a system of metaphysics, epistemology, and psychology which differs in a number of very important respects from the one we use today. These differences and the manner in

---

[1] Edmond Huguet points out that in the sixteenth century the word *facteur* is often equivalent to the modern *auteur, écrivain, poète* (*L'Évolution du Sens des Mots*, 1934, 43). The English word 'maker' had similar connotations in the Renaissance (cf. *Oxford English Dictionary*, under *maker*, 5).

[2] By René Wellek, for instance: '"invention"...a term which covers much that later criticism would have called creative imagination' (*A History of Modern Criticism*, 1955, I, 13).

which they are significant for the theory of poetry will be discussed in the later chapters of this study, after some account has first been given of the rather more straightforward concepts of divine fury, nature, art, imitation, and *naïveté*. I propose to examine also how far the concepts of invention and imagination were of service to the theorists in their attempts to find an independent justification for poetry, and to consider finally what use in this connection was made of concepts other than these two.

[2]

POETRY AS THE ART OF
SECOND RHETORIC

Perhaps the most notable characteristic of late fifteenth- and early sixteenth-century treatises on poetry is that the word 'poetry' does not occur in their titles at all. Rather are they called treatises on rhetoric: the art of second rhetoric, or of versified rhetoric—such is the standard designation at this time.[1] A second notable characteristic of these works—and, as we shall see, it is closely linked with the first—is that they are concerned almost exclusively with the technological aspects of poetry, rhymes, rhyme-schemes, stanza-forms, and so on. They contain very little that a modern reader would recognise as a theory of poetry, apart from whatever implications were contained in the frequently repeated statement that poetry is the second part of rhetoric. Just what this statement did imply we shall examine in a moment.

For the rest, however, poetry seems to be regarded quite simply as a craft and poets as craftsmen who have to conform to various complicated sets of rules and restrictions in the handling of the materials of their craft, namely words. The more complex and difficult to observe those rules are, the greater will be the skill required of the poet in order to overcome them. In other words, a great deal of attention is being paid to the outward form of poetry and, apart from a few brief recommendations as to which topics should be dealt with in short-lined stanza-forms

---

[1] An important difference must be kept in mind between present-day usage and early Renaissance usage here. Then the predominant meaning of the word 'art' was not the essentially modern one of 'skill displaying itself in perfection of workmanship', but rather 'a body or system of rules serving to facilitate the carrying out of certain principles' (*O.E.D.*, under *art*). A typical Renaissance definition of the word is given by Abraham Fraunce, *The Lawiers Logike* (1588), I, i, 1*b*: 'An art is a methodicall disposition of true and coherent preceptes, for the more easie perceiving and better remembring of the same.'

and which in long-lined stanzas, very little attention is given to the content.

We may take the so-called *Instructif de la seconde rethoricque*, probably written by Regnaud Le Queux, as a characteristic example of this type of treatise. This work, written in verse, was first published in 1501 as a *préambule* to *Le Jardin de plaisance Et fleur de Rethoricque*, and it was reprinted several times during the first half of the sixteenth century. There are ten chapters, of which the first is devoted to a definition of rhetoric and the second enumerates the ancient authors who have written on rhetoric and on poetic theory. The third makes the distinction between the two parts of rhetoric, prose and verse. With the fourth chapter we come to the consideration of poetry proper; here the seven vices of poetry are set out—*faulce proportion, impropre consonance, impropre location, redites,* too hasty taking of words with harsh sounds from the Latin, *equivoques contraintes,* and finally hiatus. From this the author passes in chapter five to the six figures of poetry, namely *synalepha* (which is more or less the same as elision), *syncope* (cutting short), *apocope* (omitting the last letter or syllable of a word), *synonyme, mots equivoques,* and *dialogue.* A figure is defined as

> impropriete
> Licenciee et aprouuee
> Par vs et par auctorite.

The sixth chapter deals with masculine and feminine rhymes, the seventh with the numbers of syllables in each line, the eighth with the arrangement of rhymes and the errors which should be avoided therein, and the ninth with the various types of rhyme, *rime léonine, rime croisée,* and so on. Finally the tenth chapter contains advice for the writing of moralities, comedies, mysteries, chronicles, romances, and histories. That the advice is not very profound, nor very precise, we may see from the following few lines concerning moralities, which I quote for the sake of the fine ring of the full rhymes:

> Item on les doit decorer
> De belles collocutions
> Icelles aussi honnorer
> De belles demonstracions

Rethoricques ornacions...
Item que lon blasme et desprise
Les vices fort en general...
Lon doit donc les vertus priser
Et des vices dire le mal
Puis les vertus auctoriser...
En parlant tousiours par honneur
En grande substancialite
Sans aucune imbecilite
Et sans remplaige de langaige
Qui nait en soy vtilite
Grande en vng chascun personnaige.[1]

A quarter of a century later things had not altered very much. Jean Molinet's *Art de Rhétorique vulgaire* of 1493 was anonymously rewritten and amplified in 1524–5 under the title of *L'Art et Science de Rhétorique vulgaire*. This treatise is really very little more than a long list of complicated rhyme- and stanza-forms (*vers dizains, vers douzains, vers quatorzains, vers tiercez, complainctes, rondeaux, virlaiz, balades, chantz royaulx, rymes equivoques*, etc., etc.), with a few brief technical remarks appended to each item, explaining the rules to be followed in the use of the device in question. Thus in the section concerned with the *rondeau*, Molinet's continuator notes: 'Encores pour plus enrichir et orner ledit rondeau, on doibt donner sentence entiere et parfaicte a la premiere ligne, et user de ryme, l'une parfaicte et masculine, et l'autre imparfaicte et feminine.' The whole is rounded off by a dictionary of rhymes.[2]

As late in the century as 1548 the *Art Poétique Françoys* of Thomas Sebillet, even though it marks a real advance over previous treatises in that it comes much closer than they had done to a serious consideration of what poetry is and what poets are doing (the title itself of the work is probably significant from this point of view), still contains a very high proportion of narrowly technical material. The second book of this treatise contains an account of 'toutes lés formes et differences dés Pöemes usurpées en l'art Pöétique François, et au passé, et au

---

[1] *Le Jardin de plaisance Et fleur de Rethoricque*, ed. E. Droz and A. Piaget (1910), t. I, fos. a iiii r° and c ii r°.

[2] See Patterson, *op. cit.* I, 195–206; E. Langlois, *Recueil d'Arts de Seconde Rhétorique* (1902), lxxiii–lxxxvii, 265–426.

présent', and Sebillet offers this to the reader 'a fin qu'entendant quéle matiére se traite mieus en cestuy cy, ou en cestuy la, et quéle forme de ryme y est plus souvent et plus proprement usurpée, tu n'ays rien que souhaitter pour t'eslever a la perfection du Pöéte'.[1] The list of 'formes et differences' is slightly shorter than that of our previous example, but it is still formidable, comprising epigram, sonnet, *rondeau*, ballad, *chant royal*, canticle ('Chant Lyrique ou Ode et Chanson'), epistle, elegy, dialogue (including eclogue, morality, and farce), *coq a l'asne*, blason, enigma, *Deploration et Complainte, Lay et Virelay*. Sebillet devotes a chapter to each of these forms, describing in some detail what matter is appropriate to them, setting out the requirements of rhyme and line-length, and discussing the various faults and elegances. Despite the important part which Sebillet acknowledged that other elements, such as inspiration, played in the composition of poetry, he was still very far from abandoning his belief in the great importance of craftsmanship and formal complexity, which could (and, as he held, should) be learnt by the poet, just as any other craftsman learns the technique of his craft. This belief was, of course, to some extent a direct inheritance from the *grands rhétoriqueurs* and their over-elaborate, oratorical, and pedantic style of writing. They had deliberately sought out difficult poetic forms, using emphatic verbal music coupled with rather stilted diction in order to produce what are largely virtuoso effects. Intricate craftsmanship had been their main concern rather than the general theory of poetry. But Sebillet was not merely following the example of his literary predecessors in this matter; another more powerful influence also encouraged him to take the same path.

Underlying the concentration upon merely technical matters was a view of poetry which effectively militated against any large-scale examination of the nature of poetic activity as something *sui generis*—namely, the traditional classification of poetry under the heading of rhetoric. Poetry was held to be simply one of the kinds of rhetoric, with the result that its nature and its objects, its ends, were determined for it. There was no need of any special theory of poetry, for that was already contained in

[1] Th. Sebillet, *Art Poetique Françoys*, ed. F. Gaiffe (1932), 102.

the general theory of rhetoric. Even from its very early days the discipline of rhetoric, as treated by Isocrates and Aristotle, had been concerned with both prose and verse. Considerations of style and diction came very close, in the hands of the rhetoricians, to fulfilling all the requirements of a technical poetics. Figures of syntax and word-order, metaphors, and all the various types of ornament which language could fashion were equally well to be found in the speeches of the orators as in the works of the poets. The verse form was simply one more rhetorical figure, or 'colour'. For poetry was considered to have exactly the same object as any other form of discourse, namely to persuade an audience either that something is so, or that it should act in a particular manner. The study of all the various devices of language and thought which enabled one to achieve those ends was called rhetoric. Medieval rhetoricians simply took over the repertory of figures from the classical manuals of rhetoric and reinforced the already strong tendency towards formalisation and bare prescription without making very much effort to examine the theoretical aspects of what they were about. Least of all was there any feeling that poetry required separate consideration.

In the late Middle Ages and the early Renaissance the 'science' of rhetoric was still usually divided into two parts. The first part dealt with the figures of speech and thought in general, the second part with those colours which are peculiar to poetry, that is, with all the possible varieties of rhyme and rhythm and with the fixed stanza-forms. The standard introductory formula for all this was a charming little *non sequitur*: 'est dicte seconde rhethorique pour cause que la premiere est prosayque.'[1] We have already noted this distinction between the two parts of rhetoric, prose and verse, in the *Instructif de la seconde rethoricque* of 1501, and find it again still later, in Gracien du Pont's *Art et Science de Rhétorique métrifiée* of 1539: 'il y a deux manieres de Rhetoricque vulgaire. L'une est dicte rhetoricque prosaicque. L'aultre rhetoricque metriffiée, c'est a

---

[1] See the anonymous treatise *Les Regles de la Seconde Rhetorique* (1411?/32); Bauldet Herenc, *Le Doctrinal de la Seconde Rhetorique* (1432), in Langlois, *op. cit.* 11, 165.

dire Rithme, laquelle se faict par vers et mettres.' *Rithme* seems to be considered superior to prose by virtue of the very difficulty and complexity of its rules: '...qu'est plus subtille et difficile, pour la subgection des regles, proportion et mesure, que la dicte prose'.[1]

As their nickname suggests, the *grands rhétoriqueurs* had made much of the idea that poetry is simply a kind of rhetoric. Georges Chastellain entitled his versified discussion of poets and poetry *Les Douze Dames de Rhétorique*. There he talks of the 'doulceur réthoricque' which all poems worthy of the name must have, and claims that he himself possesses 'en parler rhétorical saveur'. And in the series of letters accompanying *Les Douze Dames* maistre Jehan Robertet admires Chastellain for his 'élégante et haulte réthorique', and addresses him as 'cler orateur...tres-clair orateur'.[2] Another of the *grands rhétoriqueurs*, Jean Molinet, entitled his treatise on poetics *L'Art de Rhétorique*, and began: 'Rethorique vulgaire est une espece de musique appellée richmique, laquele contient certain nombre de sillabes avec aucune suavité de equisonance.'[3]

Even when, as in the case of Sebillet, a writer begins to consider the theoretical bases of poetry as well as its technical aspects, the view that poetry is a form of rhetoric still remains. Sebillet begins his discussion of poems in general with a chapter on invention, 'prémiére partie de Pöésie'. This is a direct borrowing from rhetorical terminology, and the author at once sets about justifying his use of the word: 'ne doit on trouver estrange si je donne en l'art pöétique les prémiéres parties a celle, laquéle les Rhetoriciens ont aussy nombrée premiére part de tout leur art. Car la Rhétorique est autant bien espandue par tout le pöéme, comme par toute l'oraison.' Nothing could be more clearly stated than this. Furthermore, 'l'Orateur et le Pöéte tant proches et conjoins...différent principalement en ce, que l'un est plus contraint de nombres que l'autre'. The poet has to observe a more complicated set of formal rules than the orator; otherwise they are alike. And, as the *grands rhétori-*

[1] Quoted in Patterson, *op. cit.* I, 207.
[2] *Œuvres de Georges Chastellain*, ed. de Lettenhove (1863–6), VII, 169, 178, 150, 145, 147.
[3] Quoted in Langlois, *op. cit.* 216.

19

queurs had maintained, the greater the difficulty, the greater the elegance; hence Sebillet's admiration for the punning *ryme en equivoque*. Sebillet further recommends that the young poet should study the works of the rhetoricians, together with those of the philosophers, as the proper complement of his natural abilities: 'Le surplus de l'invention qui consiste en l'art, prendra le pöete des Philosophes et Rheteurs qui en ont escrit livres propres et particuliers.'[1]

Just how hard the rhetorical tradition of poetry died we may judge from odd echoes of it which can be heard even in the theories of the Pléiade. Du Bellay, for instance, at the end of the first book of the *Deffence et Illustration* foresees that his readers will be surprised that he does not discuss the orator at the same time as he is discussing the poet. He therefore explains his reasons for not doing this: 'ne t'ebahis, si je ne parle de l'orateur comme du poete. Car outre que les vertuz de l'un sont pour la plus grand' part communes à l'autre, je n'ignore point qu'Etienne Dolet, homme de bon jugement en notre vulgaire, a formé l'*Orateur Françoys.*'[2] Du Bellay is not attempting to separate poetry from rhetoric here. It is merely that he sees no need to repeat something which has already been quite adequately done by another.

Also very revealing of the close connections between poetry and rhetoric is the chapter in another Pléiade work of theory, Jacques Peletier du Mans' *Art poëtique*, in which the author claims to discuss the 'diferancé du Poëté e dé l'Orateur'. There is no suggestion that the poet and the orator differ in their ultimate aims, or that they employ any fundamentally different techniques to achieve those aims. The two main differences which Peletier proposes are of a fairly superficial nature. First, the orator is more tied down to the particular circumstances of his case than is the poet, who can introduce a greater diversity of material into his discourse:

Voęla l'uné des principalés diferancés qu'il i a antré l'Orateur e lé Poëté, qué cétuici peùt s'ebatré an tous g'anrés d'argumans, cétuila ét

[1] Sebillet, *op. cit.* 21–2, 25–6.
[2] J. du Bellay, *Deffence et Illustration de la Langue françoyse*, ed. H. Chamard (1948), 85–6.

astreint aus chosés particulierés. Car l'Orateur né pourra pas chęrcher l'ocasion dé fęré parler les Dieus, dé treter l'Amour, les Ieus festiz, les Anfęrs, les Astrés, les regions, les chans, les prez, les fonteinés e telés beautez d'Ecriz.

Secondly, the orator has to discuss in detail a single aspect of his case in order to win over his audience for a short time; whereas the poet speaks to all eternity and need therefore deal only cursorily with the more trivial and detailed points:

lui [the poet] qui parlé a uné eternite, dǫęt seulémant toucher lé neu, lé sęgręt et lé fons d'un argumant, e parler plus resolumant, lęssant les mę́nués narracions. L'Orateur, qui parlé aus hommés presans, e lé plus souuant au peuplé, fęt assez s'il à uné accion, e uné façon con-uenablé a pouuoęr gagner ses g'ans seulémant pour uné heuré.[1]

We should notice too how the poet, like the orator, deals in *argumants*. This rhetorical terminology is still present in the 1587 preface to the *Franciade*, where Ronsard remarks that 'le Poëte heroique invente & forge argumens tous nouveaux'.[2] The twentieth-century reader might expect that it was primarily the orator's rather than the poet's business to find out persuasive arguments to convince an audience.

To regard poetry as a branch of rhetoric was in fact to make certain assertions about the objects of poetry and about the means which it employed to achieve those objects. In this 'rhetorical' view the poet, like the orator, set out to move his audience, to persuade or dissuade it of something, by making the appropriate apportionments of praise or blame. The audience would in the very nature of things seek after what was presented to it as good, and shun what was shown to be evil. This was an open encouragement to judge poetry by ethical rather than by aesthetic standards. The medieval Church had been only too ready to do this, anaesthetising poetry by making it the hand-maiden of theology, along with all the other arts. The only difference between poetry and the prose forms of oratory was

---

[1] J. Peletier, *L'Art Poëtique*, ed. A. Boulanger (1930), 83–4.

[2] P. de Ronsard, *Œuvres Complètes*, ed. P. Laumonier (1914 in progress), XVI, 336. I assume throughout that Binet's 'restoration' of this preface involved no gross distortions, semantic or doctrinal, of Ronsard's text.

that poetry, since it was written in 'numbers' forming musical harmonies, was more pleasing, more attractive to its hearers than the less *nombreux* prose. This was no small advantage, providing that it was always used for irreproachable ends. The difficulty facing the Church was that most of the poetry of classical antiquity advocated, by implication at least, a clearly non-Christian ethics. There was also the further danger that poets might provide their audiences with more earthly pleasure than celestial profit—and that was certainly not to be encouraged.

Finally, we may note that this view of poetry, namely that it provides moral teaching by means of a pleasing form (which I have linked with the theory of poetry as rhetoric), was confirmed for the sixteenth century by the literary authority of Horace. In the *Epistula ad Pisones*, known also as the *Ars poetica*, he had recommended that the poet should either please his readers or instruct them; but better still was for him to do both:

> Omne tulit punctum qui miscuit utile dulci,
> lectorem delectando pariterque monendo.[1]

This recommendation to didacticism was a commonplace of criticism in the sixteenth century, and it occurs quite frequently in the writings of the Pléiade. Ronsard himself towards the end of his treatise on 'l'Art poëtique françois' expressed the hope that 'cest abbregé te soit aggreable, & utile à la posterité'.[2] A similar combination of epithets was used by Du Bellay in the *Ode au Seigneur des Essars*:

> Des poëtiques espris
> L'utile & doulce escriture
> Comprent ce qui est compris
> Au ciel & en la nature.[3]

And he paraphrased Horace's line again when praising Caracciolo:

> Mon Caraciol, qui n'aspire
> A ces vanitez qu'on admire

---

[1] Horace, *The Epistles*, ed. A. S. Wilkins (1950), 72–3. It should be noted that Peletier translated Horace's *Ars poetica* into French verse in 1544.

[2] Ronsard, *op. cit.* XIV, 34.

[3] Du Bellay, *Œuvres Poétiques*, ed. H. Chamard (1908–31), IV, 174.

> Seulement pour l'obscurité,
> Au droit sentier nous achemine,
> Et sçait mesler en sa doctrine
> Le plaisir à l'utilité.[1]

We have to remember, of course, that Horace was himself much influenced in his ideas on poetry by the theories of the classical rhetoricians.

[1] *Ibid.* v, 359.

[3]

POETRY AS DIVINE FURY

The pressure put upon poetry to be something less than its full
self was therefore considerable in the early sixteenth century.
Either poetry was regarded primarily as a sort of intellectual
game, a display of expertise by highly accomplished craftsmen—
in which case the content really counted for very little. Or it
was required to be a sermon in verse, in which the succulent
marrow of moral instruction was hidden beneath the bark of
poetic ornament. The Pléiade considered the first attitude
towards poetry to be trivial, and the second they found far too
cramping. They were deliberately attempting, in Du Bellay's
words, to introduce 'quasi comme une nouvelle poësie'.[1] For
they were convinced, in a way that they believed the great
majority of their predecessors had not been convinced, of the
supreme intrinsic worth of poetry. The Pléiade sought to free
poetry from the obligation of conforming to extra-poetical scales
of value; poetry did not have to masquerade as ethics, or as
philosophy, or as history. It could indeed deal with all those
topics, and did so very often, but the true essence of poetry did
not lie there. Nor did it consist in the fact that poetry was
written in verse. Poetry was written in verse, to be sure, but
not everything that was written in verse was poetry. There were
poets, and there were versifiers, or rhymers. To be a versifier
was to be one of a worthless and ignorant rabble,[2] whereas to be
a poet was to follow a high and noble calling. 'Il y a autant de
différence', wrote Ronsard in the *Preface sur la Franciade* of
1587, 'entre un Poëte & un versificateur, qu'entre un bidet & un
genereux coursier de Naples, & pour mieux les accomparer,
entre un venerable Prophete & un Charlatan vendeur de

[1] Du Bellay, *Deffence*, 90.
[2] Cf. Du Bellay, *Deffence*, 173: '...vous autres si mal equipez, dont l'ignorance
a donné le ridicule nom de *rymeurs* a nostre Langue (comme les Latins appellent
leurs mauvais poëtes *versificateurs*)...'. His italics.

triacles.'[1] Poetry was no longer regarded merely as an elegant amusement, a young man's pastime, but as a career, a way of life almost, to which one dedicated onself.

A large number of factors, social, intellectual, and psychological, helped to bring about this heightened self-awareness on the part of poets in the sixteenth century. As Weber has argued, the fact that under the influence of François Ier and his sister the royal court became the centre not only of worldly elegance and luxury but also of the highest intellectual and artistic culture enabled poets to realise more fully than before their own dignity.[2] The *grands rhétoriqueurs* had had to exist on usually meagre and always extremely variable pensions whose continuance depended on the favour of a protector and on the state of the royal exchequer. Thus a large proportion of their poetic effort had to be spent on the flattery of important people, which did not produce very valuable results in terms of poetry. As court poets they were merely entertainers and chroniclers whose services were readily expendable. With the italianising of the French royal court in the early part of the sixteenth century poets became more valuable both for their prestige-value as living embodiments of learning and culture and also in their role as propagandists for the sovereign himself.[3] In addition most of the poets belonged to what might be called the *petite noblesse de province*, and although it was a class which found itself under considerable economic pressure at this time, their membership of it gave them a certain feeling of security in social terms at least. This becomes obvious if one compares the poetry of the *rhétoriqueurs* with that of Clément Marot and with that of the Pléiade. The tone of abject flattery progressively diminishes, even though it certainly does not disappear altogether. Yet poets no longer felt themselves automatically inferior to the kings and nobles to whom they addressed their poems.

More important to the Pléiade than their social status, however, was their membership of the aristocracy of the mind. The high 'odi profanum vulgus, et arceo' note so often struck by the

[1] Ronsard, *op. cit.* xvi, 335.

[2] Weber, *op. cit.* ch. ii.

[3] On this last point see G. Gadoffre's remarks in his *Ronsard par lui-même* (1960), 19 ff.

Pléiade is precisely that of the humanist supremely confident of the unique value of learning and of literature.[1] The ideal model which such men as Jean Dorat and Marc-Antoine Muret held constantly before the eyes of their students was that of the disinterested scholar and poet. The great wealth of literary material that had comparatively suddenly come to the attention of learned men was felt to be one of mankind's most precious possessions. To enter into this rich heritage, to add to it, and to enlarge it was therefore held to be a great honour and a great responsibility. It was a vocation in the most solemn sense of the word, and to fit oneself for the vocation of poet demanded the most strenuous pursuit of moral virtue. In the *Abbregé de l'Art poëtique françois* Ronsard is most emphatic about this: 'Or, pour ce que les Muses ne veulent loger en une ame, si elle n'est bonne, saincte, & vertueuse, tu seras de bonne nature, non meschant, renfrogné, ne chagrin; mais animé d'un gentil esprit, ne laisseras rien entrer en ton entendement qui ne soit sur-humain & divin.'[2] It is this virtue, the virtue that is in the poet himself and in his poetry, which constitutes the only true nobility. Poetry is a virtue, an excellence of the individual human soul, which is its own reward and its own justification. Pontus de Tyard is expressing the feelings of the whole group when he notes with a certain pride, 'Aussi est le nombre petit, et peu cognu, de ces parfaits studieux, qui plus pour l'amour de vertu embrassent le travail literaire, que pour appetit de gain, ou delectation de renommée'.[3]

Behind the close association of poetry with virtue lies the belief in the divine origin of poetry. This doctrine had been available to the Middle Ages in the writings of Horace, but it was accorded little serious examination in France until Sebillet and more particularly the Pléiade drew attention to it as an important element in poetic theory. Horace had thought of Orpheus, the first poet of all, as a priest and interpreter of the

---

[1] Cf. Du Bellay, *Deffence*, 180–1: 'Seulement veux-je admonnester celuy qui aspire à une gloyre non vulgaire, s'eloingner de ces ineptes admirateurs, fuyr ce peuple ignorant, peuple ennemy de tout rare & antique scavoir, se contenter de peu de lecteurs.'   [2] Ronsard, *op. cit.* XIV, 5.

[3] P. de Tyard, *Solitaire Premier*, ed. S. F. Baridon (1950), 3–4. See also Franchet, *op. cit.* ch. II.

gods, who civilised primitive savage man and taught him how to
live peaceably with his fellows. Through the wisdom which
Orpheus and the other early poets distilled in their works men
learnt to practise public and private virtues, to distinguish the
sacred from the profane, to build cities, and to make tables of
laws. Because of all this men began to revere the poets and their
songs as divine:

> Silvestres homines sacer interpresque deorum
> caedibus et victu foedo deterruit Orpheus....
>   fuit haec sapientia quondam,
> publica privatis secernere, sacra profanis,
> concubitu prohibere vago, dare iura maritis,
> oppida moliri, leges incidere ligno;
> sic honor et nomen divinis vatibus atque
> carminibus venit.[1]

It is this tradition which Sebillet follows in his *Art Poétique
Françoys*: 'un Orphée par la douceur de ses vers chantez avoit
illustré la gloire des plus hauts et plus puissans dieuz.' By now
the canon of divine poets has been christianised, so that Moses
is hailed as the 'premier divin Pöéte', and the list continues
with David, Solomon, and the Prophets. Sebillet also stresses
the origin of human knowledge in the divine perfection. All the
arts, since they are 'conjoins avec ceste divine perfection que
nous appellons Vertu', contain some spark of the divine fire, for
our minds are of kindred substance with the divine fire, though
of necessity incomparably less pure. Whenever a spark from the
divine fire comes near to a human mind, light is generated in the
latter and it is enabled to know the divine substance. This is
especially true in the case of the poetic art: 'comme en tous lés
ars ceste estincelle du feu divin à l'approcher de l'esprit son
semblable, rend lumiére, par laquéle ell' est évidemment
congnue; aussi en l'art Pöétique (me soit permis de nommer art
ce que plus proprement j'appelleroie divine inspiration) reluyt
elle en plus vive et plus apparente splendeur.' The parenthesis is
important here, for it introduces the neo-platonic conception of
poetry as a divine inspiration, which the Pléiade was to proclaim
with such fervour. Sebillet goes on: '...le Pöéte de vraye

---

[1] Horace, *op. cit.* 74.

27

merque, ne chante ses vers et carmes autrement que excité de la vigueur de son esprit, et inspiré de quelque divine afflation'. Through its own harmony, in fact, poetry participates in the divine harmony which sustains the universe—this is very pythagoro-platonic!—thus confirming that poets enjoy 'quelque don divin, et céleste prérogative, laquéle est clérement montrée par lés nombres dont lés Pöétes mesurent leurs carmes, la perfection et divinité desquelz soutient et entretient l'admirable machine de cest univers, et tout ce qu'elle clost et contient'.[1]

Sebillet realised that one does not become a poet simply by writing technically correct verse, but that a true poet must also have 'entendement et esprit divin pour meriter l'honneur de ce nom'. He was aware that 'ce qu'en Pöésie est nommé art... n'est rien que la nue escorce de Pöésie, qui couvre artificiéle-ment sa naturéle séve, et son ame naturélement divine'.[2] But he did not examine in any great detail the implications which this theory of 'divine afflation' held for poetry. He simply asserted that it was so, linked his statement with the saying that poets are born and not made, and passed on to a lengthy con-sideration of the very 'art' whose importance he seemed to be minimising a moment before. As we have seen, Sebillet listed and discussed a considerable number of the complicated forms beloved of the *grands rhétoriqueurs*.[3] Theoretical matters were quite neglected after the first three chapters of his treatise.

The Pléiade, on the other hand, had the greatest contempt for this kind of art, for what Du Bellay refers to as 'toutes ces vieilles poësies Françoyses aux Jeuz Floraux de Thoulouse & au Puy de Rouan: comme rondeaux, ballades, vyrelaiz, chants royaulx, chansons & autres telles episseries, qui corrumpent le goust de nostre Langue, & ne servent si non à porter temoing-naige de nostre ignorance'.[4] In the *Ode à Michel de l'Hospital* Ronsard has Jupiter tell his daughters, the Muses, that

> Vostre mestier, race gentille,
> Les aultres mestiers passera,
> D'autant qu'esclave il ne sera
> De l'art aux Muses inutile.[5]

[1] Sebillet, *op. cit.* 7–10, 11–13.   [2] *Ibid.* 10, 22–3.   [3] See p. 17.
[4] Du Bellay, *Deffence*, 108–9.   [5] Ronsard, *op. cit.* III, 141.

As we shall see later, this is not a wholesale condemnation of all art.[1] Ronsard was fully aware of the necessity for skilful workmanship even in the most 'inspired' poems. He is here protesting only against the arid formalising of the *grands rhétoriqueurs* and of their successors, the *marotiques*, 'qui pensent... avoir accomply je ne sçay quoy de grand, quand ilz ont rymé de la prose en vers'.[2] Ronsard's Muses have nothing to do with 'art penible, & miserable', for they are to be directly inspired by Jupiter:

> Affin (o Destins) qu'il n'advienne
> Que le monde appris faulcement
> Pense que vostre mestier vienne
> D'art, & non de ravissement:
> Cet art penible, & miserable
> S'elongnera de toutes pars
> De vostre mestier honorable...
> Sans plus ma saincte fureur
> Polira vostre science.[3]

The theory of divine fury had been discussed by Plato, briefly in the dialogue *Ion*, and more fully in the *Phaedrus*. Plato, however, was known to the Renaissance not in the original Greek (although the first modern edition in Greek was published in 1513, it was not widely read until much later), but rather in the Latin translations of Marsilio Ficino, which were embellished with the translator's extensive neo-platonic commentaries; these commentaries are the real source of the divine fury theory as it is expounded by the Pléiade. Of course, the idea that poetry is of divine origin was also embodied in the myth of the Muses, which was fully current among the predecessors of the Pléiade. Lemaire de Belges was using the conventional imagery associated with this myth when he talked of

> le don celestin
> De la liqueur et fontaine des Muses.[4]

In Lemaire's case it was nothing but conventional imagery, and its significance is hardly more than that of an ornament,

---

[1] Cf. pp. 46 ff.   [2] Ronsard, *op. cit.* xiv, 25.
[3] *Ode à Michel de l'Hospital*; Ronsard, *op. cit.* iii, 142, 143.
[4] J. Lemaire de Belges, *La Concorde des deux Langages*, ed. J. Frappier (1947), 18.

unrelated except in a superficial manner to what surrounds it. The Pléiade, however, laid great stress on the substance of the myth and gave it pride of place among their poetic theories. As Pontus de Tyard was to announce, 'Je veux vous declarer une grande partie de ce que les fables Poëtiques ont touché des Muses, sous l'escorce dequoy le suc et la moelle se trouve de plusieurs bonnes doctrines'.[1]

Three years after the appearance of the *Deffence et Illustration* Pontus set out the full theory of divine fury, complete with all the Ficinian glosses and a few more of his own in addition, in the *Solitaire Premier, ou, Prose des Muses, et de la fureur poëtique.* Here he makes the orthodox distinction between the two types of *aliénation*. The first is caused by 'maladies corporelles', and is 'follie et vice du cerveau'. The other is 'engendrée d'une secrete puissance divine, par laquelle l'ame raisonnable est illustrée: et la nommons, fureur divine, ou, avec les Grecs Enthusiasme...son propre est d'eslever depuis ce corps jusques aux Cieux l'ame qui des cieux est descendue dedans ce corps'. It is through divine fury, then, that the soul rises up once more to its original home and to the source of eternal bliss. The soul passed through four stages in its descent from the uppermost region of the heavens into the vile depths of a material body: 'je vous ay dit...que par quatre degrez l'ame descent, depuis le souverain *un*, commencement eternel de toute chose, et qui tient le plus haut lieu, jusques au corps, qui est le plus bas, et infime de tout'. The first was 'Angelique entendement', the second 'Raison intellectuelle', the third 'Opinion', and the fourth 'Nature' (which Pontus defines as 'celle puissance animale qui consiste en l'office de nourriture et generation'). Because there were four descending stages, there are also four ascending stages through which the soul must pass on its return journey:

Aussi pour remonter estoient necessaires quatre degrez, lesquels se peuvent comprendre en celle illustration d'Ame ou elevation d'Entendement, que je vous ay dit estre nommée fureur divine. Car la fureur divine...est l'unique escalier, par lequel l'Ame peut trouver le chemin qui la conduise à la source de son souverain bien, et felicité derniere.

[1] P. de Tyard, *op. cit.* 27.

The four varieties of divine fury are as follows:

La premiere est par la fureur Poëtique procedant du don des Muses. La seconde est par l'intelligence des mysteres, et secrets des religions sous Bacchus. La troisiesme par ravissement de prophetie, vaticination, ou divination sous Apollon: et la quatriesme par la violence de l'amoureuse affection sous Amour et Venus. . . souz ces quatre especes sont cachées toutes les plus abstraites et sacrées choses, ausquelles l'humain Entendement puisse aspirer: mesmes la vraye et certaine cognoissance de toutes les disciplines, qui si longuement (et souvent en vain) entretiennent les studieux à leur poursuite. Car il ne faut croire, que defaillant en nous l'illustration de ces raiz divins, et n'estant la torche de l'Ame allumée par l'ardeur de quelque fureur divine, nous puissions en aucune sorte nous conduire à la cognoissance des bonnes doctrines et sciences: et moins nous eslever en quelque degré de vertu pour, seulement de pensée, gouster nostre souverain bien hors des viles et corporelles tenebres esclairées de l'obscure lampe, qui nourrit son feu en l'humeur des fausses et decevantes delectations.[1]

Here poetry is incorporated into a complete metaphysical and epistemological framework, and it becomes an integral part of that framework. Poetry is not simply an optional extra, a pleasing and elegant embellishment which has nothing at all to do with the really important issues of human life. Poetry, in fact, has an essential part to play in the relations between body and soul. Because of its divine origin it is an upwards-striving power; its effect is that of sublimation, not of degradation. It is the means whereby the soul, bewildered by its sudden fall into the world of materiality and multiplicity and by its own cleaving to that world, is enabled to attain a certain harmony within itself, and to begin the long reascent into the realm of spirit:

Le fond, lequel l'Ame ruminant ça bas a rencontré, a esté le corps, auquel elle se delecte et affectionne tant fermement, que pour les divers et contraires objects rencontrez, elle est contrainte de separer, et distribuer ses puissances en diverses et contraires actions, tellement, que la superieure partie de soy est endormie, et (comme on pourroit dire) estonnée de si lourde cheute: et l'inferieure toute agitée et elancée des perturbations, d'où s'engendre un horrible discord et desordre disposé en trop improportionnée proportion. Incompatible par ce point semble estre en elle toute juste action, si par quelque

[1] P. de Tyard, *op. cit.* 10–18.

31

moien cest horrible discord n'est transmué en douce simphonie, et ce desordre impertinent reduit en egalité mesurée, bien ordonnée et compartie. Et ce faire est pour son particulier devoir la fureur Poëtique chargée, resveillant par les tons de Musique l'Ame en ce, qu'elle est endormie, et confortant par la suavité et douceur de l'harmonie la partie perturbée, puis par la diversité bien accordée des Musiciens accords chassant la dissonante discorde et en fin reduisant le desordre en certaine egalité bien et proportionnément mesurée, et compartie par la gracieuse et grave facilité de vers compassez en curieuse observance de nombres et de mesures.

This is the preliminary harmony of the soul, which is completed by 'la sainte communication des mysteres et secrets religieux'. At the next stage the union of the soul with 'l'entendement' is achieved 'par le ravissement des propheties et divinations'. Finally, when the soul is a perfect unity within itself, it can enter into the supreme Unity of Unities:

En fin, quand tout ce qui est en l'essence et en la nature de l'Ame, est fait un, il faut (pour revenir à la source de son origine) que soudain elle se revoque en ce souverain *un*, qui est sur toute essence, Chose, que la grande et celeste Venus accomplit par Amour, c'est à dire, par un fervent, et incomparable desir, que l'Ame ainsi eslevée a de jouir de la divine et eternelle beauté.[1]

This is a fine and inspiring piece of neo-platonism, and it is capped by the more detailed account of poetic fury which Pontus gives in the following section:

La fureur Poëtique procede des Muses (dy-je) et est un ravissement de l'Ame, qui est docile et invincible: au moyen duquel elle est esveillée, esmue, et incitée par chants, et autres Poësies, à l'instruction des hommes. Par ce ravissement d'Ame, j'enten que l'Ame est occupée, et entierement convertie, et intentive aux saintes et sacrées Muses, qui l'ont rencontrée docile et apte à recevoir la forme qu'elles impriment, c'est à dire, l'ont trouvée preparée à estre esprise de ce ravissement, par lequel estant esmeue, elle devient invincible, et ne peut estre souillée, ou vaincue d'aucune chose basse et terrestre: mais au contraire surmonte et surcharge toutes ces vilitez. D'avantage elle est esveillée du sommeil et dormir corporel à l'intellectuel veiller, et revoquée des tenebres d'ignorance à la lumiere de verité, de la mort

---

[1] P. de Tyard, *op. cit.* 18–20.

à la vie, d'un profond et stupide oubly à un resouvenir des choses celestes, et divines: en fin, elle se sent esmeue, esguillonnée, et incitée d'exprimer en vers les choses, qu'elle prevoit et contemple. Aussi n'entreprenne temerairement chacun de heurter aux portes de Poësie: car en vain s'en approche, et fait ses vers miserablement froids celuy, auquel les Muses ne font grace de leur fureur, et auquel le Dieu ne se monstre propice et favorable.[1]

For the rest, Pontus makes the stock assertions that divine inspiration is transmitted from the poets themselves to 'ceux qui les recitent et interpretent', and from the interpreters to the audience, and that divine inspiration enables the poets to have a knowledge of 'toutes les sciences'. For 'comment donc sans un instinct de divine fureur pourroit le bon Poëte diversifier son œuvre de tant de fleurs cueillies tres à propos au florissant verger de toutes disciplines?'[2] We may note that the *disciplines* are now regarded as a source of adornment for the poem rather than as matter to be imparted to the reader.

Pontus is perhaps not to be taken as completely representative of the Pléiade, in as much as he is far more of a thoroughgoing platonist than any other member of the group. Yet he is worth quoting at some length, since he gives an admirably comprehensive account of the total scheme of thought within which the theory of the divine inspiration of poets operates. He shows us the sort of background against which we should view the pronouncements of the other Pléiade theorists. By comparison with the *Solitaire Premier* Peletier's remarks, for instance, seem in themselves almost meagre. Yet the theme is stressed well enough. He begins by repeating Horace's comments on the civilising and moral functions performed by the first poets ('Les Poëtes ont etè jadis les mętrés e reformateurs dę la vię'), and then affirms the divine origin of poetry, demonstrating this by pointing to the myth of the Muses: 'les anciens ont fęt Apolon e les Musés presider a la Poësię, commę Dieus a unę chosę diuinę: pour montrer qu'ęlę n'à origine autrę quę celestę.' He also makes the by now conventional claim that poets reveal to men the divine laws hidden in the universe and in Nature: 'Les Poëtés sélon lę diuin Platon, sont intęrpretés des

---

[1] P. de Tyard, *op. cit.* 21–2. [2] *Ibid.* 26.

Dieus, quand iz sont an leur seinté fureur. Car eus rauiz, e abstrez des pansémans terrestrés, conçoęuét les sécrez celestés, diuins, naturęz e mondeins: pour les manifester aus hommés.'[1]

Ronsard, on the other hand, gives more or less the same neo-platonic account of divine fury that Pontus was to do in the *Solitaire Premier*, but in brief. Naturally, poetry is of divine origin:

> les vers viennent de Dieu,
> Non de l'humaine puissance.

Jupiter tells the Muses that

> Vous, par la force Apollinée
> Ravirez les Poëtes saincts,
> Eulx, de vostre puissance attaincts
> Raviront la tourbe estonnée,

and he explains to them the fourfold division of their 'mestier honorable':

> Demambré en diverses pars,
> En Prophetie, en Poësies,
> En Mysteres, & en Amour,
> Quatre fureurs, qui tour à tour
> Chatouilleront voz fantasies.

And, of course, poets interpret the gods to men:

> Ceulx la que je feindray Poëtes
> Par la grace de ma bonté,
> Seront nommez les Interpretes
> Des Dieux, & de leur volunté.[2]

However, Ronsard also stresses a point which Pontus passes over very briefly, namely the necessity for the soul to be adequately prepared to receive the divine inspiration. Not only

---

[1] Peletier, *op. cit.* 66–9.

[2] *Ode à Michel de l'Hospital*; Ronsard, *op. cit.* III, 142–5. Ronsard later makes another reference to the conception of the four *fureurs* in the poem addressed to Monsieur de Belot, *op. cit.* xv, 18:

> Car, comme dit ce grand Platon, ce sage,
> Quatre fureurs brulent nostre courage,
> Bacchus, Amour, les Muses, Apollon,
> Qui dans nos cœurs laissent un aiguillon
> Comme freslons, & d'une ardeur segrette
> Font soudain l'homme & poëte & prophette.

must the poet be free from vice, but he must have been restored to a condition of positive virtue. Divine fury enters the human heart with the speed of lightning, but only

> Pourveu qu'il soit preparé,
> Pur de vice, & reparé
> De la vertu precieuse.
> Jamais les Dieux saincts & bons
> Ne repandent leurs saincts dons
> Dans une ame vicieuse.[1]

Ronsard returned to this idea in the *Responce aux injures & calomnies*. There he described the soul of the poet being seized by 'une gentille & docte frenaisie', and added:

> Tel bien ne se promet aux hommes vicieux,
> Mais aux hommes bien nés, qui sont aymés des cieux.[2]

In the *Hymne de l'Automne*, written at about the same time, the preparations that the poet is required to undertake before he can receive the 'don de Poësie' are specified as

> oraison, jeusne, & penitence aussi,
> Dont aujourd'huy le monde a bien peu de souci.[3]

This is in fact what Pontus had required for the second stage of the divine fury, that which succeeded poetry, namely 'la sainte communication des mysteres et secrets religieux, au moyen desquels les purifications, et devotieux offices, incitent l'Ame à se r'assembler en soy-mesme, pour toute se vouer en sacrée dedication et entiere intention à la reverence, qui la prosterne devant la divinité qu'elle adore'.[4] Ronsard, we may notice, tends to widen the sphere of poetry (in the persons of the Muses) so that it includes all four stages. Nor, when he is considering it as one among four varieties of fury, does he restrict its role to that of being the first and least exalted of the four.[5] Poetry, in Ronsard's view, reaches up into the highest

---

[1] Ronsard, *op. cit.* III, 143.
[2] *Ibid.* XI, 161–2. Cf. also the passage from the *Abbregé* quoted in p. 26.
[3] *Ibid.* XII, 47.   [4] P. de Tyard, *op. cit.* 19.
[5] It is possible that Ronsard's generalisation of poetic fury was suggested to him by Ficino's commentary on the *Phaedrus* (*Platonis opera...Additis Marsilii Ficini Argumentis & Commentariis*, 1561, II; 'In Phaedrum', cap. IV); see F. A. Yates, *The French Academies of the Sixteenth Century* (1947), 82.

realms of man's intellectual and spiritual endeavour. It is the vehicle of all man's noblest aspirations, and to become a poet is to commit one's whole being to a most sacred purpose.

Such is the Pléiade's reaction against the 'miserables escritz', the 'menus fatras' of the versifiers.[1] The poet is a being 'soustenu et poussé du Dieu';[2] he is a vessel which by reason of its purity is worthy to receive emanations from the divinity and to give them forth again to the ordinary run of men in the supremely harmonious form of poetry. The theory of divine inspiration and divine fury which lies behind this view of the poet and his work is a theory which recognises the poetic activity as being essentially different from other forms of mental and communicative activity, and at the same time it is one which gives to poetry a greatly enhanced value. The poetic fury is a 'ravissement', it comes from outside the poet and it sweeps him along with it; and it enables him to go beyond the normal range of his mental powers. As Montaigne notes of the poet, 'il confesse luy mesme qu'elles ["les saillies poëtiques, qui emportent leur autheur et le ravissent hors de soy"] surpassent sa suffisance et ses forces, et les reconnoit venir d'ailleurs que de soy, et ne les avoir aucunement en sa puissance'.[3] Such a situation would in any other circumstances be exceedingly dangerous. The effect of the poetic fury upon a person is very similar to that of the unbridled passions or of madness, sweeping the reason headlong in a riotous, uncontrollable tumult. But poetic fury is redeemed, or rather it is not allowed to fall in the first place, by its divine origin. This was more than ample guarantee of its own essential value and of the value of its products. Poets have, quite literally, a 'divinité d'invention' which sets them above other men.[4]

---

[1] Ronsard, *op. cit.* xiv, 25, and xvi, 346.
[2] P. de Tyard, *op. cit.* 73.
[3] M. de Montaigne, *Essais*, ed. M. Rat (1952), i, 135.
[4] Du Bellay, *Deffence*, 40.

[4]

INSPIRATION, NATURE, AND ART

The Pléiade stressed the importance for the poet of divine inspiration, or poetic fury as personified in the beings of the Muses, in what is perhaps a rather self-consciously trail-blazing manner. Inspiration they envisaged as an element in their work which would mark them off definitively from their immediate predecessors. For the moment they measured themselves against a sort of timeless absolute; all great poetry, they were saying, requires that its author should have received inspiration from the divinity. But at the same time the Pléiade believed that the development of poetry through the ages had taken the form of a continuous degeneration, passing from the first, divine poetry of Orpheus and others, through the later, merely human poetry of the classical Greeks, and on to the disappearance or all poetry amid the 'Ignorance' of the Middle Ages. This historical account of poetry introduces into our discussion two other concepts of prime importance in sixteenth-century poetics, namely Nature and Art, and sets up a significant opposition between them.

Du Bellay makes the basic contrast, that between the 'divine' and the 'human' poets, in the poem addressed to Bertran Bergier. In the case of the former,

> la seule nature
> Sans art, sans travail & sans cure
> Fait naistre le poëte, avant
> Qu'il ayt songé d'estre sçavant...
> Aussi les vers du temps d'Orphee,
> D'Homere, Hesiode & Musee,
> Ne venoient d'art, mais seulement
> D'un franc naturel mouvement.

Later, poets did not receive such generous bounty from Nature

37

and in attempting to make good this deficiency they spoilt their
work by an excess of art:

> Depuis geinant tel exercice
> Soubs un miserable artifice,
> Ce qu'avoient de bon les premiers
> Fut corrompu par les derniers.[1]

All this Du Bellay uses as the prelude to a hyperbolic compli-
ment paid to Bergier: he is like one of the first poets, for he is
untutored and inspired.

But it is Ronsard in the *Ode à Michel de l'Hospital* who gives
the most complete exposition of the falling-away of poetry from
its original perfection. In this poem Ronsard distinguishes five
stages in the process of degeneration. First—and this was really
a preliminary stage—the Muses inspired the Sibyls with the
gift of prophecy:

> Elles...
> Vindrent...
> Parmy les peuples incongnuz
> Ou dardant leurs flammes subtiles,
> Du premier coup ont agité
> Le cuœur prophette des Sybilles,
> Epoinct de leur divinité.

At a later stage there appeared

> les Poëtes divins,
> Divins, d'autant que la nature
> Sans art librement exprimoient,
> Sans art leur nayve escripture
> Par la fureur ilz animoient.

These poets, 'Poëtes sainctz', were Eumolpos, Musaeus,
Orpheus, Hesiod, Linos, and Homer. And they were followed
by
> la jeune bande
> Des vieux Poëtes humains:
> Degenerant des premiers,
> Comme venuz les derniers,
> Par un art melancolique

---

[1] Du Bellay, *Œuvres poétiques*, v, 117–20. I would refer the reader once more
to Abraham Fraunce's definition of art quoted in p. 14, n. 1.

Trahissoyent avec grand soing
Leurs vers, esloignez bien loing
De la saincte ardeur antique.

In the following *strophe* Ronsard lists periphrastically the poets, both classical and alexandrian Greeks, whom he is thinking or under this heading. Then,

Par le fil d'une longue espace,
Apres les Poëtes humains,
Les Muses souflerent leur grace
Dessus les prophettes Romains...
Eulx toutesfois pinçant la lyre
Si bien s'assouplirent les doigs,
Qu'encor les fredons de leur voix
Jusqu'aujourdhuy l'on entent bruire.[1]

It is worth noting that Ronsard gives a further account of the last two stages at the beginning of the *Abbregé de l'Art poëtique françois*. Having discussed the first poets, he turns to a consideration of the Greeks and of their imitators, the Romans: 'les seconds poëtes que j'appelle humains, pour estre plus enflez d'artifice & labeur que de divinité. A l'exemple de ceux cy, les poetes Romains ont foisonné en telle fourmiliere, qu'ilz ont apporté aux librairies plus de charge que d'honneur, excepté cinq ou six desquelz la doctrine, accompagnée d'un parfait artifice, m'a tousjours tiré en admiration.'[2] Here Ronsard once more makes clear the contrast between art and inspiration, and, if anything, his judgement of the merely human poets and especially of the Romans is even harsher than in the *Ode à Michel de l'Hospital*.[3]

[1] Ronsard, *op. cit.* III, 148–52.
[2] Ronsard, *op. cit.* XIV, 5.
[3] There are interesting parallels to this contrast between the early, inspired poetry and the later poetry written with 'artifice & labeur' in medieval (and Renaissance) Christian epistemology. The commonly accepted view was that, whereas the Holy Ghost had instilled into the Apostles an intuitive knowledge of things, the only way for men now to acquire knowledge was by studying the arts. Furthermore, Adam in his original state of innocence had been in possession of a complete and immediate understanding of the arts; but since the Fall men have only been able to reach such understanding by dint of long and arduous efforts, and even then their understanding is imperfect (cf. Perry Miller, *The New England Mind*, 1939, 105 ff.). This is exactly the position of 'human' poets *vis-à-vis* Orpheus and Homer. The modern labelling of the sixteenth century as an age of renaissance

In the poem Ronsard goes on to describe the final degradation of poetry during the Middle Ages:

> Tandis l'Ignorance arma
> L'aveugle fureur des Princes,
> Et leurs aveugles Provinces
> Contre les Sœurs anima.
> Ja desja les enserroit,
> Mais plus tost les enferroit,
> Quand les Muses detournées
> Voyant du fer la rayeur,
> Haletantes de frayeur
> Dans le ciel sont retournées.[1]

This is indeed a familiar theme in Pléiade writing. Du Bellay had already described in the *Musagnoemachie* the struggle of his fellow-poets and their royal patrons with Ignorance, 'le Monstre hideux', and Ronsard in his own early ode in praise of Madame Marguerite had had the monster despatched in a most warlike and efficient manner by Henri II's sister.[2] In the poem under consideration, of course, this function is performed by de l'Hospital, whom Jupiter describes as

> celuy qui defera
> Les souldars de l'Ignorance.[3]

The two series of texts by Du Bellay and Ronsard which I have just quoted make the points first that ideally 'la seule nature . . . Fait naistre le poëte', and secondly that the divinity of the first poets consisted in the fact that

> leur nayve escripture
> Par la fureur ilz animoient.

That these two points were closely allied in sixteenth-century minds is made clear by Ronsard's description of the first,

tends to make us forget that at that time historical thinking was still deeply coloured by the doctrine of the Fall. The future held in store not a Triumph of Progress in the nineteenth-century manner, but the Apocalypse and the Day of Judgement. The rediscovery of the great literature of Greece and Rome served merely to confirm the teaching of the Church that the Golden Age on earth belonged to the past, not to the future.

[1] Ronsard, *op. cit.* III, 152.
[2] Du Bellay, *Œuvres poétiques*, IV, 3–26; Ronsard, *op. cit.* I, 75 ff.
[3] Ronsard, *op. cit.* III, 156.

inspired poets' work as *nayve*, for one of the main connotations of the word at the time was that of naturalness.[1] And Pontus de Tyard used the authority of Cicero to confirm the alliance in the *Solitaire Premier*:

Aussi est-ce, ce que le grand disert Romain Ciceron entendoit, disant, en faveur du Poëte Archias, que plus souvent la nature sans doctrine, que la doctrine sans la nature avoit servy et valu à la vertu et louange, appellant du nom de nature celle divine agitation, comme un peu apres il declaire, affermant par l'authorité de grands et honorables personnages, l'estude des autres choses consister en Art, preceptes, reigles, et doctrines, et le pouvoir du Poëte estre naturel, comme esveillé des forces de l'Entendement, et quasi esmeu et enflammé de quelque Esprit divin.[2]

A contrast is being made between Nature and inspiration on the one hand and Art on the other, between those abilities which are ours from birth and which are 'given' to us, and the skills which we acquire by instruction.[3] To reach an understanding of the proper division of labour between these two was one of the important objects of poetic theorising at this time, simply because sixteenth-century poets were necessarily 'human' poets, that is to say they could no longer rely exclusively upon inspiration from the divinity. It was not enough to say, as Sebillet had done, that 'Le Pöéte naist, l'Orateur se fait',[4] for an understanding of the orator's art was also very necessary to the poet, quite apart from his own inborn gifts. The poet had to express his inspired conceptions in a form of discourse which employed words; and there were a certain number of rules, or at least

---

[1] For an extended commentary on the possible connotations of the word *naïf* in the sixteenth century, see pp. 77 ff.

[2] P. de Tyard, *op. cit.* 26–7.

[3] We should note that the two main meanings of the word 'nature' in the Renaissance—'all Creation' and 'constitution of some particular thing or being'— tend to shade into each other. Yet for the most part this causes little confusion, since Nature (in the first sense) manifested itself in all things and beings, including poets, by means of their natures (in the second sense). For a discussion of the relationship between the two kinds of nature, see D. B. Wilson, *Ronsard, Poet of Nature* (1961), 1–8; a more detailed semantic study of the whole question is to be found in H. S. Wilson's article, 'Some Meanings of *Nature* in Renaissance Literary Theory', in *Journal of the History of Ideas*, II, 4 (1941), 430–48.

[4] Sebillet, *op. cit.* 25.

guiding principles, which had to be followed in composing with words. These were the rules and principles codified in the art of rhetoric.

Indeed it is in the classical theories of rhetoric that we find the origin of the attempt to assess the relative importance to the poet of Nature and of Art. Protagoras probably instigated the analysis of the requirements of an orator, but the fullest accounts have survived to us in the rhetorical treatises of Cicero and Quintilian, who both adopt the Protagoran categories of *natura, ars,* and *exercitatio.* In the *De Oratore* Cicero stresses the prime importance of what he calls 'natura atque ingenium': 'sic igitur, inquit Crassus, sentio naturam primum, atque ingenium ad dicendum vim afferre maximam.'[1] These together provide one with the essential mental and physical attributes— acumen, fertility, a good memory, a ready tongue, a pleasant voice, vigour, and an agreeable appearance—without which it is impossible to be a fine orator. These attributes can be polished and improved by art, but they cannot originally be produced in a man by art if he does not already possess them. Art Cicero understands as being the rules of rhetoric exemplified in the practice of the great orators: 'intellego...sic esse non eloquentiam ex artificio, sed artificium ex eloquentia natum.'[2] Art is the rationalisation and codification of successful practice. The final requisite is *exercitatio,* that is to say the systematic practical training of an orator in the skills of his profession. Quintilian, by contrast, tends to emphasise the value of training more than Cicero had done, although he acknowledges that natural endowment is an essential pre-requisite. Thus a moderately good orator will owe more to Nature than to Art, but perfection is to be achieved only by means of the latter: 'consummatos...plus doctrinae debere quam naturae putabo.'[3] As D. L. Clark has written, 'It seems quite appropriate that both Cicero and Quintilian, while agreeing that art and nature are both necessary, should show a special bias in allotting the preponderance. Cicero, the orator, would rather like to consider himself a

---

[1] Cicero, *De Oratore,* Loeb edn. (1942), i, 80.
[2] *Ibid.* i, 100.
[3] Quintilian, *Institutio Oratoria,* Loeb edn. (1953), i, 348.

genius; while Quintilian, professor of rhetoric, would tend to appreciate the full value of instruction in his subject.'[1]

We have already seen how closely amalgamated the theories of poetry and of rhetoric still were in the sixteenth century. And so it is only to be expected that the Nature *versus* Art debate should be carried on in terms of poetry as well as in terms of rhetoric. The near-identification of inspiration with Nature which we have just noted in Ronsard and in Pontus de Tyard represents the attempt of sixteenth-century poets to incorporate the neo-platonic theory of divine fury into the traditional rhetorical scheme of *natura, ars, exercitatio*.[2] We have now to examine the different manifestations of this attempt at eclecticism in the writings of the Pléiade and their predecessors.

We may turn first to Sebillet's image of the bark and the sap which he used to express the relationship between art in poetry and the divine nature that it covers.[3] Even though he divides his discussion most unevenly between this essentially divine soul and the technicalities of its integument, he does stress the close interdependence in the poet himself of natural endowment and acquired art. It is essential, he says, for the poet to have a certain 'subtilité et sagacité de l'esprit, laquéle si Dieu a déniée à l'homme, pour neant se travaillera-il de dire ou faire en despit de Minerve: singuliérement en l'art de pöésie, que lon tient communément et bien, se parfaire plus de nature que

[1] 'The Requirements of a Poet', in *Modern Philology*, xvi, 8 (1918), 81. The idea that art perfects Nature was to become a commonplace of Renaissance thought. In the literary context this could refer to rhetorical theory, as we have just seen, and also to Aristotelian theories of art, according to which art improves upon Nature by making manifest the universals inhering in it. It is a notion found in educational theory; Cardinal Sadoleto, for instance, maintains that the reason why we should undergo a literary training is so that we might perfect the rough and unfinished form which we receive from Nature (*De Liberis recte instituendis*, 1533). And it is also a conception familiar to jurists, again on Ciceronian authority: 'la vraye raison [*raison* is used here to mean a system of rational principles of action upon which laws can be based], laquelle n'est autre chose, sinon la nature menée et reduitte à sa perfection, ainsi que Ciceron le demontre en ses livres qu'il a escrit *des Loix*' (Guy de Brués, *Premier Dialogue contre les nouveaux Academiciens*, ed. P. P. Morphos, 1953, 99).

[2] Plato himself had distinguished between the poet and the orator on the grounds that the former is inspired. For the orator he follows the Protagoran pattern, making his excellence depend partly upon natural ability and partly upon art (*Phaedrus*; *The Dialogues of Plato*, transl. B. Jowett, 1953 edn., iii, 178).

[3] See p. 28.

d'art'. Nevertheless, he continues, art is essential to the poet in order that he may be able to build on the foundation laid by Nature. And to acquire this art the poet must study the philosophers and the rhetoricians, and steep himself in the works of both the 'bons et classiques pöetes françois' and also the 'plus nobles Pöetes Grecz et Latins'.[1] In other words, there must be Nature *plus* art.

This had been Horace's attitude. For him it was a moot point whether a good poem owed more to Nature than to art:

> Natura fieret laudabile carmen an arte
> quaesitum est.

Helpful co-operation between the two was the proper solution:

> ego nec studium sine divite vena
> nec rude quid prosit video ingenium; alterius sic
> altera poscit opem res et coniurat amice.[2]

At the end of the fifteenth century and the beginning of the sixteenth the balance was weighted most emphatically in favour of *ars* and *studium*. But by the time Du Bellay was writing the *Deffence* the neo-platonic divine fury theories seem to have begun to reverse the position, for he felt it necessary to devote a whole chapter to the contention that 'le naturel n'est suffisant à celuy qui en Poësie veult faire œuvre digne de l'immortalité'. Du Bellay agreed that poets are born poets, 'car cela s'entend de ceste ardeur & allegresse d'esprit qui naturellement excite les poëtes, & sans la quele toute doctrine leur seroit manque & inutile', and he agreed with 'les plus scavans' that 'le naturel' could do more without 'la doctrine' than doctrine without nature.[3] Perhaps he would even have agreed with Pontus's claim that 'le naturel [est] tousjours en l'homme, meilleur que l'artifice'.[4] But his sense of intellectual superiority would not allow him to concede that Nature could do everything alone: 'ce seroit chose trop facile, & pourtant contemptible, se faire eternel par renommée, si la felicité de nature donnée mesmes

[1] Sebillet, *op. cit.* 24–5.   [2] Horace, *op. cit.* 75.
[3] Du Bellay, *Deffence*, 103–5.
[4] P. de Tyard, *Le Second Curieux*, in *The Universe of Pontus de Tyard*, ed. J. C. Lapp (1950), 128.

aux plus indoctes etoit suffisante pour faire chose digne de l'immortalité.'[1] *Mesmes aux plus indoctes*—that is the key phrase. In the poem pillorying *Le Poëte Courtisan* Du Bellay reaffirmed by means of heavy sarcasm his conviction that 'le seul naturel' cannot make a great poet:

> . . . il suffit icy [at court] que tu soyes guidé
> Par le seul naturel, sans art et sans doctrine,
> Fors cest art qui apprend à faire bonne mine.
> Car un petit sonnet qui n'a rien que le son,
> Un dixain à propos, ou bien une chanson,
> Un rondeau bien troussé, avec une ballade
> (Du temps qu'elle couroit) vault mieux qu'une Iliade. . .
> La court te fournira d'argumens suffisans,
> Et seras estimé entre les mieulx disans,
> Non comme ces resveurs, qui rougissent de honte
> Fors entre les scavans, desquelz on ne fait compte.[2]

The Pléiade poets were very conscious that they were taking part in a revival of learning, and from their scholarly heights they looked down upon the flock of ignorant, undisciplined court rhymers. The works of the latter, they stated, would disappear from people's memories on the author's death, or even earlier. Only a poet in whom natural 'ardeur et allegresse d'esprit' was backed up by skill in 'art' and by solid learning could hope to produce a work which all posterity would treasure. To achieve such heights demanded a life of strenuous effort, not the life of a 'poëte courtizan' immersed in social trivialities, but a life of dedication and austerity: 'qui desire vivre en la memoire de la posterité, doit comme mort en soymesmes suer & trembler maintesfois, & autant que notz poëtes courtizans boyvent, mangent & dorment à leur ayse, endurer de faim, de soif & de longues vigiles.' The Pléiade's high ideal was the poet whom Du Bellay apostrophised at the beginning of his chapter 'Du long poeme francoys':

ò toy. . . doué d'une excellente felicité de nature, instruict de tous bons Ars & Sciences, principalement naturelles & mathematiques, versé en

---

[1] Du Bellay, *Deffence*, 105.
[2] Du Bellay, *Œuvres poétiques*, vi, 132–3.

tous genres de bons aucteurs Grecz & Latins, non ignorant des parties & offices de la vie humaine, non de trop haulte condition, ou appellé au regime publiqu', non aussi abject & pauvre, non troublé d'afaires domestiques, mais en repoz & tranquilité d'esprit, acquise premierement par la magnanimité de ton couraige, puis entretenue par ta prudence & saige gouvernement, ò toy (dy-je) orné de tant de graces & perfections.[1]

Peletier, too, was much concerned with the relationship between Nature and Art. He made the familiar Renaissance point that the arts reside in Nature and are communicated to man by it: 'les Ars...sont chosɇs trop celestɇs pour déuoɇr ętrɇ atribueɇs a l'imaginacion humeinɇ. Les sémancɇs an sont an cetɇ grandeur dɇ Naturɇ: laquelɇ ocultɇmant e insansiblɇmant les à fęt antrer an l'esprit des mortęz.' But Peletier was interested in this relationship more from the point of view of the poetic product than from that of the poet himself. He distinguished between 'fond' and 'forme', equating Nature with the one, and Art with the other: 'Naturɇ donnɇ la disposicion, e commɇ unɇ matierɇ: l'Art donnɇ l'operacion, e commɇ la formɇ.' Nature provides the material and an indication of what is to be made of it; art then looks after the actual fashioning: 'Naturɇ ouurɇ lɇ chemin, e lɇ montrɇ au doę: l'Art conduit, e gardɇ dɇ sɇ déuoyer....An sommɇ, la Naturɇ bien démandɇ lɇ sécours e la mein artisanɇ: E l'Art, nɇ peut rien sans lɇ naturęl....Ensi, Naturɇ, sera difusɇ par tout son ouuragɇ: e l'Art męlè par toutɇ sa Naturɇ.' Art and Nature are thus each dependent upon the other in the production of a work of poetry; they are 'conjurateurs' who singly can achieve but little. Perhaps Nature is the more important of the two, since 'les Ars sont an notrɇ puissancɇ, pouruù qué nous eyons la faueur dɇ Naturɇ', whereas the converse is not true. Yet we must always remember that 'telɇ felicite ęt naturęlɇ: męs an partiɇ aquisitiuɇ'.[2]

We have already seen something of Ronsard's attitude towards art, namely his scorn for 'l'art aux Muses inutile' of the versifiers.[3] But later, in the *Hymne de l'Automne*, he acknow-

---

[1] Du Bellay, *Deffence*, 106, 127–8.
[2] Peletier, *op. cit.* 65, 74–5, 137, 216.   [3] Cf. p. 28.

ledged that a poet should be endowed with both fury and art
together, and was grateful that such had been his own case:

> Le jour que je fu né, le Daimon qui preside
> Aux Muses me servit en ce monde de guide...
> Me donna pour partage une fureur d'esprit,
> Et l'art de bien coucher ma verve par escrit.[1]

Similarly, art would be of great importance to the epic poet
whom the French nation awaited so eagerly: '[il] aura une
bouche sonnant plus hautement que les autres...[il] aura
l'esprit plus plein de prudence & d'advis, & les conceptions plus
divines, & les paroles plus rehaussées et recherchées, bien
assises en leur lieu par art & non à la volée.' In fact, Ronsard
seems almost to amalgamate art and divine inspiration when he
asserts of a particular narrative technique that 'tel art plus
divin que humain est particulier aux Poëtes'.[2] Already in the
Abbregé he had pointed out that the first conception of a poem
'despend d'une gentille nature d'esprit', but that the organisa-
tion of that conception depends on 'artifice, estude et labeur'.[3]
And on more than one occasion in the preface to the *Franciade*
just cited he links 'artifice' and 'un bon esprit naturel' as the
twin requirements of an epic poet.

It is obvious that Ronsard is now talking about a completely
different sort of art, or artifice, from that of the versifiers.
Indeed he even condemns them for their lack of art, and com-
plains that in the trivial poetic forms which they cultivate there
is no room for *artifice* to show itself: 'Ces versificateurs se
contentent de faire des vers sans ornement, sans grace & sans
art, & leur semble avoir beaucoup fait pour la Republique,
quand ils ont composé de la prose rimée...versificateur[s],
composeur[s] d'Epigrammes, Sonnets, Satyres, Elegies, &
autres tels menus fatras, ou l'artifice ne se peut estendre.'[4] We
are now in the 1580's, and the versifiers are not using the same
forms as they did in the 1540's, but the Pléiade's scorn for their
'episseries' is as biting as ever. Genuine art, for Ronsard and for
Du Bellay, is concealed art, the art which cannot be appreciated

[1] Ronsard, *op. cit.* XII, 46.
[2] *Preface sur la Franciade*, 1587; Ronsard, *op. cit.* XVI, 337, 345.
[3] *Ibid.* XIV, 14.   [4] *Ibid.* XVI, 336, 346.

by the ignorant. Thus in the *Responce aux injures & calomnies* Ronsard makes the point that the art of true poets does not seem to be an art at all to the versifiers:

> Les Poëtes gaillards ont artifice à part,
> Ils ont un art caché qui ne semble pas art
> Aux versificateurs, d'autant qu'il se promeine
> D'une libre contrainte, où la Muse le meine.[1]

True art is a non-art to the uninitiated; the poet is constrained to observe the requirements of the art, but paradoxically by this constraint he achieves freedom. And again in the final preface to the *Franciade* Ronsard speaks of 'le Poëte bien advisé, plein de laborieuse industrie' and of his art, more divine than human, 'lequel de prime face est caché au Lecteur, s'il n'a l'esprit bien rusé pour comprendre un tel artifice'.[2]

Ronsard did not minimise the importance of *labeur* in the writing of poetry. That, so he claimed, was why he preferred to use the ten- or eleven-syllable line rather than the alexandrine in the *Franciade*:

Nos vers communs de dix à unze syllabes...pour estre courts & pressez, contraignent les Poëtes de remascher & ruminer plus longue-ment: & telle contrainte en meditant & repensant fait le plus souvent inventer d'excellentes conceptions, riches paroles & phrases elabourées, tant vault la meditation, qui par longueur de temps les engendre en un esprit melancholique, quand la bride de la contrainte arreste & refreint la premiere course impetueuse des fureurs & monstrueuses imagina-tions de l'esprit.[3]

But *contrainte* and *longue meditation* were not all; in addition the poet must constantly correct and polish his work in the light of his critical intelligence: 'Tu seras laborieux à corriger & limer tes vers, & ne leur pardonneras non plus qu'un bon jardinier à son ante, quand il la voit chargée de branches inutiles ou de bien

---

[1] Ronsard, *op. cit.* xi, 160; cf. Du Bellay in the *Regrets*: 'L'artifice caché, c'est le vray artifice' (*Œuvres poétiques*, ii, 167). *Gaillard* in Ronsard's passage has the sense of 'industrious, skilful', as in the proverb cited by Cotgrave: 'Ouvrier gaillard cele son art—the industrious worker prostitutes not his art' (R. Cotgrave, *A Dictionarie of the French and English Tongves*, 1611).

[2] Ronsard, *op. cit.* xvi, 336–7.

[3] Ronsard, *op. cit.* xvi, 348.

peu de prouffict.'[1] Du Bellay had also drawn his readers' attention to the part played by what he called *émendation* in poetic composition, once the violence of the original 'enthusiasm' has abated: 'L'office d'elle [*émendation*] est ajouter, oter, ou muer à loysir ce que cete premiere impetuosité & ardeur d'ecrire n'avoit permis de faire. Pourtant est il necessaire... les [one's writings] remettre à part, les revoir souvent, & en la maniere des ours, à force de lecher, leur donner forme & façon de membres.'[2]

The poet must be endowed with a certain natural ability— 'la faueur dé Naturé', as Peletier called it. He must be *vertueux* so that he may be worthy to receive the gift of divine inspiration, and divine inspiration will give him access to fields of knowledge, both terrestrial and celestial, which he could not otherwise enter. But he must also be *laborieux, industrieux* in mastering the techniques of the poetic art so completely that the art contained in his work is not apparent except to true connoisseurs. This, allowing for individual differences of emphasis, is a fair summary of the Pléiade's views on the poet in his relationship to inspiration, to Valéry's 'trouvailles', and to Nature, to what is given, on the one hand, and to art, craftsmanship, the 'assez long travail' of filling in the blanks between the 'trouvailles', on the other.[3] The problems which naturally arise when one considers poets and poetry from this point of view—namely what precisely does the poet receive from Nature and from inspiration, what are the forms of art appropriate to poetic expression, how is the artificial form made to express the inspired content, how far may the poet go in altering the first inspiration for the sake of achieving a pleasing form, and so on— are all important questions, even though nowadays we may feel them to be based on a distinction, that between form and content, of rather questionable validity. The sixteenth-century theorists of poetry were well aware of the importance of these questions, and they made considerable attempts to find answers to them. Yet the problems posed by the interrelationships of inspiration,

---

[1] *Abbregé; ibid.* XIV, 6–7.   [2] Du Bellay, *Deffence*, 170–1.
[3] See Valéry's foreword, 'Au Sujet du Cimetière Marin', to Gustave Cohen, *Essai d'Explication du Cimetière Marin* (1933), in particular pp. 25 and 28.

Nature, and art were not the only ones discussed by Renaissance theorists. These three concepts were relatively stable in themselves, and it was largely a matter of determining the proper balance between known ingredients. But the current theory of poetry, and of art as a whole, was making use of another concept which was far more unstable, far more controversial than any of these three. This was the concept of imitation, which I shall discuss in the following two chapters.

[5]

IMITATION OF NATURE

Like most terms used by aestheticians, imitation has more than one meaning. The sixteenth century recognised two main contexts in which the word could be used. First it designated the relationship between the poem and a 'subject' derived in some way from things which exist, from Nature, however interpreted; and secondly it described the use made by contemporary writers of the literary models contained in the works of the ancient Greeks and Romans, and to a lesser extent in the works of the modern Italians. Poetry was widely acknowledged to be an imitation of Nature, but it was not at all clear what exactly was meant by 'Nature', nor whether the poet imitated all the time or only some of the time, nor what was the status of his imitation when he had produced it. Again, poets were urgently recommended to imitate the best works of the ancients, but there was a wide divergence of opinion as to what constituted proper imitation. Did it consist of dealing with the same subjects as the Greek and Roman poets, or of using equivalent stanza-forms to theirs, or of taking over their figures of speech, their 'ornaments', and incorporating them into one's own work, or was it rather a reliance on vague reminiscences of one's reading? We may well share the feeling of puzzlement which Count Ludovico expressed in the first book of Castiglione's *The Courtier*: 'Many will judge...and talke...of following [*della imitazione*], but they cannot doe mee to understand...wherein following consisteth. Nor why thinges taken out of Homer or any other, are so well couched in Virgill, that they appeare rather amplified than followed.'[1]

Imitation, then, is a term which did double duty in the sixteenth century. Let us deal first with the more philosophical of the two senses, that in which poetry is said to be an imitation

[1] B. Castiglione, *The Book of the Courtier*, Everyman's Library (1948), 64–5.

of Nature. This view of poetry began its literary life with Plato. Plato maintained in the *Republic* and in the *Laws* that the arts of painting, poetry, music, and sculpture are all imitations. But in the light of Platonic metaphysics, these arts are not first-degree imitations, not one step removed from reality, but two, for they are imitations of entities which are themselves imitations. The only true reality for Plato consisted of the eternal, unchanging Ideas, which are of an intellectual and non-material nature. Reflecting these eternal Ideas, and substantially different from them, is the world of the senses, the world of appearances, which is material, ever-changing, and transitory. Finally, there is a third category of manifestations, which in turn reflect the material world; these comprise shadows, the images seen in water or in mirrors, and the fine arts. In the *Republic* Socrates argues that we ought to distinguish, for instance, three sorts of beds. There is first the eternal Idea of the bed, the 'essence of the bed', formed in and by the mind of the divine creator. Then there is the material bed made by the carpenter, who copies as best he can the original Idea of the bed—which he can only dimly perceive. Lastly there is the image of the bed produced by the painter. Socrates then poses the question of what name we should give to the maker of this third bed:

I think, he said, that we may fairly designate him as the imitator of that which the others make.

Good, I said: then you call him whose product is third in the descent from nature an imitator?

Certainly, he said.

And so if the tragic poet is an imitator, he too is thrice removed from the king and from the truth; and so are all other imitators.

That appears to be so.[1]

Since they imitate appearances and not Ideas, works of art occupy a very lowly position in the hierarchy of being. They are thrice removed from the source of all Truth, all Goodness, and all Beauty.[2]

---

[1] Plato, *op. cit.* II, 471.

[2] The neo-platonists of the Renaissance, however, did not share Socrates' poor opinion of the fine arts, for they did not look at Plato's metaphysics from the same point of view as the master had done. Plato placed himself on the level of the Ideas,

Plato's definition of poetry as imitation was taken over by Aristotle: 'Epic poetry and Tragedy, as also Comedy, Dithyrambic poetry, and most flute-playing and lyre-playing, are all, viewed as a whole, modes of imitation.' Aristotle, however, was careful to cut away Plato's metaphysical superstructure, so that calling poetry an imitation was no longer unconditionally to condemn it. Works of art were still held to copy 'things' in some way, but in the Aristotelian scheme this implied nothing about their relative status on the scale of being. Imitation became that which distinguished the arts from all other forms of human activity, so that the poet's imitation was no longer made to suffer by comparison with other, nobler kinds of imitation. Aristotle went even further in the rehabilitation of poetry, for he traced poetic imitation back to man's natural tendency to imitate (apparent from earliest childhood), to his capacity for learning by imitation, and to the pleasure he finds in imitating and in learning:

to be learning something is the greatest of pleasures not only to the philosopher, but also to the rest of mankind, however small their capacity for it; the reason of the delight in seeing the picture is that one is at the same time learning—gathering the meaning of things, e.g. that the man there is so-and-so; for if one has not seen the thing before, one's pleasure will not be in the picture as an imitation of it, but will be due to the execution or colouring or some similar cause.[1]

and from these lofty heights he looked down (in both senses) on the world of appearances, which lay immeasurably far below. Material appearances mirrored the Ideas, but they could not become transformed in any way which would enable them to bridge the gap separating them from the Ideas. Ficino's neo-platonism, on the other hand, started in the world of appearances and strove to raise them up into the world of Ideas. The dynamic emphasis in this neo-platonism may have been produced by an admixture of Aristotle's conceptions of Becoming with Plato's account of Being. According to the Florentine neo-platonists the fine arts, by imitating (at however many removes) the Idea of the True, the Good, and the Beautiful, were making the first step on the ladder which leads from the ever-changing, imperfect world of appearances up into the world of perfect and immutable Being. Through the contemplation of beauty in particulars the soul is drawn upwards (the direction in which it is its nature to move), until it attains to the contemplation of the one universal beauty, which is in God. This, of course, is the metaphysical scheme underlying Pontus de Tyard's account of the successive stages through which the soul passes when it is 'ravished' by divine fury.

[1] *De Poetica*; *The Works of Aristotle*, ed. W. D. Ross (1908–52), XI, 1447*a*, 1448*b*.

Man's instinct for imitation is thus closely connected with his desire for knowledge.

But the imitations produced by the arts are not merely plain copies of whatever the artist passively observes existing in material reality. For from the perception of many particulars the mind naturally derives single, general concepts, or universals. These are the true objects both of knowledge and of art. The philosopher tries to achieve knowledge of the eternally enduring universals inherent in the particulars, which exist only at a certain moment in time. The artist, on the other hand, tries to represent particulars in such a way that the universals embodied in them are revealed more clearly than they are in 'real life'. Thus poetry is 'more philosophical and of graver import' than history, 'since its statements are of the nature rather of universals, whereas those of history are singulars'.[1] Poetry thus moves on a higher plane of truth than the mere copying of material actuality. It improves upon Nature in that it sets in sharp relief the universals inhering in Nature, while still preserving the particulars intact. This is the basis of Aristotle's argument that the poet should relate not events which have in fact taken place, which already exist *in actu*, but probable events, those which might happen, which exist *in potentia*. Thus the *vraisemblance*, the not-yet-actual, of art is of a higher order of being than the *vérité* of actual things.

This is a theory of art whose validity and value rest upon a specific metaphysical and epistemological system. If the rather subtle relationship between the particulars and the universals is misunderstood or, worse still, ignored completely, the theory loses most of its force. And this is in fact what happened. Quite quickly Aristotle's view of imitation as the process whereby the universals are made manifest in particulars was coarsened into the view that imitation should aim at achieving merely a vivid representation of particulars, in order that the hearer may be moved exactly as though he were actually present at the scene described, or 'imitated'. Certainly vivid representation was the highest sense which Horace gave to imitation (though more often, perhaps, Horace thought of imitation as the following of

---

[1] Aristotle, *op. cit.* XI, 1451*b*.

traditions established by the poets of the past), and Aristotle's literary theories were known to the Middle Ages mainly in the pale reflections of them presented in Horace's *Ars poetica*. The *De Poetica* was only resurrected and translated into Latin early in the sixteenth century (it reached the Paris presses in 1538), and only gradually did the deeper significance of the Aristotelian theory of poetry come to be more fully understood. One of the chief obstacles to a complete understanding was precisely the trivialisation of the concept of imitation to which I have just referred. Only with Ronsard can we be said to approach the genuine Aristotelian sense of the term, and even then we do not yet have the full theory of universals and particulars.

Sebillet did not describe poetry as an imitation in the Aristotelian sense at all. Du Bellay in the *Deffence* refers only once to the relationship of the poetic art with its subject-matter, Nature, but he does not use the word 'imitation' to describe that relationship: 'j'estimeroy' l'Art pouvoir exprimer la vive energie de la Nature.'[1] Imitation for Du Bellay concerns the poet's relations with other poets, not with Nature.

Peletier also considered the 'expression' of Nature to be the proper aim of poetry, and this, he claimed, could not be achieved by anyone writing in a language which was not his own: 'quand à ceux qui totalement se uouent et adonnent à une langue peregrine...il me semble qu'il ne leur est possible d'atteindre à cette naiue perfection des anciens non plus qu'à l'art d'exprimer Nature, quelque ressemblance qu'il i pretende.'[2] In the *Art Poëtique* he remarks, promisingly, 'Il faut donq qué lé Poëté soȩt imitateur dé la Naturé', but the development is disappointing: 'e qu'il ȩt ses sesons. Son etudé, séra son yuȩr: son inuancion, séra son Printans: la composicion, son Ete: sa

---

[1] Du Bellay, *Deffence*, 80.

[2] Preface to the translation of Horace's *Ars poetica*; Peletier, *op. cit.* 228–9. The word *exprimer* leaves unanswered the question of how well Aristotelian imitation of Nature by Art was understood. That Art 'expresses' Nature might mean that it makes explicit that which is implicit in Nature, and this is fairly close to Aristotle's meaning. But more probably it was taken to mean that Art represents Nature in lively (i.e. expressive, or 'speaking') pictures (cf. p. 73, n. 2). This supposition is perhaps confirmed by the other contexts in which *exprimer* occurs in Peletier's work; e.g. 'lé dù a la Comparȩson...ȩt d'eclȩrcir, exprimer e rȩpresanter les chosȩs commé si on les santoȩt' (Peletier, *op. cit.* 130).

reputacion, son Automné.' This is pretty, but not very enlightening. More interesting is the later comment that 'L'Art bien
imité la Naturé tant qu'il peùt: męs il né l'ateint jamęs'.[1] This is
a clear regression to the Platonic attitude towards imitation,
without the benefit of neo-platonic dynamism. Imitations are
merely copies, which by definition are necessarily inferior to
their originals. Art is therefore on a lower plane of reality than
Nature, and can never be anything other than the shadow-image
of Nature, imperfect and incomplete. In removing this dictum
from its context, however, we have accorded it more importance
than Peletier did himself. In actual fact he was using it as a
sentence, or apophthegm, to support his contention that one can
express oneself more perfectly in one's native tongue ('Nature')
than in a language which has been learnt ('Art').

Peletier also proposed imitation of Nature as the method to
be adopted in composing 'l'Euuré Heroïqué'. Not only should
the poem as a whole be 'lé miroęr. . .du Teatré dé cé mondé',
but the development of the action and the varying of the style
should also be modelled upon Nature. And he concluded his
treatise with the recommendation that the poet should 'con-
tampler les viués imagés des chosés dé la Naturé'.[2] The
presence here of the word 'viué' would seem to suggest that we
are dealing with the vivid representation theory rather than
with the more subtle kind of imitation which Aristotle had
described.

Pontus de Tyard felt that the arts imitate Nature in that they
make unity out of multiplicity. Nature brings together the dis-
cordant elements of the world in such a way that harmony and
beauty are produced: 'Nature a accordé comme une musique, &
temperé les diversitez, & dissemblables principes & elemens de
tel balancement, que leur discorde accordée fait ceste belle &
parfaite masse du monde.' The arts are based on the same
principle: 'Les arts, imitans nature, apparient si proprement les
dissemblables, qu'ils ne semblent estre qu'un.' But for Pontus
the dissimilars only *seem* to be one. In the case of the arts we are
dealing only with the world of appearances, and to a platonist,
even to a neo-platonist, that is an illusory, deceitful world. We

---

[1] Peletier, *op. cit.* 75, 113.   [2] Peletier, *op. cit.* 201, 221.

have to be wary of it: 'La peinture attrempe, & destrempe si discretement une proportionnée confusion de couleurs, blanche, rouge, jaune, verte, noire, que ses images contrefaits ressemblent les vrais corps, jusques à tromper le jugement des yeux.'[1] We should notice here the opposition which Pontus sets up between the images (already a derogatory term in the context of platonism) and the objects they copy. Or rather the images do not copy the 'vrais corps', they only resemble them. They are 'contrefaits', fashioned on the model of the original objects, but also counterfeit, not the real things, and made with intent to deceive. Yet in any case the 'vrais corps' have only a relative measure of truth in that they are material, not intellectual entities, and the 'jugement des yeux' is only a very limited sort of judgement, since it is a judgement of the senses, and not of the intellect.

Whatever may be the exact value given to the concept of imitation, the idea that poets imitate was fairly widespread in the sixteenth century. As Claude Fauchet was made to remark in Louis Le Caron's dialogue on poetry, 'les Poëtes ne trouuent rien, qui ne soit conuenable à leur imitation'.[2] With Ronsard, however, we come to a somewhat fuller understanding of the theory that poetry is an imitation of Nature. In the preface to the *Odes* of 1550 he asserted that 'Je suis de cette opinion que nulle Poësie se doit louer pour acomplie, si elle ne ressemble la nature'. Yet this is only secondarily a statement of Ronsard's views about the relationship between art and Nature. Primarily Ronsard is using it as an argument in support of his belief that poetry should have 'copieuse diversité'. Poetry should strive to resemble Nature because Nature displays a great profusion and variety of material, and it is in this rich diversity that its beauty consists: 'laquelle ne fut estimée belle des anciens, que pour estre inconstante, & variable en ses perfections.' Thus Ronsard expects that his own poetry, which he considers 'tant varie', will probably be 'facheuse aus oreilles de nos rimeurs, & principalement des courtizans, qui n'admirent qu'un petit

---

[1] P. de Tyard, *Le Premier Curieux*, in *The Universe of Pontus de Tyard*, 122.

[2] *Les Dialogues de Loys Le Caron* (1556), fo. 146 r°.

sonnet petrarquizé, ou quelque mignardise d'amour qui continue tousjours en son propos'.[1]

In the *Abbregé*, however, Ronsard comes nearer to the Aristotelian doctrine of imitation. Weber points out that despite the earlier translations 'la *Poétique* d'Aristote ne commence à exercer une influence en France qu'à partir de 1561 par l'intermédiaire de la poétique latine de Jules César Scaliger, qui en diffuse les principes'.[2] Certainly this seems to be the first time that we find the essentially Aristotelian concept of *vraisemblance* introduced into a discussion of poetry as imitation: 'Tout ainsi que le but de l'orateur est de persuader, ainsi celuy du Poëte est d'imiter, inventer, et representer les choses qui sont, qui peuvent estre, ou que les anciens ont estimé comme veritables.'[3] Ronsard has accepted Aristotle's contention that poetry should depict that which is possible, that which is in potentiality. But for the moment potentiality is merely one of three categories in which the material of poetic imitation, invention, and representation can be classed, along with actuality and good authority. Two years later, in the 1567 version of the *Abbregé*, Ronsard adopted the Aristotelian point of view in full. He amended the final phrase of the sentence I have just quoted to read, 'les choses qui sont, ou qui peuvent estre, vraisemblables'. Things in a state of potentiality, or likeness to the truth of actuality, are now the only materials which it is appropriate for the poet to handle.

By 1572 Ronsard is making a definite contrast between *la vérité*, i.e. actual facts, which are the proper material of History, and *le vraisemblable*, which is the proper material of Poetry:

Encore que l'Histoire en beaucoup de sortes se conforme à la Poësie, comme en vehemence de parler, harangues, descriptions de batailles, villes, fleuves, mers, montaignes, & autres semblables choses, où le Poëte ne doibt non plus que l'Orateur falsifier le vray, si est-ce quand à leur sujet ils sont aussi eslongnez l'un de l'autre que le vraysemblable est eslongné de la verité. L'Histoire reçoit seulement la chose comme elle est, ou fut, sans desguisure ny fard, & le Poëte s'arreste au vraysemblable, & à ce qui peut estre.

---

[1] Ronsard, *op. cit.* I, 47.
[2] Weber, *op. cit.* I, 124.   [3] Ronsard, *op. cit.* XIV, 13.

Thus it is Ronsard's firm conviction that 'le Poëte qui escrit les choses comme elles sont ne merite tant que celuy qui les feint & se recule le plus qu'il luy est possible de l'historien'. Ronsard repeats this point in the last preface to the *Franciade*: 'le Poëte heroïque...a pour maxime tres-necessaire en son art, de ne suivre jamais pas à pas la verité, mais la vraysemblance, & le possible: Et sur le possible & sur ce qui se peut faire, il bastit son ouvrage, laissant la veritable narration aux Historio-graphes.'[1] He is well aware that if the poet rejects 'truth' as the proper material for his work, then he is in grave danger of being convicted by the moralists of propagating untruth. The medieval Church had been only too ready to ascribe to poets, with Socrates, 'a fault which is fundamental and most serious... the fault of saying what is false',[2] and the objection was still frequently made in the sixteenth century. The result is that just as in the 1572 preface Ronsard had made it clear that even though the poet goes to 'le vraysemblable' for his subject-matter, he must be sure, like the historian, not to 'falsifier le vray', so here too he warns us that neither the historian nor the poet should ever 'mentir contre la verité de la chose'. *Le vraisemblable*, for all its not being truth, i.e. what is or has been, is nevertheless not automatically untruth, i.e. what has not been or cannot be. *Le vraisemblable* conforms to the true nature of things and depicts, or makes actual in images, or represents, what things contain in potentiality. Thus *le vraisemblable* brings out the universals in particulars. It conforms to the actual truth of the particulars and through this truth it expresses at the same time the potential truth of universals.

There is a well-ravelled semantic knot here, in which a number of different senses of 'truth' are all referred to by the same word. The basic difficulty is that, broadly speaking, the polarity of *actus* and *potentia*, which, as Owen Barfield remarks, 'had carried perhaps half the weight of the philosophical thought of the Western mind through all the centuries that elapsed between Aristotle and Aquinas',[3] was no longer felt to be a valid distinction in the sixteenth century. There were no longer

---

[1] Ronsard, *op. cit.* XVI, 3–4, 336.   [2] Plato, *op. cit.* II, 222.
[3] O. Barfield, *Saving the Appearances* (1957), 93.

two planes of existence as there had been for medieval thinkers, one the plane of actuality, the here-and-now, the other the plane of potentiality, the not-yet-manifested—but only one plane, that of the here-and-now. If a thing did not exist in the actual, material world, then it did not exist at all. Apart from God and the revealed truths of the Christian religion (which constituted a special case), there was held to be no reality, no truth, other than the actual objects of our perception. The weakening, or coarsening, of Aristotle's ideas can be seen in the movement of thought from 'potentiality' to 'possibility', where the idea of an existent (unexercised) power, which is expressed in the Latin *potentia* (though less forcefully than in the Greek δύναμις which it translates), is watered down to that of mere accidental perhaps-ness.[1] In my own account I have superimposed the terms potential and actual upon Ronsard's discussion of *vrai-semblance*. Ronsard himself talks of 'le vrai' on the one hand and 'le possible' on the other, and simply by adopting these terms he is placing himself at an immediate disadvantage. Everything which is not *le vrai* must necessarily be inferior to it, must necessarily be 'untruth'. Certainly this is so from the point of view of the platonists, and thanks to the exclusion of the potential from the plane of reality, which I have just described, it tends also to be the case for non-platonists. To say that the poet is concerned with the *vraisemblable* is to admit that poetry is a seeming truth, an appearance which is necessarily remote from, and an inaccurate image of, the ideal original, or that it is a 'non-truth', with no guarantee of correspondence with things as they really are.

Without the metaphysical framework on which it so closely depends Aristotle's imitation-theory of poetry is easily trivialised into either the representation of what is merely possible, or the imitation of picturesque details of Nature. Just how far Ronsard has allowed himself to go in these directions we may see from the following passages, both taken from the 1587 *Preface sur la Franciade*:

Or, imitant ces deux lumieres de Poësie [Virgil and Homer], fondé & appuyé sur nos vieilles Annales, j'ay basti ma *Franciade*, sans me

[1] See Barfield, *op. cit.* 136.

soucier si cela est vray ou non, ou si nos Roys sont Troyens ou
Germains, Scythes ou Arabes: si Francus est venu en France ou non:
car il y pouvoit venir, me servant du possible, & non de la verité.
C'est le faict d'un Historiographe d'esplucher toutes ces considerations,
& non aux Poëtes, qui ne cherchent que le possible.[1]

One feels that, for the moment at least, Ronsard is not over-
much concerned with the truth that is in the possible, and that in
this mood it would be only too easy for him to produce something *monstrueux*, which he normally despises so thoroughly.

His imitation of Nature is not much better:

Tu imiteras les effects de la Nature en toutes tes descriptions, suyvant
Homere. Car s'il fait bouillir de l'eau en un chaudron, tu le verras
premier fendre son bois, puis l'allumer & le soufler, puis la flame
environner la panse du chaudron tout à l'entour, & l'escume de l'eau se
blanchir & s'enfler à gros bouillons avec un grand bruit, & ainsi de
toutes les autres choses. Car en telle peinture, ou plustost imitation
de la nature consiste toute l'ame de la Poësie Heroïque.[2]

This is simply making the listener feel he is actually present at
the camp-fire, and valuable as this process may be in bringing
poetry into contact with life as it is actually lived and with
Nature as it actually exists, it is rather less than Aristotle's true
meaning. It may produce a poetry of particulars, rather than a
poetry of universals-in-particulars, and it is the latter which
Aristotle seems to have intended. The danger of the former kind
of poetry is that particulars may be gathered together and
minutely described without there being conveyed any sense of
the universal significance which lies behind them. We may be
thankful that in spite of his theorising Ronsard avoided this
danger in such a large proportion of his work.

Perhaps the above quotations represent merely a momentary
lapse on his part. It is interesting to notice that thirty years
earlier Le Caron had put into Ronsard's mouth a rather more
subtle account of the relationship between *le possible*, *le vraisemblable*, and *la vérité*: 'Le poëte...doit...comme rapportant
ses conceptions à l'vniuersité des choses discourir ce qui a peu
estre fait, ou a esté vrai-semblable, ou grandement necessaire,
& le descrire de telle perfection, que rien ne soit en lui qui n'ait

[1] Ronsard, *op. cit.* XVI, 340.   [2] *Ibid.* 345.

sa bienseance tant admirable, que la verité semble plustost
l'auouer sien que le fait mesme.'[1] Here the idea is expressed
that poetry represents a truth which is in some sense more true
than the truth of fact and of actuality, and this approaches more
closely to Aristotle's meaning than do Ronsard's own words.
Yet the concept embodied in 'ce qui a peu estre fait', the concept
of might-have-been-ness, is still, I feel, something of a falling-
away from the Aristotelian 'potentiality'.

[1] Le Caron, *op. cit.* fo. 134 r⁰.

[6]

IMITATION OF MODEL AUTHORS

The two passages from the *Preface sur la Franciade* which I quoted at the end of the previous chapter give us some indication of Ronsard's ideas about the imitation of Nature. They also introduce us to the second sense of imitation, that of imitating other authors. This kind of imitation constituted one half of the foremost problem of mid-sixteenth-century literature in France, namely how to draw the maximum benefit from the great works of the past whilst at the same time achieving self-expression for one's own *vulgaire*. Although French writers were fully aware of the importance of modelling their own work upon that of the ancient Greek and Roman authors—for that was the finest literature they knew—they were also determined to win immortality on their own account. In the sixteenth century a number of scholars and writers in France (and in other countries of Western Europe) spent a great deal of energy in persuading their more conservative fellows that the vernaculars were inherently just as capable of expressing the noblest and most profound thoughts of men as were Greek and Latin. Admittedly, in their present state the vernaculars could not compete for richness and elegance with the classical languages. But nothing more was required than that all learned men (and in this category were included poets) should write in their native tongue—which had the supreme advantage of being natural to them—rather than affect an artificial Latin. French scholars should be proud to use the French language, and should not contemn it as a crude, barbarous tongue, unfitted to express their lofty conceptions. Through being used the language would become more flexible and more elegant. And in addition it should be deliberately enriched, not only by exploiting the grea resources of the various dialects and of the technical vocabularies of the trades, but also, and perhaps more importantly, by manufacturing new words on the pattern of Greek and Latin originals. It was the duty of Frenchmen to cultivate their own language in order to make it the equal of the ancient tongues. The only reason why it was not their equal already was that in the past Frenchmen had sadly neglected their obligations. It was now high time that the fault was remedied.

This is the argument that Du Bellay is presenting in the first three or four chapters of the *Deffence*, when he pours scorn on 'la sotte arrogance & temerité d'aucuns de notre nation, qui n'etans rien moins que Grecz ou Latins, deprisent & rejetent d'un sourcil plus que stoïque toutes choses ecrites en François', and on 'l'etrange opinion d'aucuns scavans, qui pensent que nostre vulgaire soit incapable de toutes bonnes lettres & erudition'. Later he asserts that 'nostre Langue Françoyse n'est si pauvre, qu'elle ne puysse rendre fidelement ce qu'elle emprunte des autres, si infertile, qu'elle ne puysse produyre de soy quelque fruict de bonne invention, au moyen de l'industrie & diligence des cultivateurs d'icelle'.[1] In other words, anything originally written in another language can be quite adequately translated into French, and in addition works of value can quite well be written in French in the first place. Here are the twin objects of Renaissance literary endeavour: imitation, for translation is the most direct form of imitation, and invention.[2]

The general advice to study diligently the ancient authors was a traditional recommendation to would-be poets. Horace had urged study of the Greeks, especially Homer, as an essential part of one's training in the poetic art, and his successors in the Middle Ages supplemented the Greeks with the Romans, and with Virgil and Ovid in particular. In the sixteenth century, when the field of classical literature had been so greatly extended, these exhortations were made with redoubled insistency. Thus Peletier in the preface to his translation of Horace's *Ars poetica* asserted that 'c'est chose toute receue et certaine qu'homme ne sauroit rien ecrire qui lui peut demeurer à

[1] Du Bellay, *Deffence*, 14, 29.

[2] On this point see also Peletier's preface to his translation of Horace's *Ars poetica*, and Estienne Pasquier, *Choix de Lettres sur la Littérature la Langue et la Traduction*, ed. D. Thickett (1956), 75–83.

honneur, et uenir en commandation uers la posterité sans l'aide et appui des liures Grecz et Latins'.[1] Sebillet had made substantially the same point when he wrote of the poet that 'encor pourra-il grandement locupléter et l'invention et l'économie [of the poem], de la lecture et intelligence des plus nobles Pöétes Grecz et Latins'.[2] Yet neither Peletier nor Sebillet explained in detail just how this familiarity with the ancients was to be utilised by the modern poet in producing his own compositions. Translation was presumably one possible method, for Sebillet devoted a whole chapter to this genre, alleging that 'la Version ou Traduction est aujourd'huy le Pöéme plus frequent et mieus receu des estimés Pöétes et des doctes lecteurs'. In Sebillet's opinion translation was a highly praiseworthy branch of literature: 'vrayement celuy et son œuvre meritent grande louenge, qui a peu proprement et naïvement exprimer en son langage, ce qu'un autre avoit mieus escrit au sien, aprés l'avoir bien conceu en son esprit', and he proceeded to lay down a number of very sound principles which should guide the translator in his work.[3]

But the poets of the Pléiade were convinced that translation alone was not sufficient if the writer intended to win honour for 'nostre vulgaire' and immortality for himself and his work. 'Celuy donques qui voudra faire œuvre digne de prix en son vulgaire, laisse ce labeur de traduyre', Du Bellay advised.[4] Translation was too close, too servile an imitation to produce anything of lasting value as literature. True imitation involved a more complex process than that, and one which it was not at all easy to define. A series of very important chapters in Du Bellay's *Deffence* is concerned with this very problem of determining what is the nature of right imitation. The main disadvantage of translations, as far as Du Bellay was concerned, was that they could not help being partial and incomplete renderings of their originals. Each language had its own particular quality, which, since it was unique, could not be expressed perfectly in any other language. This objection Du Bellay put forward in the course of his discussion of 'eloquution', or eloquence,

---

[1] Peletier, *op. cit.* 228.   [2] Sebillet, *op. cit.* 28.
[3] *Ibid.* 187–8.   [4] Du Bellay, *Deffence*, 41–2.

dont la vertu gist aux motz propres, usitez, & non alienés du commun
usaige de parler, aux methaphores, alegories, comparaisons, simili-
tudes, energies, & tant d'autres figures & ornemens, sans les quelz
tout oraison & poëme sont nudz, manques & debiles: je ne croyray
jamais qu'on puisse bien apprendre tout cela des traducteurs, pour ce
qu'il est impossible de le rendre avecques la mesme grace dont
l'autheur en a usé: d'autant que chacune Langue a je ne scay quoy
propre seulement à elle, dont si vous efforcez exprimer le naif en une
autre Langue, observant la loy de traduyre, qui est n'espacier point
hors des limites de l'aucteur, vostre diction sera contrainte, froide,
& de mauvaise grace.[1]

This was most clearly true in the case of poetry. Translators of
poetry Du Bellay would call 'traditeurs' rather than 'traducteurs',
'veu qu'ilz trahissent ceux qu'ilz entreprennent exposer'. He
himself would avoid translating the works of poets,

à cause de ceste divinité d'invention qu'ilz ont plus que les autres, de
ceste grandeur de style, magnificence de motz, gravité de sentences,
audace & varieté de figures, & mil' autres lumieres de poësie: bref
ceste energie, & ne scay quel esprit, qui est en leurs ecriz, que les
Latins appelleroient *genius*. Toutes les quelles choses se peuvent
autant exprimer en traduisant, comme un peintre peut representer
l'ame avecques le cors de celuy qu'il entreprent tyrer apres le naturel.

By translation, then, it was impossible to reproduce the 'je ne
scay quoy' which characterised another language, and conversely it was also impossible to express in translations the
'je ne scay quoy' of one's own language in its fullest and freest
form. It was for this reason that Du Bellay described translation
as 'chose laborieuse & peu profitable, j'ose dire encor' inutile,
voyre pernicieuse à l'acroissement de [la] Langue'.[2]

Yet imitation of some sort was the proper way to enrich a
language, to make it more copious and more varied in its means
of expression. After all, it was by imitating the Greeks that the
Romans had enriched their Latin tongue. Du Bellay pictured
them 'immitant les meilleurs aucteurs Grecz, se transformant en
eux, les devorant, & apres les avoir bien digerez, les convertis-
sant en sang & nouriture, se proposant, chacun selon son
naturel & l'argument qu'il vouloit elire, le meilleur aucteur,

---

[1] Du Bellay, *Deffence*, 35–6.   [2] *Ibid.* 40–2.

dont ilz observoint diligemment toutes les plus rares & exquises vertuz, & icelles comme grephes. . .entoint & apliquoint à leur Langue'.[1] This is the famous *innutrition* metaphor to which Faguet has drawn our attention.[2] French writers must now follow the example of the Romans and 'illustrate' their native tongue by imitating the great literature of the classical past. Du Bellay affirmed quite categorically that 'sans l'immitation des Grecz & Romains nous ne pouvons donner à nostre Langue l'excellence & lumiere des autres plus fameuses', and that 'le moyen de l'enrichir & illustrer. . .est l'immitation des Grecz & Romains'. Imitation was for Du Bellay the most important aspect of the art of poetry, as opposed to those elements which originated in inspiration and in invention. 'Car il n'y a point de doute,' he writes, 'que la plus grand' part de l'artifice ne soit contenue en l'immitation, & tout ainsi que ce feut le plus louable aux Anciens de bien inventer, aussi est ce le plus utile de bien immiter, mesmes à ceux dont la Langue n'est encor' bien copieuse & riche.' But to imitate an author in the right way was not a simple matter: 'entende celuy qui voudra immiter, que ce n'est chose facile de bien suyvre les vertuz d'un bon aucteur, & quasi comme se transformer en luy, veu que la Nature mesmes aux choses qui paroissent tressemblables, n'a sceu tant faire, que par quelque notte & difference elles ne puissent estre discernées.'[3]

Imitation of this sort, whose aim was to achieve as nearly as possible identity with the author imitated, differed from translation in that by this method a poem was never taken over into the other language exactly as it stood. Smaller elements of the poem, however, such as pithy sayings, or words even, might well be borrowed and used without alteration: 'ce n'est point chose vicieuse, mais grandement louable, emprunter d'une Langue etrangere les sentences & les motz, & les approprier à la sienne.' Yet the true imitator would take care not to copy the superficial mannerisms of his model, he would not 'faire comme ceux qui, voulans aparoitre semblables à quelque grand seigneur, immiteront plus tost un petit geste & façon de faire vicieuse de

---

[1] *Ibid.* 42–3.
[2] E. Faguet, *Seizième Siècle: Études Littéraires* (undated), 214–15.
[3] Du Bellay, *Deffence*, 45–6, 90, 102.

luy'. His aim would be to render the 'vertuz & bonnes graces' of his author, and in order to do that he must feel a certain kinship with him. Du Bellay recommended that the imitator should 'sonde[r] diligemment son naturel, & se compose[r] à l'immitation de celuy dont il se sentira approcher de plus pres. Autrement son immitation ressembleroit celle du singe.'[1]

The distinction is very finely drawn between translation and imitation, both in Du Bellay's theory and in his practice. Some of the sonnets published in *L'Olive* the year after the *Deffence* appeared can hardly be regarded as anything but straight-forward translations of petrarchist and ariostan originals.[2] Du Bellay's contemporaries were quick to point out that he was not living up to his own principles of imitation. One of the first attacks came from Guillaume Des Autelz. In his *Replique aux furieuses defenses de Louis Meigret* of August 1550 he made a very sharp dig at Du Bellay on this score:

En premier lieu, ie ne suis pas de l'auis de ceux, qui ne pensent point que le François puisse faire chose digne d'immortalité de son inuen-tion, sans l'imitation d'autrui: si c'est imiter desrober vn sonnet tout entier d'Arioste, ou de Petrarque, ou vne ode d'Horace, où ilz n'ont point de proprieté, mais comme miserables emphyteotaires recon-noissent tout tenir auecques redeuance des Seigneurs directz, et ne different en rien des translateurs qu'ilz mesprisent tant, sinon en ce qu'ilz laissent ou changent ce qu'il leur plait: quelque immodeste plus librement diroit ce qu'ilz ne peuuent traduire. Mais ie pense qu'il y ha bien à dire, à considerer en quoy gist l'artifice, et la grace d'vn bon auteur, pour s'efforcer de l'ensuiure par semblable chemin: et à luy desrober du tout son inuention, ses mots, et ses sentences.[3]

If what is really a translation claims to be something more, to be a higher and more subtle form of imitation, then it is theft, alleges Des Autelz.

Du Bellay at once defended himself against this charge in the preface to the second edition of *L'Olive* with the following rather ingenuous query:

[1] Du Bellay, *Deffence*, 46–7, 106–7.
[2] See Chamard's footnotes to *L'Olive*, in *Œuvres poétiques*, I, e.g. pp. 28–9, 47–8, 52.
[3] G. Des Autelz, *Replique aux furieuses defenses de Louis Meigret* (1551 edn.), 58–9.

Si, par la lecture des bons livres, je me suis imprimé quelques traictz en la fantasie, qui apres, venant à exposer mes petites conceptions selon les occasions qui m'en sont données, me coulent beaucoup plus facilement en la plume qu'ilz ne me reviennent en la memoire, doibt on pour cest raison les appeller pieces rapportées? Encor' diray-je bien que ceulx qui ont leu les œuvres de Virgile, d'Ovide, d'Horace, de Petrarque, & beaucoup d'aultres, que j'ay leuz quelquefois assez negligemment [the nonchalance of this phrase is a fine piece of lifemanship!], trouverront qu'en mes escriptz y a beaucoup plus de naturelle invention que d'artificielle ou supersticieuse immitation.[1]

Imitation, then, was largely a matter of unconscious reminiscence; and in any case (here Du Bellay abruptly sidestepped to avoid being driven any further into this uncomfortable corner), invention was more important than imitation.

Certainly, in his theorising Du Bellay is not very clear on the issue of imitation. His pronouncements compare rather unfavourably with those, for instance, of Marcus Hieronymus Vida, the Italian whose *Poeticorum ad Franciscvm Francisci Regis Franciae Filium, Delphinum, libri III* had been published in Rome more than twenty years earlier, and yet seem strangely enough to have been practically ignored by the Pléiade.[2] Vida was most specific in his recommendations as to how the young poet should imitate the ancients. He should take over the form of a phrase, or an image, or even sometimes the words themselves; but he should always—and this is the important point— give them a new application, a new sense, so that they are taken beyond their original significance and given a further depth and richness. Vida was advocating a form of literary allusiveness

[1] Du Bellay, *Œuvre poétiques*, I, 19–20.
[2] A number of commentators allege that Vida's *art poétique* was eagerly read by the Pléiade poets. Morçay and Müller, *op. cit.* 263, speak of it as a book 'dont les hommes de la Pléiade firent grand cas'; Clements, *op. cit.* 196, claims that it was 'a handbook for the Pléiade'. Chamard is more circumspect; for him it was simply a work 'très en vogue à la Renaissance' (Du Bellay, *Œuvres poétiques*, VI, 130, n. 3). But either the statements are left unsubstantiated, or reference is made to Du Bellay's two bare mentions of Vida in the *Deffence* and in *Le Poëte Courtisan*. It seems to me that these are insufficient evidence to justify the assertions quoted. I have been unable to find further evidence which would justify them, and in fact the striking difference in quality between Pléiade accounts of the process of imitation and Vida's account leads me to suspect that the former did not read Vida with any great care.

which, combined in fitting proportion with material of one's own invention, would, so he claimed, produce work of lasting value.[1] Du Bellay was never as explicit as this, and when he discussed the details of imitation he seems always to have talked as though it were a question of taking over material from the ancients unchanged. This, of course, is precisely where his theory is open to objection. Yet occasionally in practice he was able to produce the best sort of imitation. The famous sixth sonnet of the *Antiquitez de Rome*—'Telle que dans son char la Berecynthienne...'—is a case in point.[2] Here the passage imitated, from the sixth book of the *Aeneid*, has been completely 'converti en sang & nouriture', so that it contributes its own full share of meaning to Du Bellay's poem. The Virgilian allusion provides an echo of genuinely heroic expectations modified by a bitter dramatic irony, for the glories of Rome's world-wide dominion which Anchises foretells contrast sadly with the evidence of ruin, both physical and spiritual, which Du Bellay has found in modern Rome. Yet the poem is still successful even if the reader does not recognise the exact allusion.

Succeeding writers took up the theoretical discussion of imitation at the point where Du Bellay had left off, without, however, achieving a very much clearer conception of it than he had done. In the *Art Poëtique* Peletier, like Du Bellay, recommended translation as a means of enriching one's language: 'les Traduccions quand ęlés sont bien fętés, peuuęt beaucoup anrichir unę Languę. Car lę Traducteur pourra fęrę Françoęsę unę belę locucion Latinę ou Grecquę: e aporter an sa Cite, auęc lę poęs des santancęs, la majeste des clausęs e elegancęs dę la languę etrangerę.' He also stressed the difficulty of the translator's task: 'les Traduccions...sę font par art...e sont telęmant artificielés, quę la loę an ęt antanduę dę peu dę g'ans.'[3] Yet he seems to have been considerably less critical of translations of poetry than Du Bellay. More interesting, however, is the chapter which deals specifically with imitation as such. Peletier begins by showing, with Aristotle, that to imitate is in man's nature, and concludes from this that it is right for poets to take

---

[1] Vida, *Opera* (1537), 294–7.   [2] Du Bellay, *Œuvres poétiques*, ii, 9.
[3] Peletier, *op. cit.* 106–7.

as their models the great authors of the past. Thus Homer and Virgil should be used as standards by which to judge other poets (and also oneself, of course); to this extent they should be imitated. But imitation has only a limited value: 'Il né faut pas pourtant qué lé Poëté qui doét excéler, soét imitateur jure ni perpetuél. Eins sé proposé non seulémant dé pouuoér ajouter du sien, mes ancorés de pouuoér feré mieus an plusieurs poinz.' The poet should not be content merely to imitate his model, but should add something of his own, and also improve upon the original. For the fact was that imitation was the lazy, timid man's way of writing, and no great work could be produced by it: 'Par seulé imitacion rien né sé fét grand: c'ét lé fét d'un hommé pareceus e dé peu dé keur, dé marcher tousjours aprés un autré. Celui séra tousjours dérnier, qui tousjours suiura.' One must imitate only in moderation: 'Je conseilhé a tous bons espriz, d'étré sobrés imitateurs, e fins....Car, quelé gloéré i à qué dé suiuré un chémin tout fét e tout batu.'[1] True glory consisted not in following but in pressing forward and extending the path that others have only started.

Ronsard himself had comparatively little to say on the subject of the imitation of literary models. To be sure, he urged that the young poet should familiarise himself thoroughly with the works of 'good poets': 'Tu seras studieux de la lecture des bons poëtes, & les apprendras par cœur autant que tu pourras', he advised, for 'la leçon des bons & anciens autheurs' is an important foundation for one's own invention.[2] Already in the preface to the 1550 volume of *Odes* he had acknowledged that he himself deliberately set out to imitate the 'naive douceur' of Horace and to 'suivre Pindare', and he proclaimed himself 'imitateur des poetes Grecs', in that he 'redi[t] souvent memes mots, memes sentences, & memes trais de vers'.[3] The precise method which the poet should employ in order to turn his reading to good account in his own work Ronsard did not specify. His theory of imitation—and his practice does indeed conform to it—seems to be contained in the image of the poet as a bee, passing from flower to flower and gathering sweet food

---

[1] Peletier, *op. cit.* 96 and 103.
[2] Ronsard, *op. cit.* xiv, 6.   [3] *Ibid.* i, 44–5, 55.

from each. This is the image that Ronsard used towards the end of the poem *Hylas*, when he described himself as selecting the finest passages from the books he read and then fashioning them into some work of his own:

> Mon Passerat, je resemble à l'Abeille
> Qui va cueillant tantost la fleur vermeille,
> Tantost la jaune: errant de pré en pré
> Volle en la part qui plus luy vient à gré,
> Contre l'Hyver amassant force vivres.
> Ainsy courant & feuilletant mes livres,
> J'amasse, trie & choisis le plus beau,
> Qu'en cent couleurs je peints en un tableau,
> Tantost en l'autre: & maistre en ma peinture,
> Sans me forcer j'imite la Nature.[1]

This image of the bee seems to have been a favourite one with Ronsard, for he used it on a number of other occasions besides this (in the *Epistre à Charles, Cardinal de Lorraine*, for example, and again in the *Responce aux injures & calomnies*).

What is especially interesting in this passage from *Hylas* is that here Ronsard brings together the two senses of imitation which I have been discussing in this chapter and the last. The poet takes his 'colours' from others, and yet at the same time he claims to be representing Nature. What has in fact happened is that the model authors have become a norm for the imitation of Nature, for they are believed to have already discovered the best ways of expressing Nature in poetry. Therefore by imitating the ancient literature as exactly as he can the modern poet will approach most closely to the perfect imitation of Nature. Thus, paradoxically, imitation of the ancients is in itself imitation of Nature. In fact it is in one sense the best thing that the modern poet can do, to follow in the tracks of the ancients, for their paths are the right ones. This view of imitation gives rise to the confusion which Saintsbury condemned as one of the worse points in Horace's literary doctrine. Horace, he pointed out, urged the poet to ' " be like the best of your predecessors, stick to the norm of the class, do not attempt a perhaps impossible and certainly dangerous individuality." In short the false *mimesis*—

---

[1] Ronsard, *op. cit.* xv, 252.

imitation of previous art—is mixing herself up more and more with the true *mimesis*, representation of nature.'[1]

The distance between the 'true mimesis' and the 'false mimesis' is not, however, as great as might appear at first sight. At one extreme, the extreme of true mimesis, is the Aristotelian conception of poetic imitation as a selection of elements from reality, or experience, or Nature, and a representation of them in such a way that the inner significance, the universality inherent in them, is made apparent. This theory of imitation raises poetry to a higher level of being than that of mere fact. Poetry in this light appears as an improvement upon Nature, since it goes beyond the mere particulars to express the universal meaning which they contain. I have suggested, however, that in the sixteenth century the essential premisses to Aristotle's doctrine of imitation, namely his metaphysical and epistemological theories of universals and particulars, were largely ignored. As a result the Aristotelian theory of imitation was grossly simplified, so that imitation ceased to be the significant selection of materials from Nature, and became instead representation of Nature for its own sake. Poetry, it was held, should be a speaking picture,[2] it should paint so lively a portrait of Nature that the viewer believed himself to be actually present at the scene described.

At the other extreme, the extreme of false mimesis, stand the predominantly philological interests of the early humanist editors, who stressed above all else in the ancient literatures the perfection of form and expression. For them style was the element in a literary work which was most worthy of imitation. Modern writers should strive to reproduce that noble elegance and rich variety which were characteristic of the best Greek and

---

[1] G. Saintsbury, *A History of Criticism and Literary Taste in Europe* (1949), I, 226–7.

[2] Du Bellay, for instance, *Œuvres poétiques*, v, 68, asserted that

l'escritture [of the poet]
N'est qu'une parlante peinture.

The remark is made again in Le Caron's dialogue on poetry: '...la poësie, laquelle nous appellons la viue ou parlante peinture' (Le Caron, *op. cit.* fo. 147r°). Plutarch was apparently the first to popularise this saying of Simonides (see M. H. Abrams, *The Mirror and the Lamp*, 1953, 33).

Roman authors. Obviously, this involved detailed examination of the individual excellences of the styles to be imitated, and also a consideration of what styles were proper to different subject-matters, to different speakers, to different occasions, and so on. One step more and the two kinds of mimesis, true and false, can meet. Vividness of representation—the sense in which imitation of Nature was currently interpreted—was felt to be largely a matter of style, that is, it depended very much on what types of sentence-structure and what figures of speech were used, and on the choice of vocabulary: the very matters, in short, with which the humanist imitators of the ancients were concerned. Given the belief that the ancient writers were the most skilful exponents of their art the civilised world had yet known (and this was certainly an article of literary faith among scholars during the early part of the sixteenth century), no conflict could possibly arise between the attempt to imitate Nature and the attempt to imitate the ancients. Thus in the sense in which the sixteenth century understood the words, there was nothing untoward in Ronsard's assertion that by taking 'le plus beau' from a number of different books, and composing what he borrowed into a single picture, he was imitating Nature. Nature was to be seen not through Ronsard's own eyes, but through the eyes of previous poets.

Yet the Pléiade also derived a more particular benefit from their imitation of the ancients, one which was very much in the spirit of the literary allusiveness recommended by Vida, even though they did not have as precise a theoretical conception of it as he had done. Du Bellay in his enthusiastic urging of the young poet to familiarise himself thoroughly with the works of the Greeks and Romans had written: 'Ly donques & rely premierement (ò Poëte futur), feuillette de main nocturne & journelle les exemplaires Grecz & Latins...qu'il n'y ait vers, ou n'aparoisse quelque vestige de rare & antique erudition.'[1] The last phrase is the important one, for it indicates clearly that the Pléiade wanted to give their work a definite flavour of tradition, almost as a sort of guarantee of its value. In this way, despite the fact that they were writing poetry which was 'new',

---

[1] Du Bellay, *Deffence*, 113.

they could still enjoy the security of being associated with accepted literary authority. In addition they wanted to offer their readers the pleasure of recognising the allusions to classical literature and lore. In the beginning the Pléiade set their sights high, and were extremely erudite, even to the point of being hermetic. Typical of this stage are the *Amours* which Ronsard wrote for Cassandre; for the full understanding of these sonnets the commentary by Muret which was appended to the 1553 edition was more or less indispensable.[1] Later—and this was surely as much in response to the pressure of their public as a reflection of their own poetic needs—they became more 'open', and began to rely almost entirely on allusions which they knew would be clear to their readers, thus giving them the pleasure of recognising the familiar, rather than demanding from them the effort of understanding the abstruse. In Du Bellay's *Regrets*, for instance, the allusions are for the most part to well-known stories; the Ulysses sonnets are obvious examples of this, and in other sonnets there appear such familiar figures as Prometheus, Achilles and his lance, Orpheus, Theseus, Pylades and Orestes, and so on.[2] By the time we come to Ronsard's *Sonets pour Helene* in 1578 the poet is relying on a single main allusion, to Helen of Troy. Yet this still has the striking effect of adding an extra dimension to the feelings which Ronsard portrays.[3]

A discussion of the extent to which a poet, or any other writer, is entitled to assume that his readers will be familiar with works of literature other than the one which is now in front of them would be irrelevant to the present subject. I will merely point out that, while language is in an obvious sense something which we all share, the individual words cannot help but carry with them echoes of their use on other occasions, and that these 'other occasions' are necessarily different for each one of us. When a writer deliberately alludes to other literature, he is referring his readers to an experience of words which he hopes

[1] See the footnotes in Ronsard, *op. cit.* IV, 5–179 *pass.*

[2] Du Bellay, *Œuvres poétiques*, II, 60, 62, 68, 76–7, 102, 106, 156–7.

[3] An excellent account of what effects a Renaissance poet could and could not achieve by means of allusion to the classical literatures is given by Weber in his discussion of the theme of Ulysses and the storm as it appears in Du Bellay's *Regrets* (Weber, *op. cit.* I, 434–8).

they will have more or less in common, in order that he may take advantage of and control the echoes of those words. By relying on this shared experience he can indicate how his own words are to be taken and what associations are appropriate to them. Allusiveness is thus a valuable literary technique, and we must acknowledge that the Pléiade were able to exploit it with a fair measure of success, despite the unsatisfactory nature of their theorising about it.

[7]

'NAÏVETÉ' IN POETRY

Successfully to imitate the ancients was, however, only one half of the poet's task, and the half belonging to artifice at that. The poet was also required to be spontaneous and 'natural' in the presentation of his material. This again was what constituted, in part at least, the excellence of the ancients. Their poetry was *naïf*, it was simple (to all outward appearances), natural, not unnecessarily elaborate or artificial. We must of course distinguish here between the *naïveté* which had been a characteristic of the 'divine' poets, and the *naïveté* which could be achieved by merely human poets. The poetry of the former had been '[une] nayve escripture' because those men were endowed by Nature with the ability to give forth their inspiration in the form of song as soon as they received it, without having to seek the aid of art. The human poets, however, received their inspiration in a fragmented form, and they were not able immediately and 'naturally' to transform it into poetry. If they were to achieve *naïveté* at all, they could do so only by means of all the long and careful work involved in the processes of art; their ideal would be '[l']art caché qui ne semble pas art'.[1] That is why Ronsard writes, towards the beginning of the 1572 preface to the *Franciade*, that 'j'ay patronné mon œuvre... plustost sur la naive facilité d'Homere que sur la curieuse diligence de Virgile'.[2] Strictly speaking, this was an impossible ambition, since the truly Homeric *naïveté* was now forever beyond the reach of men. But a 'human' approximation to it had been achieved in the past, and it was the intention of the Pléiade to achieve it once more in their own works. Ronsard himself, for instance, acknowledged his imitation in the *Odes* of what he described as the 'naive douceur' of Horace.[3]

[1] See p. 48.
[2] Ronsard, *op. cit.* XVI, 5. The word *curieux* is used here, as often in the sixteenth century, with the sense of *soigneux*.　　　　　　　[3] *Ibid.* I, 44.

There was another sense in which poetry had to be *naïf*, one which we can best express by saying that the poet was expected to be faithful to his own nature, to his own individuality as a poet. This sense of *naïveté* is important in sixteenth-century literary criticism and theorising, for it indicates a growing awareness of the value of what we would nowadays call 'originality', the value of what one has found or made for oneself, as opposed to the traditional, to what one has received from other poets. Clearly, these ideas can be linked with the notion—already fully established in sixteenth-century poetics—of the poet as an inspired being, favoured at intervals with visitations from the Muses. Indeed, it is possible to regard the sixteenth-century conception of *naïveté* as a prefiguration, in some measure, of that group of ideas about the poet and his work which eventually, in the late eighteenth and early nineteenth centuries, crystallised into the Romantic theory of 'original genius'.[1]

---

[1] The term 'originality' was not itself brought into use until after the sixteenth century. Originality helped to introduce connotations of 'hitherto non-existent, newly created, produced for the first time ever', which were not present in the earlier concept of *naïveté*. A person who has originality is one who is capable of originating or creating new things. *Naïveté*, on the other hand, refers only to the ability to represent Nature in a spontaneous, 'natural' way. In the sixteenth century *original* (in its adjectival sense) and *originalité* hardly existed. *Original* was normally used as a noun, and was the antonym of *copie*. Bernard Palissy, for instance, points out that 'une pourtraiture qui aura esté contrefaite à l'exemple d'une autre pourtraiture, la contrefacture ou pourtraiture qui aura esté faite, ne sera jamais tant estimée comme l'original sur lequel on aura prins le pourtrait' (*Les Œuvres de maistre Bernard Palissy*, ed. B. Fillon and L. Audiat, 1888, I, 78). And Amyot in his translation of Plutarch's *Lives* speaks of 'Andronicus le Rodien', who, 'aiant par ses mains recouuré les originaux [of Aristotle's works], les meit en lumiere & escriuit les summaires que nous auons maintenant' (J. Amyot, *Les Vies des Hommes Illustres Grecs & Romains...Translatees de Grec en Francois*, 1559, fo. 328 rº). Yet this early meaning was quite soon extended to something like our modern one, for in the second half of the seventeenth century the ultra-purist Bouhours reported that the use of *original* in the expressions 'esprit original' and 'auteurs originaux' had become quite common. Bouhours himself, however, questioned the elegance of this usage (D. Bouhours, *Remarques nouvelles sur la langue françoise*, 1682, 3me éd., 121–2). Yet Fontenelle in 1728 was writing of Newton's *Principia* that 'Tout le monde fut frappé de l'esprit original qui brille dans l'Ouvrage, de cet esprit créateur' (B. de Fontenelle, *Éloge de M. le Chevalier Neuton*, 1728, 8), and by the time Voltaire wrote his *Remarques sur les Pensées de M. Pascal* in 1738, the usage seems to have become fully established: 'Il y a très-peu d'hommes vraiment originaux, presque tous se gouvernent, pensent et sentent par l'influence de la coutume et de l'éducation' (*Œuvres complètes de Voltaire*, 1818, XX, 238).

In the Renaissance, however, the word *naïf* did not have quite
these high ambitions. Most simply, to describe something as
naïf was to indicate that it was connate with its possessor,
'apporté en naissant', or 'natif'. Thus Montaigne writes of
'joueurs de comedie': 'vous les voyez sur l'eschaffaut faire une
mine de Duc et d'Empereur; mais tantost apres, les voyla
devenuz valets et crocheteurs miserables, qui est leur nayfve et
originelle condition.'[1] And Ronsard, enthusing over some
particularly fine passages in the *Aeneid*, refers his reader to
'mille autres telles ecstatiques descriptions, que tu liras en un si
divin aucteur, lesquelles te feront Poëte, encores que tu fusses
un rocher, t'imprimeront des verves, & t'irriteront les naifves
et naturelles scintilles de l'ame que des la naissance tu as
receues, t'inclinans plus tost à ce mestier qu'à cestuy-la'.[2]

Indeed *naïf* was more or less equivalent to *naturel*, but with
the added suggestions of genuineness and 'rightness', in the
sense of particular appropriateness. Cotgrave's synonyms are
(*inter alia*) 'naturall, right, proper, true, no way counterfeit'.
Light is interestingly cast upon the connotations of the word by
the company it keeps in the following passage by Rabelais,
where he is complaining about Dolet's unauthorised edition of
Gargantua and *Pantagruel*, and urges us not to take 'la faulse
monnoye pour la bonne, et la forme fardée pour la nayve, et la
bastarde et adulterine edition du present œuvre pour la legitime
et naturelle'.[3]

As a noun, *le naïf* signified the true and natural character of
something, free of all adornment and affectation. Ronsard was
almost punning when he used the word to describe the sculptor
at his work:

> L'un grave en bronze & dans le marbre à force
> Veut le naif de Nature imiter.[4]

The sculptor imitates Nature as it really is, he represents its
true self and also its 'naturalness', that is the spontaneous and
direct expression of its own self. We have already met this
conception of the unique and natural character of a thing in

---

[1] Montaigne, *op. cit.* I, 291.   [2] Ronsard, *op. cit.* XVI, 333.
[3] Quoted in Morçay & Müller, *op. cit.* 143.
[4] Ronsard, *op. cit.* II, 3.

connection with the 'defence' of the vernaculars. Du Bellay had pointed out the impossibility of expressing 'le naif' of one language in another without seeming 'contraint, froid, & de mauvaise grace'.[1] This 'naif' was the 'je ne scay quoy', the unique quality which distinguished one language from another. Therefore, he urged, let us seek to express 'le naif' of our own tongue—'sa nayfve proprieté si copieuse & belle', as he described it in the second preface to *L'Olive*[2]—instead of wasting our energies on the impossible task of trying to render the distinctive qualities of Greek or Latin into French.

Peletier was also of the opinion that the neo-Latin poets would be no more successful than the mere translators in attaining to *naïveté*, for they were still using a language which was not native or natural to them; thus they could never express themselves with complete naturalness, nor could they express Nature itself in the way that the ancients had been able to do: 'Quand à ceux qui totalement se uouent et adonnent à une langue peregrine...il me semble qu'il ne leur est possible d'atteindre à cette naiue perfection des anciens non plus qu'à l'art d'exprimer Nature.'[3] Peletier returned to this point in his own *Art Poëtique*: 'Lé Poëté pourra il jamęs ętré parfęt, auquel ęt denieé la perfeccion du langagé auquel il doet ecriré, qui n'ęt qué l'un des moindrés instrumans dé son metier? Car il ęt certein, qu'uné Langué aquisitiué n'antré jamęs si auant an l'antandémant commé la natiué.' All the more reason, then, to write in French, since 'les Musés vienét apresant pour habiter an Francé: męs non point pour trouuer des hótés, vetuz d'acoutrémans peregrins...elés veulét lé naif e la puréte qué produit la tęrré ou elés vienét habiter'.[4]

Barthélemy Aneau in the *Quintil Horatien* is even prepared to question the value of being versed in the ancient languages at all, on the grounds that they might well inhibit the poet's *naïveté*: 'sans lesquelles langues n'ont pas laissé aucuns d'estre tresbons poëtes & paradventure plus naïfz, que les Grecaniseurs, Latiniseurs & Italianiseurs en Françoys.'[5] And Pontus de Tyard

---

[1] See p. 66.   [2] Du Bellay, *Œuvres poétiques*, I, 15.
[3] Preface to the translation of Horace's *Ars poetica*; Peletier, *op. cit.* 228–9.
[4] Peletier, *op. cit.* 113–15.   [5] Quoted in Du Bellay, *Deffence*, 102, n. 1.

was making a similar point in the *Second Curieux* when he asserted that 'chacun exprime en sa langue naturelle plus naifvement les imaginations de son esprit, qu'en un langage aprins, tant prompt & familier le puisse-il avoir'.[1]

Naïveté, therefore, was the (unique) essence of a language, which could be exploited to the full only by native speakers of that language, and it was also a quality of the best poetry— naturalness, spontaneousness, and rightness. The *naïveté* of poetry was held to derive not only from the nature and the naturalness of the language, but also from the nature and the naturalness, the 'naive grace', of the poet himself. This is one of the considerations which lie behind the repeated demands by the theorists of the Pléiade that the poet should be 'de bonne nature', and that he should have 'cé qué la naturé peut donner'.[2] If poetry is to be *naïf*, if it is to express the nature of the poet, we must be sure that the poet's nature is worthy to be expressed, and sufficiently virtuous to be a suitable lodging for the Muses. We have already noted Ronsard's insistence that the poet shall have 'une ame... bonne, saincte, & vertueuse', that he shall be 'de bonne nature, non meschant, renfrogné, ne chagrin; mais animé d'un gentil esprit', and that he shall allow nothing to enter his mind which is not 'sur-humain & divin'.[3] From the pure soul will flow poetry that is true to Nature in all senses of the word.[4] It will represent the richness and diversity of the phenomena of the natural world, it will have the simplicity and unaffectedness of the 'natural' man, it will be the sound product of a properly functioning human intelligence, and not the unreal, pretentious fancies of a disordered mind which seeks to raise itself out of its rightful place in the universal scheme of things.

These are the points that Ronsard made in the last preface to the *Franciade*, when he presented to the reader his ideal of 'une naifve & naturelle poësie':

Tu enrichiras ton Poëme par varietez prises de la Nature, sans extravaguer comme un frenetique. Car pour vouloir trop eviter, & du

[1] P. de Tyard, *Le Second Curieux*, 128.

[2] Ronsard, *op. cit.* XIV, 5; Peletier, *op. cit.* 97.

[3] See p. 26.

[4] Cf. Peletier, *op. cit.* 97: 'L'ofiçé d'un Poëté ét dé donner...a toutés ['choses'] leur naturel e a leur naturel toutés.'

tout te bannir du parler vulgaire, si tu veux voler sans consideration
par le travers des nues, & faire des grotesques, Chimeres & monstres,
& non une naifve & naturelle poësie, tu seras imitateur d'Ixion, qui
engendra des Phantosmes au lieu de legitimes & naturels enfans.[1]

Du Bellay too was implicitly making a call for poetry to be *naïf*
when he maintained in the second preface to *L'Olive* that 'en
mes escriptz y a beaucoup plus de naturelle invention que
d'artificielle ou supersticieuse immitation'.[2] Poetry should be
natural, that is simple and unartificial, and it should also be one's
own, the independent product, or 'invention', of one's own
nature—not something acquired from others and given out
again at second hand.

This stress upon *naïveté* in poetry forms part of the Pléiade's
whole concern with the true nature of poetic activity. The
major effort of the theorists of the Pléiade was directed towards
determining the proper interrelationships, within the context of
poetic activity, between the various elements I have been discussing in the preceding chapters—between the technical pre-
cepts and artifices of the 'art' of poetry and the rapture of
divine fury, between acquired rules and natural, spontaneous
expression, between the first inspiration and the subsequent
labeur of correction, between imitation of Nature and imitation
of the ancients, and, most important of all, between imitation
of other writers and the poet's own independent work. It was
not enough simply to follow others, certainly not to follow
earlier writers in one's own language, and it was not enough
even to enrich one's language by following exactly (i.e. by
translating) the best works written in other languages. Imitation had to be of such a kind that the poet could yet be *naïf*, true
to his own natural language and true to his own natural self.

Yet to decide how this was to be achieved presented a number
of difficulties. In Ronsard's preface to the 1550 volume of *Odes*
we have one attempt at a solution. Here the poet asserted his
complete independence of his fellow-countrymen, in as much as
he was using the ode-form. He claimed proudly to be 'le
premier auteur Lirique François'; but at the same time he

---

[1] Ronsard, *op. cit.* XVI, 334.   [2] Du Bellay, *Œuvres poétiques*, I, 20.

acknowledged that he had been guided by 'les etrangers', and principally by Horace and Pindar. He begins by suggesting that if praise is due to those who carefully and dutifully follow in the steps of others, then we should laud all the more highly the poet who treads an unknown path: 'Si les hommes tant des siecles passés que du nostre, ont merité quelque louange pour avoir piqué diligentement apres les traces de ceus qui courant par la carriere de leurs inventions, ont de bien loin franchi la borne: combien davantage doit on vanter le coureur, qui galopant librement par les campaignes Attiques, & Romaines osa tracer un sentier inconnu pour aller à l'immortalité?' Among earlier French poets Ronsard has found no one whom he deems worthy of imitation, and so he has turned away from them:

Je me suis eloigné d'eus, prenant stile apart, sens apart, euvre apart, ne desirant avoir rien de commun avecq' une si monstrueuse erreur. Donques m'acheminant par un sentier inconnu...je puis bien dire (& certes sans vanterie) ce que lui-meme [Horace] modestement temoigne de lui,

> Libera per vacuum posui vestigia princeps,
> Non aliena meo pressi pede.[1]

Such was Ronsard's claim to be a pioneer in French poetry. In the same year Guillaume Des Autelz had also urged French poets in this direction in his *Replique aux furieuses defenses de Louis Meigret*:

Je voudrois moy, que nostre Poëte François fust parfaitement familier aux bonnes lettres, et aux bons auteurs principalement ceux qu'il voudroit imiter: i'entens quand il voudroit choisir vn genre de poëme desia vsité: mais s'il auoit plus hault courage, estant instruict de toute bonne doctrine, qui l'empeschera de faire sortir de la France, chose que ny l'arrogante Grece, ny la curieuse Romme, ny la studieuse Italie n'auoient encores veu? De qui ont esté imitateus les Grecs? qui mesme interroguez sus ce iamais ne respondoient rien: les Latins (combien que leur plus grand honneur, comme de gens ne s'osans fier en leur force, soit en l'imitation) n'ont ilz pas trouué vn genre nouueau et inusité de poeme, c'estasauoir la nouuelle satyre? mais les Italiens gens d'esprit plus aigu, ont reietté les inuentions estrangeres pour adherer aux leurs propres....Donq puis que nous admirons les

[1] Ronsard, *op. cit.* I, 43–5.

Sonnets, les Chans, les Triomphes de Petrarque, où nous ne pouuons dire qu'il ayt specialement imité aucun auteur Grec ny Latin: Pourquoy desperons nous d'en faire autant ou plus?[1]

A few years later, in the *Regrets*, Du Bellay was also to disclaim imitation and to avow his intention simply to be himself:

> Je ne veulx feuilleter les exemplaires Grecs,
> Je ne veulx retracer les beaux traicts d'un Horace,
> Et moins veulx-je imiter d'un Petrarque la grace,
> Ou la voix d'un Ronsard, pour chanter mes Regrets
> . . .
> Je me contenteray de simplement escrire
> Ce que la passion seulement me fait dire,
> Sans rechercher ailleurs plus graves argumens.[2]

And we have already noted Peletier's warning about the limited value of imitation, and his recommendation to 'ajouter du sien'.[3]

Yet in all their discussions of this nature there is one very important term which sixteenth-century theorists of poetry used perhaps more frequently than any other. That is the word 'invention', which has appeared a number of times in the passages I have quoted in the course of the last few pages. When the poet invents, he is doing the exact opposite of imitating other authors—even though he may have trained his own powers of invention precisely by imitating them. For invention is the most personal, the most individual, the most *naïf* part of the process of making poetry. This is surely one of the reasons why *invention* is a concept upon which the theorists of the Pléiade laid considerable emphasis. 'Le principal poinct est l'invention', asserted Ronsard, and went on: 'laquelle vient tant de la bonne nature que par la leçon des bons & anciens autheurs.' We are already familiar with the concepts of 'la bonne nature' and of 'la leçon des bons & anciens autheurs'. We have yet to examine the additional concept of invention. A few pages further on from this passage Ronsard introduces another term, familiar enough in modern discussions of poetry,

---

[1] Des Autelz, *op. cit.* 59–60.
[2] Du Bellay, *Œuvres poétiques*, II, 55.   [3] See p. 71.

but which we have hardly come across at all so far in our consideration of sixteenth-century theorising—namely 'imagination'. 'L'invention', he states, 'n'est autre chose que le bon naturel de [l']imagination.'[1] These, as I have already pointed out, are to my mind two of the difficult concepts of sixteenth-century poetic theory. Since the difficulty for the twentieth-century reader consists almost entirely in the fact that sixteenth-century connotations of the words differ markedly from his own, I propose to devote the bulk of what remains to a detailed study of the semantic areas occupied by *invention* and *imagination* at that time.

[1] Ronsard, *op. cit.* xiv, 5–6, 12–13.

[8]

INVENTION AND IMAGINATION:
THE SIXTEENTH CENTURY AND AFTER

Nowadays the term 'invention' has almost disappeared from the vocabulary of poetic theory (though it still tends to be used quite frequently *à propos* of novels and novelists, theirs being the inventive, fictive art *par excellence*). A modern critic does not normally talk about the 'inventions' of a poet, nor about the 'invention' displayed in his poetry, unless perhaps he is talking about the invention of new poetic forms. Yet in earlier ages invention had a much wider significance than this. Certainly the modern critic does not use the word in connection with poetry written from the time of the Romantics onwards, and he uses it of earlier poetry only when he is very deliberately employing the contemporary theoretical terminology.[1] Yet, as is indicated by the mention of the Romantics, this is a comparatively recent development. The concept of invention, of finding the material of art in Nature, had always been closely connected with the 'classical' theory that all art is in some sense an imitation of Nature. It was only in the late eighteenth and early nineteenth centuries, with the triumph of the 'romantic' view of art as an independent product of the human mind, that invention was superseded by the concepts of genius, originality, and creative imagination.[2]

Yet invention had been a central term in literary doctrines throughout the entire period from Cicero in the first century B.C.

[1] M. H. Abrams, for instance, in *The Mirror and the Lamp* discusses the 'psychological criticism, in the tradition of Hobbes and Hume...that was dominant prior to Coleridge' in two chapters entitled 'The Psychology of Literary Invention'.

[2] The indices to the two volumes of Wellek's *History of Modern Criticism* provide some testimony of the virtual extinction of the term 'invention' in the course of the romantic revolution in literature. The index to the first volume, which deals with 'The Later 18th Century', contains a dozen references to Invention. In the index to the second volume, however, which is concerned with 'The Romantic Age', Invention does not appear at all.

right up to the beginnings of Romanticism at the end of the eighteenth century. Voltaire, for example, still used the word quite frequently in his discussions of literature. One instance occurs in the *Essai sur la poësie épique,* where he contrasts the talent of Addison with the genius of Shakespeare: 'Le grand sens de l'auteur de Caton, et ses talens qui en ont fait un secrétaire d'état, n'ont pu le placer à côté de Shakespeare. Tel est le privilège du génie d'invention, il se fait une route où personne n'a marché avant lui.'[1] Another example of the use of *invention* is to be found in the article *Génie* in the *Questions sur l'Encyclopédie,* where the word appears again in association with talent and genius:

Ce terme de *génie* semble devoir désigner non pas indistinctement les grands talens, mais ceux dans lesquels il entre de l'invention. C'est surtout cette invention qui paraissait un don des dieux, cet *ingenium, quasi ingenitum,* une espèce d'inspiration divine. Or, un artiste, quelque parfait qu'il soit dans son genre, s'il n'a point d'invention, s'il n'est point original, n'est point réputé génie; il ne passera pour avoir été inspiré que par les artistes ses prédécesseurs, quand même il les surpasserait.[2]

In the late 1780's André Chénier wrote a poem dealing specifically with poetic theory, and he entitled it *L'Invention.* Chénier, however, in keeping with his recommendation to imitate the writers of antiquity, was being rather self-consciously archaic in his choice of terminology.[3] But the term was still current enough in 1797 for Rivarol to use it in an important passage in his treatise *De l'Homme intellectuel et moral.* He is defining genius, and explains that 'le génie des idées est le comble de l'esprit: le génie des expressions est le comble du talent...le génie est donc ce qui engendre et enfante: c'est, en un mot, le don de l'invention'.[4]

In these passages invention appears in the very pre-romantic setting of genius engendering original works, and if nowadays we do ever talk of literary invention, this is probably the sort of

[1] Voltaire, *op. cit.* vii, 280.   [2] Voltaire, *op. cit.* xxv, 212.

[3] 'Sur des pensers nouveaux faisons des vers antiques', he wrote, 'Et sans suivre leurs pas imit[ons] leur exemple' (A. Chénier, *Œuvres complètes,* ed. G. Walter, 1950, 127, 130).

[4] A. Rivarol, *Œuvres complètes* (1808), i, 125.

context in which we most readily place it. But it is quite the wrong context to take when considering invention in the sixteenth century. To be sure, the idea that invention is an inborn quality which the gods bestow upon those destined to become poets was current long before Voltaire. Sebillet expressed exactly the same idea in 1548, and we may be sure that he was by no means the first to do so. The link between invention and the individual visitations of divine inspiration was also of long standing, although perhaps it had not previously been quite as close as Voltaire made it. Again Sebillet, albeit somewhat apologetically, referred to poetry in one breath both as divine inspiration and as art: 'me soit permis de nommer art ce que plus proprement j'appelleroie divine inspiration.' And for Sebillet, as for all other theorists of poetry in the sixteenth century, invention was the first and most important part of the *art poétique*.[1]

There is, however, a very significant difference between the eighteenth century's concept of literary invention and that of the sixteenth century. Voltaire quite clearly regarded invention as a process of *making*, for he says that the poet of genius is one who makes for himself a completely new path, a path which has never before existed, into a region where no man has yet trodden. Ronsard, on the other hand, had thought of invention as being a kind of *finding*. In the preface to his first volume of *Odes*, he encouraged the would-be poet to follow his example and to 'tracer un sentier inconnu pour aller à l'immortalité'.[2] In sixteenth-century French *tracer* had the sense of 'to tread' or 'to follow', rather than 'to mark out' (which is the usual meaning in modern French), so that in this phrase Ronsard is implying that the poet's path is already there, it is already made, and needs only to be discovered.[3] Immortality will be achieved

---

[1] Sebillet, *op. cit.* 21. [2] Ronsard, *op. cit.* I, 43.
[3] Compare the entries under *tracer* in the dictionaries of Cotgrave and of Littré (*Dictionnaire de la Langue Française*, 1878). Ronsard offers another good example of the use of the word in the *Derniers Vers*:

> Le chemin deserté que Iesuchrist trouua...
> C'est vn chemin facheux borné de peu d'espace,
> Tracé de peu de gens....

(*Œuvres de P. de Ronsard*, ed. Ch. Marty-Laveaux, 1887–93, VI, 302.)

by the poet who first seeks out and explores the as yet unknown path. This is a fundamental alteration in the metaphor and its meaning which we should not ignore. In a later chapter I will discuss from a more general standpoint the significance of the sixteenth-century view of invention in the field of epistemology.[1]

In Ronsard's view, as we have seen, poetry was a form of imitation, and as such it involved the invention, or finding out, of appropriate material, of which the poet then made a copy in words. During the course of the eighteenth century, however, poetry came to be regarded not so much as a straightforward imitation of external Nature, in part or in whole, but rather as a rearrangement of the internal thought-elements to form new wholes. This change in the conception of the nature of poetry, which laid new emphasis upon the free activity of the poet's mind, was obviously related to the eighteenth century's pre-occupation with the problems of epistemology and with the investigation of the complex processes of human thought. The most widely held psycho-epistemological theories were usually variations on the view that ideas, or images, constituted the basic units of thought, and that these were either derived from sensations, or formed part of the mind's innate furniture. Within this general framework literary theorists concentrated especially on the question of images. They were encouraged in this by the long rhetorical tradition, stemming from Cicero and Quintilian, which had emphasised the importance to literature of images, in as much as by their vividness they moved the hearer just as though he were actually present at the scene described.[2] One result of this concern was that the mental faculty which handled images, namely the imagination, came to have a greatly increased importance in theories of literature from the eighteenth century onwards.

Eighteenth-century psychologists distinguished two kinds of imagination. One was closely associated with the memory, and this Condillac, for instance, defined as 'l'opération qui réveille les perceptions en l'absence des objets'. The other kind of imagination was a power which made novel combinations of ideas, 'une opération, qui, en réveillant les idées, en fait à notre gré des combinaisons toujours nouvelles'.[1] The two kinds of imagination were commonly referred to as passive and active. These are the terms which Voltaire used in the *Encyclopédie* article: 'Il y a deux sortes d'imagination: l'une, qui consiste à retenir une simple impression des objets; l'autre, qui arrange ces images reçues et les combine en mille manières. La première a été appelée imagination passive; la seconde active.'[2] In the *Logique* of 1780 Condillac explained how this process worked in the case of the poet:

Lorsque, par la réflexion, on a remarqué les qualités par où les objets diffèrent, on peut, par la même réflexion, rassembler dans un seul les qualités qui sont séparées dans plusieurs. C'est ainsi qu'un poète se fait, par exemple, l'idée d'un héros qui n'a jamais existé. Alors les idées qu'on se fait sont des images qui n'ont de réalité que dans l'esprit; et la réflexion qui fait ces images prend le nom d'*imagination*.[3]

Voltaire considered imagination to be responsible for almost everything in the composition of a poem: 'C'est par elle qu'un poëte crée ses personnages, leur donne des caractères, des passions, invente sa fable, en présente l'exposition, en redouble le nœud, en prépare le dénoument.'[4]

Nowadays poetic imagination is normally thought of as *de facto* creative imagination. A typical modern exposition is that of A. R. Chisholm, glossing Mallarmé: 'Poetic imagination is a series of creative acts, corresponding to the incessant Creation which furnishes the starting-point of poetic activity, namely the external phenomena out of which ideas and images are made.'[5] The poet is a creator, one who brings into existence poems, images, meanings—the results of his creation can have many different names. But the poet has not always been a creator. In the sixteenth century, and probably for some time afterwards as well, he was simply a maker, a *facteur*.[6] The dis-

---

[1] E. B. de Condillac, *Œuvres philosophiques*, ed. G. Le Roy (1947–51), I, 28.

[2] Voltaire, *op. cit.* xxv, 492.   [3] Condillac, *op. cit.* II, 385.

[4] Voltaire, *op. cit.* xxv, 494. For a detailed account of the part played by imagination in poetry according to Voltaire, see the complete article on *Imagination* in the *Encyclopédie*.

[5] A. R. Chisholm, 'Mallarmé: "Victorieusement fui le suicide beau..."', in *French Studies*, xiv, 2 (1960), 156.

[6] See E. Huguet, *Dictionnaire de la langue française du seizième siècle* (1925 in progress), under *facteur*.

tinction here between creating and making is an important one, I think. The reasons for its importance are well summarised by Barfield in his book *History in English Words*:

'Creare' was one of those old Latin words which had been impregnated through the Septuagint and the Vulgate with Hebraic and Christian associations; its constant use in ecclesiastical Latin had saturated it with the special meaning of *creating*, in divine fashion, out of nothing, as opposed to merely human *making*, which signified the rearrangement of matter already created, or the imitation of 'creatures'. The application of such a word to human activities seems to mark a pronounced change in our attitude towards ourselves.[1]

It marks also, I would suggest, a change in our attitude towards God as Creator, and towards the process of creation itself. In the sixteenth century divine creation was something mysterious and quite beyond the realm of man's comprehension. Later, however, God was gradually reduced to the status of a skilled craftsman, a watchmaker who had constructed and set in motion the cosmic clock in such a way that it would continue to function of its own accord without any further prompting on His part. If this was all that creation was, then there was nothing so inconceivable or mysterious about it. In that case men were creators too. Thus, in proportion as God's creative activity came to be 'explained' in terms of self-perpetuating mechanical laws, the general concept of creative activity tended to be released from its hitherto exclusive associations with the divinity. At the same time men's view of the nature of their own human activity of 'making' began to approximate more and more to the idea of creative activity. Creation was still a creation *ex nihilo*; but now man was capable of this as well as God. In the sphere of mental activity, this change in attitude affected particularly the faculty of imagination, since imagination was after all the 'making' power of the mind. The imagination made images; gradually it began to create them instead.

Voltaire, however, had been careful to point out that the active imagination cannot truly be called creative: 'L'imagination active...rapproche plusieurs objets distants, elle sépare ceux qui se mêlent, les compose et les change; elle semble créer

---

[1] O. Barfield, *History in English Words* (1956 edn.), 202, his italics.

quand elle ne fait qu'arranger.'[1] The imagination does not produce any new images, any new basic units of thought. It merely takes those which are already present in the mind, separates them from other units of thought with which they were associated in the original sensations, and joins them together in new ways.

Yet thirty-odd years later Rivarol, while making the same distinction between 'imagination passive' and 'imagination active', had no hesitation in qualifying the second as *créatrice*.[2] Half a century after Rivarol Baudelaire was able in his review of the Salon of 1859 to endow imagination, which was for him 'la reine des facultés', with the power of creation in a very real and solemn sense: 'elle a créé le monde (on peut bien dire cela, je crois, même dans un sens religieux).... Elle décompose toute la création, et, avec les matériaux amassés et disposés suivant des règles dont on ne peut trouver l'origine que dans le plus profond de l'âme, elle crée un monde nouveau, elle produit la sensation du neuf.' And a little further on he quotes in support of his own position (and translates) the passage from Mrs Catherine Crowe's *The Night Side of Nature* in which she discusses 'the *constructive* imagination'—Baudelaire renders this by 'l'imagination *créatrice*', and the italics are his—and defines it as 'a much higher function [than "fancy"]... which, in as much as man is made in the likeness of God, bears a distant relation to that sublime power by which the Creator projects, creates, and upholds his universe'. The imagination, in Baudelaire's view, does not simply produce images or copies of external reality, but feeds on it, digests it, and transforms it into something new: 'Tout l'univers visible... est une espèce de pâture que l'imagination doit digérer et transformer.'[3] Invention, either in the by now outmoded sense of finding, or in the pejorative senses of making up and fabricating (Littré's 'action de supposer, de controuver, mensonge') which tended to attach themselves more and more closely to the word during the eighteenth and nineteenth centuries, would be quite out of place

---

[1] Voltaire, *op. cit.* xxv, 494.   [2] Rivarol, *op. cit.* i, 115.
[3] Ch. Baudelaire, *Œuvres complètes*, ed. Y.-G. Le Dantec (1956), 773, 776, 780.

in contexts such as these.[1] Invention did still have a favourable sense at this time, but that tended to be confined almost exclusively to the sphere of contriving useful mechanical devices, and it would thus have been just as inappropriate here as the other two senses.

The Baudelairean type of creative imagination is one with which we are quite familiar today in the context of literary theories. In England the concept was firmly established in the theoretical vocabulary by Coleridge. Yet in France, according to Margaret Gilman, 'the more exalted conception [of imagination] never seems to have taken root'.[2] The same writer also maintained that the word *imagination* has occurred remarkably seldom in French poetic theory and criticism since Baudelaire.[3] It may well be, as she suggested, that imagination is being superseded by some other concept or group of concepts, in the same way that imagination and creativeness superseded invention.

Yet a certain concept of imagination had already been incorporated into literary theory long before August Wilhelm Schlegel, Schelling, and Coleridge transformed it into the creative faculty *par excellence*. Since imagination was regarded in rather different lights in the sixteenth century and in the nineteenth, it is valuable, I think, to consider in what ways the two concepts of imagination do differ. Logan Pearsall Smith once wrote that 'it would be vain to seek in the psychology and criticism of that time [the Renaissance] any clear definition of the meaning of the term *imagination*'.[4] Despite this warning I shall attempt in subsequent chapters to examine the meaning of the term 'imagination' in the Renaissance, not indeed in order to produce a clear definition (terms which can be clearly defined are rarely as interesting as those which cannot), but rather in order to describe the areas of thought within which the word then

---

[1] Voltaire, however, could still associate invention with imagination: 'Ce don de nature ["génie"] est imagination d'invention dans les arts, dans l'ordonnance d'un tableau, dans celle d'un poëme' (*op. cit.* xxv, 494).

[2] M. Gilman, *Baudelaire the Critic* (1943), 124.

[3] M. Gilman, 'From Imagination to Immediacy in French Poetry', in *Romanic Review*, xxxix, i (1948), 30.

[4] L. P. Smith, *Words and Idioms* (1933), 74.

operated. Similarly, I shall attempt to illuminate, even if I do not necessarily delimit, the areas of meaning which were covered by the term 'invention'. Although this is a word very commonly found in sixteenth-century writings on literary theory, it has been so seldom used in literary contexts during the past hundred and fifty years or more that it would seem to be a necessary task to re-examine in some detail the full meaning of invention in earlier ages. It is to be hoped that from this extended study of the two concepts and others we shall be able to obtain some insight into the problems with which Pléiade thought was faced in its attempt to achieve a definitive defence of poetry.

INVENTION, RHETORIC,
AND POETRY

In modern English we tend to confine the meaning of invention to 'newly discovered contrivance or device', or 'discovery of a new contrivance or device', and in this we are usually thinking of mechanical contrivances. The first two definitions of the modern verb 'invent' in Chambers's *Twentieth Century Dictionary* (1959 edn.) are as follows: 'to devise or contrive: to design for the first time', and the first meaning of 'invention' according to the same dictionary is 'contrivance'. The examples of usage given in the *Nouveau Petit Larousse Illustré* (1949 edn.) make it quite clear that the same is also true for the modern French word *invention*. *Invention* means first and foremost 'faculté, action d'inventer', and the example given of the word's use in this sense is 'l'invention du paratonnerre est due à Franklin'. The same emphasis on gadgetry appears in the entry under *inventer*. *Inventer* signifies 'imaginer le premier quelque chose de nouveau', and as an example of usage in this meaning we are offered the following sentence: 'Gutenberg inventa l'imprimerie.' The presence of the words *faculté* and *imaginer* in these two definitions might lead us to expect that there will be some stress upon invention as a mental process. In fact, as the examples show, the mental aspects of invention tend to be left on one side. 'L'invention du paratonnerre' is *action*, not *faculté*, and *imaginer* is hardly a good synonym for *inventer* in the sentence quoted. Invention seems to be mainly concerned with (mechanical) devices. The word can indeed be used to refer to a mental activity, but then it takes on the highly derogatory implications of untruth, intention to deceive, and so on. An invention is 'a deceit', a 'mensonge inventé pour tromper', to invent is equivalent to 'supposer, controuver, imaginer une

chose qu'on donne comme réelle'. 'Inventer une fausseté'—
the noun follows quite naturally after such a verb.[1]

Let us, however, trace the word back some way into the past,
and consider its semantic condition when it appeared in classical
Latin as the verb *invenio*, with its noun *inventio*, and again later
in sixteenth-century France, which is the portion of its history
that interests us particularly in this study. As the form of the
word indicates, *invenio* originally meant 'I come into *(in/venio)*,
I come to, come upon, light upon', and so 'I find'.[2] In the beginning, then, the word could signify a simple physical finding.
Lewis & Short provide us with a convenient instance of this use
from the schoolboy's deskside book, Caesar's *De Bello Gallico*:
'naves reliquas paratas ad navigandum atque omnibus rebus
instructas invenit.'[3] This sense of invention as a physical,
material finding has in fact been retained in modern French, but
only in connection with the finding of religious relics, and in
particular with the finding of the True Cross in the fourth
century by St Helena, mother of Constantine the Great. 'The
Invention of the Holy Cross' is a well-established festival in the
calendar of the Catholic Church. But in classical Latin *invenio*
was also used to refer to a mental finding or coming upon.
Again we can illustrate this from Caesar: 'inveniebat ex
captivis, Sabim flumen ab castris suis non amplius milia
passuum decem abesse.'[4] Here *inveniebat* signifies more than a
finding by accident; it is rather a finding *out*, a seeking and discovering, an ascertaining or learning. The idea of a deliberate
intention and effort of the mind has been introduced.

This brings us to a very important sense of *invenio* and its
derivatives in classical Latin, that which Lewis & Short refer to
as the 'orator's faculty of invention', and which they exemplify

[1] See the dictionaries cited, and also Littré under *inventer* and *invention*. Since
the above was first written it has come to my notice that the newly re-edited *Petit
Larousse* (1959) does in fact omit the word *faculté* from its definition of *invention*.
Furthermore *imaginer* appears only under the pejorative senses of *inventer*; the
first meaning is given as 'trouver, créer le premier quelque chose de nouveau'.
The difference between *trouver* and *créer* indicates accurately the distance which the
concept of invention has travelled in the course of its semantic history. The entry
also forms an interesting comment on the concept of creation.

[2] Cf. C. T. Lewis & C. Short, *A Latin Dictionary* (1933), under *invenio*.

[3] Caesar, *De Bello Gallico*, Loeb edn. (1946), 238.   [4] *Ibid.* 110.

in Quintilian's phrase, 'tanta in eo inveniendi copia et eloquendi facultas'.[1] In the classical manuals of rhetoric, such as those of Cicero and Quintilian, invention appears as one of the five divisions or parts of the rhetorical art. The five parts are Invention, Disposition (i.e. proper arrangement of the material of the speech), Elocution (or, as we would say, eloquence), Memory, and Delivery (which are self-explanatory). Of these, Invention is the first in order of use, and also the first in order of importance. It is, in Cicero's words, 'princeps omnium partium'.[2] It is also, according to the pseudo-Ciceronian *Rhetorica ad Herennium*, the most difficult to master: 'De oratoris officiis quinque inventio et prima et difficillima est.'[3]

Cicero gives us a neat definition of invention in general, regarded as a power of the mind, when in the first Tusculan disputation he speaks of 'illa vis quae investigat occulta, quae inventio atque cogitatio dicitur'.[4] Invention is the investigating power of the mind, that which seeks out the hidden causes and reasons of things: it is the power which undertakes the seeking-out of matters which are not ready to hand. *Invenire* is no longer something passive, no longer the event of happening upon a thing by accident; now it is something active, something deliberate and intentional, not so much a simple finding as a finding by seeking. It is to be noted also that in contrast with modern usage there is no suggestion that the invention produces untruths; if anything, the reverse is the case, for it is concerned with finding out about things which are themselves 'true', in the sense that they already exist.

When we come to invention in the art of oratory, however, where a case has to be argued and an audience to be persuaded, the definition is slightly modified: 'Inventio est excogitatio rerum verarum aut veri similium quae causam probabilem reddant.'[5] The writer, in accordance with the practice of all special pleaders, does not stipulate that the power of invention shall always be exercised upon what is true; orators often invent

[1] Quintilian, *op. cit.* IV, 40.
[2] Cicero, *De Inventione*, Loeb edn. (1949), 20.
[3] *Ad C. Herennium de Ratione Dicendi*, Loeb edn. (1954), 58.
[4] Cicero, *Tusculan Disputations*, Loeb edn. (1950), 72.
[5] *Ad Herennium*, 7.

matters which are only *like* the truth, for their concern is to make a case seem likely and probable, likely and probable enough, that is, to convince their hearers. As long as this view of invention is supported by an Aristotelian or pseudo-Aristotelian theory of verisimilitude, no harm will be done. If it is not so supported, however, invention is in great danger of being accused of producing merely non-truth, that is to say lies. This is what did in fact happen in the course of time, with the result that today, as we have noted, invention retains only its 'bad' senses when it is thought of as an 'excogitatio'.[1]

Elsewhere, in the *Topica*, Cicero explains more fully what he means by rhetorical invention. Every kind of systematic argumentation, he says, has two parts, one concerned with the invention of arguments, the other with the judgement of their validity: 'Cum omnis ratio diligens disserendi duas habeat partis, unam inveniendi alteram iudicandi...'. We should notice that invention is here considered to form part of an orderly system of thought. Cicero is at pains to stress this point. He describes Aristotle's *Topica* as 'disciplinam inveniendorum argumentorum, ut sine ullo errore ad ea ratione et via perveniremus, ab Aristotele inventam'. *Disciplina, ratio*—these are important words, for they underline the orderliness and the rational method which are held to be the bases of rhetorical invention. Later Cicero explains the advantage of being systematic in these matters: 'Ut igitur earum rerum quae absconditae sunt demonstrato et notato loco facilis inventio est, sic, cum pervestigare argumentum aliquod volumus, locos nosse debemus; sic enim appellatae ab Aristotele sunt eae quasi sedes, e quibus argumenta promuntur.'[2] Invention, or finding, is simpler if the paths leading to the things hidden, to the *occulta*, are clearly marked. Obviously it is a good thing if the mind does not have to waste time and effort on any aimless, undisciplined meandering, but can follow a rationally organised method of invention. This is provided by the so-called 'places', the headings or categories under which any matter may be discussed. I shall

---

[1] For an account of what I call here the 'Aristotelian theory of verisimilitude' and of the equation of verisimilitude with untruth, see pp. 53 ff.

[2] Cicero, *Topica*, Loeb edn. (1949), 382, 386.

examine this system of 'places', or 'topics', in a later chapter.[1]
What happens is that the orator simply runs through the established list of 'places', and picks out those which are appropriate
to his present subject: 'Faciet igitur hic noster orator...ut,
quoniam loci certi traduntur, percurrat omnis, utatur aptis,
generatim dicat, ex quo emanant etiam qui communes appel-
lantur loci.'[2] The objects of invention are still hidden and they
still have to be sought out, but the way to them is now fully
signposted.

I have discussed the concept of invention as it is found in the
rhetorics of Cicero and Quintilian rather than trace it back
through Aristotle to Plato and beyond, simply because the
Ciceronian and Quintilianian scheme of rhetoric was that known
and used by the Middle Ages and the Renaissance. George of
Trebizond's *Rhetoricorum libri V*, for instance, published in the
second half of the fifteenth century, are closely modelled on
Cicero's rhetorical treatises and lay especial emphasis on the
places of invention. And if we look at Pierre Fabri's *Grant et
vray art de pleine Rhetorique*, which had six editions between 1521
and 1544, we shall find a fairly exact reproduction of the classical
definition of rhetoric: 'Rethorique donc est...l'art pour suader
ou dissuader en sa matiere, et la disposer par parties, et
chascune aorner par beaux termes, et la retenir par ordre en
memore, et bien la pronuncer', together with a basically
Ciceronian, though somewhat embellished, account of invention: 'Combien que plusieurs conditions soient requises a vng
facteur, la principalle c'est l'inuention, car sans inuention subtille
plaisante et nouuelle, le facteur ne sçaura deduire sa matiere
plaisante ou utille, et est principalle et necessaire pour trouuer
ses raisons, prouuer ses faitz, pour suader et dissuader.'[3] The
remainder of the treatise is similarly based upon the Ciceronian
tradition of rhetoric.

I have already pointed out that classical antiquity did not
make any clear distinction between rhetoric and poetry, and that
this tendency persisted throughout the Middle Ages and well on

---

[1] See pp. 127 ff.
[2] Cicero, *Orator*, Loeb edn. (1952), 340.
[3] P. Fabri, *Le grant et vray art de pleine Rhetorique*, ed. A. Héron (1889), I, 15, 18.

into the Renaissance.[1] As Edmond Faral noted, the sources for the doctrine embodied in the treatises on poetry of the twelfth and thirteenth centuries which he studies are to be found mainly in Cicero's *De Inventione,* the *Rhetorica ad Herennium,* and Horace's *Epistula ad Pisones.*[2] Since the influence of rhetorical theory was predominant in the field of poetics, it was quite natural that the technical terms of rhetoric should come to be applied to poetry also. To the field of poetic theory was transferred the fivefold division of Invention, Disposition, Elocution, Memory, and Delivery (though usually the last two sections were omitted, as being proper only to the orator in his activity of speech-making). Ronsard, for instance, still entitled three sections of the *Abbregé* of 1565 'De l'Invention', 'De la Disposition', and 'De l'Elocution'. And just as the importance of invention had been heavily stressed in the rhetorical treatises, so it was in poetic theory also. Invention for Ronsard was 'mere de toutes choses', and he urged the would-be poet to ensure that he had 'les conceptions hautes, grandes, belles, & non trainantes à terre. Car le principal poinct est l'invention.'[3] The phrase is by now quite familiar to us.

Sebillet had expressed much the same idea fifteen years before this in his *Art Poétique Françoys.* Chapter III in the first book of that treatise is entitled 'De l'invention, premiere partie de Pöésie', and there the point is at once made that 'le fondement...du Pöéme ou carme, est l'invention'. A few lines later Sebillet emphasises the importance to the poet of a schooling in rhetorical theory, and points to the special position of invention: 'Supposé donc que celuy qui se veut exercer en la Pöésie françoise, soit autrement bien versé et entendu en toutes les parties de Rhétorique, il doit toutesfois estre plus expert en l'invention, comme celle qu'il ha particulièrement plus commune avec l'Orateur: et de laquéle résulte toute l'elegance de son pöéme.' Sebillet, however, does more than claim that invention is simply the first part of the art of poetry. Invention itself,

[1] See pp. 17 ff.

[2] E. Faral, *Les Arts poétiques du XIIe et du XIIIe siècle: Recherches et Documents sur la Technique Littéraire du Moyen Age* (1924), 99.

[3] Ronsard, *Œuvres complètes,* xiv, 5–6, 13. As I suggested earlier, the Pléiade had reasons of their own for emphasising this point (see pp. 84–5).

he says, depends in the first place upon a certain quality of the mind, and this is a gift from God: 'Le premier point de l'invention se prend de la subtilité et sagacité de l'esprit, laquéle si Dieu a déniée à l'homme, pour neant se travaillera-il de dire ou faire en despit de Minerve.' Yet there is more to invention than the possession of this gift of 'subtilité et sagacité de l'esprit'. Invention, in Sebillet's view, is also to some extent a question of art, and this art the poet must seek in the works of the philosophers and of the rhetoricians: 'Le surplus de l'invention qui consiste en l'art, prendra le pöéte des Philosophes et Rheteurs qui en ont escrit livres propres et particuliers.' Excellent training for the invention is also provided by study of other authors: 'L'invention, et le jugement compris soubz elle se conferment et enrichissent par la lecture des bons et classiques pöétes françois...encor pourra-il [the poet] grandement locupléter et l'invention et l'économie, de la lecture et intelligence des plus nobles Pöétes Grecz et Latins.'[1]

Of course Sebillet was not the only theorist to link invention with particular qualities of the poet's mind, and to recommend the imitation of model authors as a method of improving one's own powers of invention. Peletier was saying something very similar in the preface to his translation of Horace's *Ars poetica* when he referred to 'l'inuention et disposition, lesquelles uertuz ne s'acquierent que par long usage et continuation de lire'.[2] Later, in his own work on poetic theory, Peletier made the familiar division of the *art poétique* into 'Inuancion, Disposicion e Elocucion'; he also laid the obligatory stress upon the pre-eminence of invention: 'Elé ét repandué par tout lé Poémé, commé lé sang par lé cors dé l'animal: dé sorté qu'élé sé peùt apéler la vié ou l'amé du Poémé.' Once invention had given to the poem its life and its soul, then beauty and dignity could be added to it by the process of disposition, which consisted of 'uné ordonnancé e ag'ansémant des chosés inuanteés'.[3]

Meanwhile Du Bellay, writing not specifically about poetry but about 'bien dire' in general, makes the full rhetorical division into five parts, 'l'invention, l'eloquution, la disposition, la memoire & la pronuntiation'. He too pointed out the prime

---

[1] Sebillet, *op. cit.* 21–8.   [2] Peletier, *op. cit.* 227–8.   [3] *Ibid.* 88.

importance of invention: 'cete copie & richesse d'invention, premiere & principale partie du harnoys de l'orateur'.[1] Du Bellay was discussing orators here, but he also used the rhetorical terminology, including 'invention', in his discussions of poetry without any sense of strangeness. The terminology of rhetoric occurred naturally in the context of poetic theorising, for it was the tool which sixteenth-century theorists and critics had inherited from their classical and medieval predecessors.

Yet by considering *invention* merely as a technical term of rhetorical theory, I have appreciably narrowed the area of meaning which the word normally covered in the sixteenth century. Let us now look at some of the more general connotations which the concept of invention possessed for sixteenth-century writers and readers in France.

[1] Du Bellay, *Deffence*, 32–4.

$\begin{bmatrix} 10 \end{bmatrix}$

INVENTION IN
THE SIXTEENTH CENTURY

I do not propose to draw up a list of all the occasions on which
the term 'invention' is used by sixteenth-century French
writers. For my present purposes it will be sufficient if I am
able to give a representative selection which will illustrate the
main areas of meaning covered by the word at that time,
emphasising in particular those connotations which have been
discarded since the sixteenth century. The illustrations of usage
which I shall cite are taken from a period overlapping the
theoretical activity of the Pléiade by a number of years on both
sides. For convenience's sake many examples will be taken from
Montaigne's *Essais*, even though he happened to be writing
some twenty or twenty-five years after Ronsard produced the
Abbregé de l'art poëtique françois. Montaigne touches on such a
large variety of topics in so many spheres of human knowledge
and interest that his work is an unparalleled source of information concerning sixteenth-century semantic usage. Since one oɪ
Montaigne's main interests was thinking about the operations
of the human mind, I shall draw upon him freely for illustrations
of the use of *invention* in that context, which is very important
for our examination of the place of invention in poetic theory.
Montaigne, however, is at no point attempting to evolve any
novel theory of invention, nor to dispute the currently held view
of invention. He accepts the terms and concepts which are used
to discuss the operations of the mind exactly as he finds them.
His purpose is simply to question the value and the reliance
placed upon those operations; the validity of the concepts themselves as effective tools for thinking about the way in which the
mind works he takes for granted. Thus no revolution in the concept of invention divides Montaigne from Ronsard and the
Pléiade. In talking of *invention* Montaigne is quite obviously

dealing with a group of ideas which he considers to be familiar
to his readers, and which requires no special elaboration on his
part. Therefore Montaigne never deliberately sets out to
explain what he means by *invention*; there was no need for him
to do so.[1] Apart from Montaigne, I shall lay under contribution
especially those authors who write about literature and literary
theory.

It is difficult to determine the exact point in its history at
which the word 'invention' took on the familiar modern sense
of 'contrivance', or 'discovery, production of contrivances'.
There are indications, however, which may encourage us to
think that it was used with this sense at an earlier date than the
dictionaries seem to suggest.[2] For by 1535 Rabelais, re-
counting the events of Gargantua's infancy, could write that
'à un an et dix moys...par le conseil des medecins on com-
mença le porter, et fut faicte une belle charrette à boeufs par
l'invention de Jehan Denyan'.[3] And in a later chapter, when he
described 'comment Gargantua employoit le temps, quand l'air
estoit pluvieux', he noted that among other things the giant and
Ponocrates 'aprenoient et consideroient l'industrie et l'invention des mestiers'.[4] Fifteen years later Du Bellay was using the
word in very much the same context when he advised the
would-be poet to familiarise himself with the works of craftsmen: 'Encores te veux-je advertir de hanter quelquesfois, non
seulement les scavans, mais aussi toutes sortes d'ouvriers &
gens mecaniques, comme mariniers, fondeurs, peintres, en-
graveurs & autres, scavoir leurs inventions, les noms des

---

[1] The same will be true in the case of *imagination* (see ch. 14 and 15).

[2] Neither F. Godefroy (*Dictionnaire de l'ancienne langue française et de tous ses
dialectes du IXe au XVe siècle*, 1937–8) nor E. Huguet (*Dictionnaire de la langue
française du seizième siècle*) lists *invention* with this sense. Godefroy deliberately
omits words and meanings which have been retained in modern French, whilst
Huguet, although claiming—with some diffidence, it must be admitted—to note
earlier instances of 'retained' words and meanings than have been recorded by
other lexicographers, does not do this in the case of *invention*. The earliest citations
in Littré are taken from Montaigne. (In English, the first example quoted by the
O.E.D. is dated 1531.)

[3] *Œuvres de François Rabelais*, ed. A. Lefranc (1912 in progress), I, 78.

[4] Rabelais, *op. cit.* II, 238. A further instance is to be found when Picrochole's
'gouverneurs' advise him that his castle 'nous semble assez forte, tant par nature
que par les rampars faictz à vostre invention' (*ibid.* II, 292).

matieres, des outilz, & les termes usitez en leurs ars & metiers, pour tyrer de la ces belles comparaisons & vives descriptions de toutes choses.'[1]

Certainly the usage was already well established by Montaigne's time, for he speaks quite readily of '[le] miracle de l'invention de nostre artillerie', or of '[la] dangereuse invention des gehenes', 'l'invention...de quelque tissu de cotton', and so on.[2] More specifically, Montaigne connects the term *invention* with the production of engines of war. He refers to Julius Caesar's 'inventions à bastir ponts et engins', or observes of the 'engins que Dionysius inventa à Siracuse à tirer gros traits massifs et des pierres d'horrible grandeur' that they 'representoient de bien pres nos inventions'.[3] But Montaigne, like Rabelais before him, used the word also for a device in a rather more general sense. For instance, the means which Cecinna adopted in order to get news back to his family when he was away from home is described as an *invention*. So too is the sumptuary law enforced by Zeleucus in an attempt to 'corrige[r] ...les meurs corrumpues des Locriens'.[4] Rabelais had used the word of a particular 'maniere de prognosticquer': 'l'invention admirable de Pythagoras, lequel, par le nombre *par* ou *impar* des syllables d'un chascun nom propre, exposoit de quel cousté estoient les humains boyteulx, bossus, goutteux, paralytiques, pleuritiques, et aultres telz malefices en nature',[5] and also of the abuses practised by 'papelars et faulx prophetes, qui ont par constitutions humaines et inventions depravées envenimé tout le monde'.[6]

These examples are in fact quite close in meaning to the modern 'invention du paratonnerre'. But what if we stand in the sixteenth century and look in the other direction, back towards classical Latin? What of Cicero's 'vis quae investigat occulta', the active power of the mind which seeks out things hidden? We do not have to look very far to find the word used in this Ciceronian context. There is something of it (with a specifically

---

[1] Du Bellay, *Deffence*, 172.
[2] Montaigne, *op. cit.* II, 40, and III, 136, 139.
[3] *Ibid.* I, 72, 324.   [4] *Ibid.* II, 402, and I, 300.
[5] Rabelais, *Le Quart Livre*, ed. R. Marichal (1947), 166.
[6] Rabelais, *Œuvres*, IV, 296-7.

literary flavour) in Rabelais's expression of gratitude to the Cardinal de Chastillon at the head of the *Quart Livre*: 'par vostre exhortation tant honorable, m'avez donné et couraige et invention.'[1] But, in a more precise sense, Montaigne refers on one occasion to the mental power of invention in terms of the ability to produce instances in support of one's argument; he notes that 'apres que nostre invention a esté eschaufée, elle descouvre un nombre infiny de pareils exemples' in illustration of the point we are trying to make.[2] This, of course, is the invention of the rhetoricians, the first part of the orator's art, which demands familiarity with the 'places', the 'topics' of argument.

We have already seen that Sebillet links the rhetorico-poetic process of invention with certain qualities or aptitudes of the mind, with its 'subtilité' and its 'sagacité'.[3] Montaigne provides us with a number of rather more detailed examples of this usage. The fact that he has a poor memory, he remarks, explains why his 'parler' is 'court', for 'le magasin de la memoire est volontiers plus fourny de matiere que n'est celuy de l'invention'.[4] Montaigne is pointing out that it is easier simply to repeat what one has already heard other people say—'les inventions et opinions estrangieres'—than to work out one's own thoughts. But I think it is important to notice that he seems to regard both memory *and* invention as storehouses. This takes us back once more to the etymological meaning of invention as a 'coming-into'. The concept behind *invention* is not so much that of producing something entirely new, *ex nihilo* as it were, but rather that of coming into and revealing for the first time something which already exists, and which we can already speak of as being in some sense *'emmagasiné'*.

On another occasion, when Montaigne is describing himself as a young man, he asserts that 'l'esprit, je l'avois lent, et qui n'alloit qu'autant qu'on le menoit; l'apprehension, tardive; l'invention, lasche; et apres tout, un incroiable defaut de memoire'. Here again it is the capacity for active, productive thought which he is referring to, the faculty which goes beyond mere *apprehension*. In Montaigne's view, however, the power of

[1] Rabelais, *Le Quart Livre*, 10. [2] Montaigne, *op. cit.* I, 347.
[3] See p. 101. [4] Montaigne, *op. cit.* I, 31.

invention is not something on whose possession man should congratulate himself. This, of course, is in keeping with his emphasis upon the unstable and erratic nature of the human mind: 'Certes, c'est un subject merveilleusement vain, divers et ondoyant que l'homme.' It is therefore no surprise, when we read of our ideas of God, that 'Non seulement fausses, mais impies aussi et injurieuses sont celles que l'homme a forgé de son invention'. And it is Montaigne's conviction that man has enough 'incommoditez necessaires' in this world without his invention adding any more to this tally.[1]

The word *invention*, however, was used not only for the mental power itself, not only for the faculty of invention, but also for the product of that faculty's activity. We have seen something of this use already, when we noted Montaigne's phrase 'les inventions et opinions estrangieres'. A person's *inventions* are his thoughts or ideas, but more specifically those which he has produced on his own account, and not merely taken over from other people. A good illustration of this sense of *invention* is to be found in Pierre de la Primaudaye's *Academie françoise*, in a passage where the author is discussing the way in which men's mental powers depend, as far as the material they handle is concerned, upon things existing outside the mind in the external world, and thus ultimately upon God: 'L'homme ne peut penser, imaginer, ne faire aucune chose, de laquelle il n'ait quelque commencement & quelque fondement en nature & és œuvres de Dieu, desquelles il prend puis apres ses inventions.'[2] The beginning of all thought, of all imagination, and of all making is in Nature, that is, in the works of God. For us the important point here is that La Primaudaye calls the results of thinking, imagining, and making all by the same name. They are all inventions, for they are all, in a sense, 'findings' in Nature. There is confirmation for this interpretation of the word in a passage occurring a few

[1] Montaigne, *op. cit.* I, 5, 189; II, 206, and III, 104.

[2] P. de la Primaudaye, *L'Academie françoise* (1615 edn.), 105. La Primaudaye is another author writing a few years after the main theoretical activity of the Pléiade (the first two volumes of the *Academie* appeared in 1577 and 1580, respectively) whose work provides useful examples of sixteenth-century semantic usage. Large sections of his book are encyclopaedic in character, and are more concerned with furnishing a sort of *état présent* of the knowledge of the time than with attempting to extend it in any way.

chapters later, when La Primaudaye states that 'la fin de tout discours de l'entendement pretend ou à l'invention, ou conclusion de la chose qu'on cerche'.[1] Here, quite clearly, *invention* has retained much of its etymological connotation.

Montaigne frequently uses *invention* in this sense of 'idea, thought'. He describes the most fundamental metaphysical ideas of the philosophers as *inventions*, without there being any necessarily disparaging overtones in the word itself (although they are sometimes present in the total context in which the word occurs). However little credence, he says in the *Apologie de Raimond Sebond*, we may be inclined to give to the 'Atomes ...Idées et...Nombres' of Epicurus, Plato, and Pythagoras, respectively, yet these philosophers did 'promen[er] leur ame à des inventions qui eussent au moins une plaisante et subtile apparence', and they should receive due praise for that. The various theories of the nature of the universe are so many *inventions*, that is to say ideas or conceptions made by man. Again, Epicurus spoke on his deathbed of the pleasures of the soul which his own philosophical *inventions* afforded him. Aristotle's conception of the human soul was, in Montaigne's opinion, 'une autant froide invention que nulle autre', and altogether the philosophers 'se sont esbatus de la raison comme d'un instrument vain et frivole, mettant en avant toutes sortes d'inventions et de fantasies'.[2] Here it is evident that *invention* is becoming a derogatory term in its own right, and is steadily moving towards the modern senses of *mensonge*, 'deceit', and so on.

In these examples the word *invention* has stood for idea or thought in a very general sense. But there was also a more specific use of the word, which has particular relevance to the field of literature. Montaigne—and he is certainly not alone in this—uses *invention* to mean 'idea' especially when it is a question of an idea expressed in some written form. Thus, in his account of the way in which he uses *emprunts* from other authors he claims that 'es raisons et inventions que je transplante en mon solage et confons aux miennes, j'ay à escient ommis parfois d'en marquer l'autheur'. In another passage he points out that

[1] La Primaudaye, *op. cit.* 124.   [2] Montaigne, *op. cit.* II, 204, 242, 246, 334.

one should not rely entirely on 'les armes d'autruy'; it is a bad thing to 'conduire son dessein...sous les inventions anciennes rappiecées par cy par la'. Or again, he observes that it is a simple matter to admire in general terms a page of Virgil, but that it requires a genuine critical sense to be able to show in detail, 'poisant les mots, les phrases, les inventions, une apres l'autre', how that page actually achieves its excellence.[1]

Here we have been dealing with the 'ideas' of other writers; but Montaigne also refers to his own ideas in the same terms. He states, for instance, that he does not spend time polishing up his *inventions* once he has set them down: '[je] laisse...courir mes inventions ainsi foibles et basses, comme je les ay produictes, sans en replastrer et recoudre les defauts.'[2] Du Bellay was using the word *invention* in a similar context when he marvelled at 'l'etrange opinion d'aucuns scavans, qui pensent que nostre vulgaire soit incapable de toutes bonnes lettres & erudition: comme si une invention pour le Languaige seulement devoit estre jugée bonne ou mauvaise'.[3] The *invention* is quite clearly the content, the thought which is clothed in words. In much the same way, Estienne Pasquier reproached Turnèbe for his 'advis que nostre langage est trop bas pour recevoir de nobles inventions'. In the same letter he put forward the view that Frenchmen should not write in Latin to save foreigners the trouble of learning French: 'Que s'ils ont affaire de nos inventions, qu'ils les viennent chercher chez nous, & qu'ils apprennent nostre vulgaire, si par nos escrits il se rend digne d'estre appris.' Pasquier used the word again in discussing with Ronsard the problems of revising one's work in the light of what other people are likely to think of it: 'C'est ce qui nous perd en la reformation de nos œuvres: car pendant que nous estimons que ce qui desplaist à l'un, plaist à l'autre, nous penserions nous coupper un doigt, si nous retranchions quelque chose de nos inventions.'[4]

This sense of invention as an idea expressed in words was applied especially frequently to poetry. The 'invention' of a poem was the 'idea', the conception which the poem embodies.

---

[1] Montaigne, *op. cit.* II, 84, I, 157, and III, 169. [2] *Ibid.* I, 156.
[3] Du Bellay, *Deffence*, 14. [4] Pasquier, *op. cit.* 6, 75, 77.

This is the case in Dolet's praise of Marot, when he recommends the poem *L'Enfer* 'tant pour l'inuention singuliere que pour les descriptions merueilleuses qui y sont'.[1] So too with Montaigne, when he refers to his delight in the 'facilité et inventions' of '[le] bon Ovide', or discusses the qualities necessary to a good poem, laying particular emphasis upon the value of the *inventions* which it contains: 'Je ne suis pas de ceux qui pensent la bonne rithme faire le bon poëme...si les inventions y rient, si l'esprit et le jugement y ont bien faict leur office, voylà un bon poëte, diray-je.' Or again, he alludes to the *inventions* of poetry concerning a Golden Age, which are far surpassed by the actual way of life of certain 'nations... barbares...fort voisines de leur naifveté originelle': 'il me semble que ce que nous voyons par experience en ces nations la, surpasse...toutes les peintures dequoy la poësie a embelly l'age doré et toutes ses inventions à feindre une heureuse condition d'hommes.' And Montaigne remarks of Homer that 'non seulement aucunes races particulieres, mais la plus part des nations cherchent origine en ses inventions'.[2] Ronsard himself had used exactly the same terminology; it was the accepted currency of the age: 'Tu seras plus songneux', he warned the poet in the *Abbregé*, 'de la belle invention et des motz, que de la ryme, laquelle vient assez aisément d'elle mesme apres quelque peu d'exercitation.' Elsewhere in the same work he impresses upon us that 'la poësie ne peut estre plaisante ny parfaicte sans belles inventions, descriptions, comparaisons'.[3]

This last comment of Ronsard suggests a further important use of the word *invention*, namely as a term of praise to designate a certain quality in a poem, which can perhaps be regarded as a mixture of our 'originality' and 'technical skill'. That is probably the main connotation of the word in Barthélemy Aneau's defence of the old poetic forms against Du Bellay's contempt: 'noz poëmes les plus beaux & les plus artificielz, comme rondeaux, balades, chans royaux, virlais...qui toutefois en toute perfection d'art & d'invention excedent tes beaux sonnets

---

[1] *Les Œuvres de Clément Marot*, ed. G. Guiffrey (1875–1931), ii, 157.
[2] Montaigne, *op. cit.* i, 185, 235, and ii, 86, 480.
[3] Ronsard, *Œuvres complètes*, xiv, 10, 18.

& odes'. And a little later he again emphasises the 'merveil-
leuse invention' displayed in these forms.[1] Montaigne too
praises the sonnets of La Boetie, which he is sending to the
Comtesse de Guissen, for their 'invention et gentillesse'.[2]
Sebillet had used the word when he was praising the work of
Scève: 'la Délie de Sceve, Pöéme d'autant riche invention qui
pour le jourd'huy se lise'.[3] And as one last instance we may
take Montaigne again: 'Sentez lire un discours de philosophie:
l'invention, l'eloquence, la pertinence frape incontinent vostre
esprit et vous esmeut.'[4] Invention is here one of the qualities
which go to make up the excellence of any piece of writing, prose
or poetry.

I would like to round off this survey of the main connotations
of the word *invention* for the sixteenth century by returning to
the sense of 'production', or 'discovery', with which I began.
Then it had been a question of inventing (mechanical) contrivances. Now it is a matter of inventing poetic forms. Thus
Lemaire de Belges in the *Concorde des deux Langages* wrote that,
in the temple of Venus,

> La recite on, d'invention saphicque,
> Maint noble dit, cantilennes et odes,
> Dont le stille est subtil et mirificque.[5]

Some years later Sebillet stated: 'L'éclogue est Gréque d'invention, Latine d'usurpation, et Françoise d'imitation.'[6] And later
still Barthélemy Aneau defended the good name of the old
French poetic forms on the grounds that 'ces nobles poëmes
sont propres & peculiers à [la] langue Françoise, & de la sienne
& propre & antique invention'.[7] Therefore the individual poetic
forms themselves are also to be called *inventions*. Molinet's
continuator wrote in the *Art et Science de Rhetorique* of the
doublette (alternate couplets of masculine and feminine
rhymes) that 'ceste mode et invention...a trés parfaict et entier
accent'.[8] We find the word again in Guillaume Des Autelz's

---

[1] B. Aneau, quoted in Du Bellay, *Deffence*, 109, n. 1, and 120, n. 5.
[2] Montaigne, *op. cit.* I, 212.   [3] Sebillet, *op. cit.* 33.
[4] Montaigne, *op. cit.* III, 228.
[5] Lemaire de Belges, *op. cit.* 19.   [6] Sebillet, *op. cit.* 109.
[7] B. Aneau, quoted in Du Bellay, *Deffence*, 109, n. 1.
[8] Langlois, *op. cit.* 270.

reply to Du Bellay's scornful dismissal of the older forms: 'encores ne tiens ie si peu de conte de noz anciens François, que ie mesprise tant leurs propres inuentions que ceux qui les appellent espisseries, qui ne seruent d'autre chose que de porter temoignage de nostre ignorance.'[1] And Du Bellay uses the same terminology himself when he praises the sonnet as '[une] non moins docte que plaisante invention Italienne'.[2]

Yet quite apart from the specific poetic forms, poetry itself was also to be thought of as an invention, along with all the other arts and sciences, all the other branches of knowledge which in the course of time man had discovered and found, that is, 'invented'. Du Bellay in the *Deffence* alleged that 'la poësie (comme dit Ciceron) a eté inventée par observation de prudence & mesure des oreilles'.[3] In these things lie its 'commencement &...fondement en nature & es œuvres de Dieu', as La Primaudaye would put it.[4] Or again, Antoine de Harsy in 1574 began his dedication to the *Œuvres poëtiques* of Mellin de Saint-Gelais with the sentence 'qve la poësie...soit une inuention belle & gentile: voire grandement recreatiue & plaisante, il est assez notoire, & n'y a (comme i'estime) bon esprit qui aucunement en doute'.[5]

Invention, then, is a term which had a wide range of meaning in the sixteenth century. In its material senses it had already acquired the modern connotations of producing devices, and in its non-material, mental senses we can perhaps detect the beginnings of a movement towards the implications of untruth and deception. Yet the word was still very closely connected with its classical Latin past, in which invention designated a certain faculty of the mind, without any implication that this was a faculty which deliberately set out to disguise or to conceal the truth of things. By the sixteenth century, however, this classical Latin area of meaning had itself been considerably extended. Besides being the mental power, *invention* was the activity of the power, and also the end-product of the activity. In the discussion of poetry the term *invention* was used to refer

---

[1] Des Autelz, *op. cit.* 60–1.   [2] Du Bellay, *Deffence*, 120.
[3] *Ibid.* 167.   [4] La Primaudaye, *op. cit.* 105.
[5] B. Weinberg, *Critical Prefaces of the French Renaissance* (1950), 237.

to a number of different entities, qualities, and processes. Poetry itself had been invented by man; the various stanza- and verse-forms were the inventions of poets; invention was perhaps the most important of the mental powers which the poet used when composing his poetry; the activity of this power was itself the process of invention, and it resulted in the bringing forth of individual inventions, which were embodied in words; if the poem was felt to be a good poem, then invention was one of the qualities which it displayed. I have already examined certain sections of this chain against the specific background of rhetorical theory. In the next two chapters I will attempt to show how the wider connotations of the term *invention* affected its application to the field of poetic theory.

[11]

INVENTION AND POETRY AS FICTION

At the time of the Pléiade, as we have just seen, invention was a concept which had associations with practically the whole range of man's activities as a maker: with man as a maker of all kinds of material objects, from cloth to artillery, with man as a 'thinker-up' of ways of doing things, with man as a maker of thoughts, from the most trivial and the most casual to the most sublime and the most subtle, and finally—somewhere between the two, in a region which participates in both the material and the mental realms—with man as a maker of literary artifacts. The term *invention* could be applied to everything which is directly involved in these processes, to the mental faculty itself, and to the 'thing' made, whatever its nature; invention was subject, verb, and object in turn.

In most discussions of the nature of poetry in sixteenth-century theoretical writings *invention* appears to be one of the key terms used. Sebillet was using the standard vocabulary of sixteenth-century poetic criticism when he referred to 'la pure et argentine invention' of the ancient poets, or when he warned his readers that 'peu proficte le vide son des vocables, soubz lesquelz n'y a rien de solide invention'.[1] In these particular examples, however, the author does not elaborate upon the implications of the term *invention* for his own view of poetry. But there are other instances which are probably more enlightening. Pontus de Tyard, for example, makes the opposition between the understanding and reciting of poetry, and the composition or 'invention' of it: 'N'est il pas tout evident, que si l'entendement humain n'est capable par Fortune ou par Art, de bien entendre et reciter la Poësie jà escrite, à plus forte raison la mesme invention luy sera (s'il n'est aidé que de ces deux moyens) deniée?'[2] Sometimes we find that invention is con-

[1] Sebillet, *op. cit.* 22, 188.   [2] P. de Tyard, *Solitaire Premier*, 26.

trasted, more specifically, with translation. Thus, in the Epître-préface to Jean de Morel which introduced a volume of poems published in 1552, Du Bellay wrote: 'Afin que le tout puisse rencontrer quelque plus grande faveur, je commenceray, non par œuvres de mon invention, mais par la translation du quatriesme livre de l'*Eneide*, qu'il n'est besoing recommander d'avantage, puis que sur le front elle porte le nom de Vergile.' [1] Sebillet too, in deploring 'ceste penurie d'œuvres grans et Heroiques', had suggested that this was due either to 'faute de matiére', or to 'ce que chacun des Pöetes famés et savans aime mieus en traduisant suivre la trace approuvée de tant d'eages et de bons espris, qu'en entreprenant œuvre de son invention, ouvrir chemin aus voleurs de l'honneur deu a tout labeur vertueus'.[2]

More usually, however, invention was set against imitation, taken in the sense of following literary models. Guillaume Des Autelz, countering Du Bellay's theory of imitation in the *Replique aux furieuses defenses de Louis Meigret*, stated the opposition between invention and imitation most emphatically: 'En premier lieu, ie ne suis pas de l'auis de ceux, qui ne pensent point que le François puisse faire chose digne de l'immortalité de son inuention, sans l'imitation d'autrui.' [3] Later the same year, in his preface to the second edition of *L'Olive*, Du Bellay defended himself against the charges of too slavish imitation by making exactly the same contrast: 'Ceulx qui ont leu les œuvres de Virgile, d'Ovide, d'Horace, de Petrarque...trouverront qu'en mes escriptz y a beaucoup plus de naturelle invention que d'artificielle ou supersticieuse immitation.' [4] Both in translation and in imitation the poet is drawing upon other authors for his material. When he invents, on the other hand, he is relying entirely upon himself. He becomes the first to tread a particular poetic path, and all credit and honour are due to him for that primacy.

The Pléiade always insisted that it was incumbent upon the poet not to stop short at the level of imitation, but to go on to the higher stage of invention. Pontus de Tyard in the *Solitaire Premier* heavily underlined this obligation to produce inde-

---

[1] Du Bellay, *Œuvres poétiques*, I, 20. [2] Sebillet, *op. cit.* 187.
[3] Des Autelz, *op. cit.* 58. [4] Du Bellay, *Œuvres poétiques*, I, 20.

pendent *inventions*. He is discussing in a fairly general way 'la maniere, et l'ordre parfait, moyennant lesquels l'on parvient à l'intelligence accomplie des doctrines et sciences', but since he claims that these are 'subtilement celé[s]' beneath the order of the names of the Muses, we are probably justified in assuming that poetry is to be included among the 'doctrines et sciences':

il est trespertinent que l'on adjouste quelque chose du sien à la discipline, que l'on tient en memoire, et que l'on l'enrichisse de ses propres inventions: non toutesfois qu'il soit permis de s'esgarer temerairement en ses inventions, et indifferemment les approuver: mais bien, apres avoir avec la dexterité de l'entendement tournoyé autour des choses inventées...discerner, avec jugement bien instruit, les bonnes des frivoles: et rejettant cestes, choisir les bonnes et louables.[1]

A point to be noticed here is the way in which Pontus insists that invention must be strictly supervised. He does not allow it complete freedom of action; the judgement must always be at hand to review the productions of the invention, so that only 'les bonnes et louables' are retained. I shall return to this aspect of invention later in connection with the imagination. For the moment, however, I would like to point out Pontus' evident conviction that fundamentally invention is a valuable form of mental activity, even if it is perhaps only in the sense that invention provides the materials upon which the higher faculties of understanding and judgement exercise their functions. This emphasis upon the positive sides of invention seems to me to be a characteristic note in the Pléiade's treatment of the subject.

I have suggested at the beginning of this chapter that in the sixteenth century the idea of invention was closely connected with the idea of 'making'. There is a distinction to be made here, I think, between 'making' and 'making up'. In contemporary usage, as we have seen, both of these ideas are contained separately in the concept of invention. As soon as the word leaves the realm of material things and is applied to the non-material, mental realm, it becomes a making up rather than a making, a fabrication of untruths rather than a manufacture of

[1] P. de Tyard, *Solitaire Premier*, 54–6.

things which are useful. Ever since the time of Plato poetry had been regarded as a making up, as lying, and poets as liars. This attitude was still fully current in the sixteenth century. Pontus de Tyard, for instance, had the narrator in *Le Premier Curieux* put forward the view that 'Les poëtes...honorent leurs escrits de mensonges, & les remplissent de tout ce qu'ils pensent esmouvoir la delectation & l'admiration aux humaines pensées; puis quelle foy requiert celuy duquel la profession est tant fabuleuse, qu'il n'ose selon les preceptes de son art representer une verité, si elle n'est revestue de robe de mensonge?'[1] In all ages poets had endeavoured to defend themselves against these charges. Boccaccio spoke for all poets when he explained in the *Genealogia Deorum Gentilium* that 'poets are not liars... poetic fiction has nothing in common with any variety of falsehood, for it is not a poet's purpose to deceive anybody with his inventions'.[2] Jacques Legrand in the fifteenth century gave a more detailed account of what poets were aiming to achieve with their 'fictions': 'Finis ergo poetarum non est mentiri, vel irritare: sed ex similitudinibus rerum vnam pro alia intelligere et ita veritati semper intenta ficto sermone suum conceptum exprimere.'[3]

Usually, however, poetry had been defended not from the point of view of what poets were trying to achieve, but from the point of view of the effects that their works would have on the readers. That is to say, it was a defence on specifically didactic grounds; the so-called 'untruths' of poetry were alleged to contain moral lessons, to set forth 'vne reprehention de vice, ou remonstrance de vertu'.[4] But in the sixteenth century renewed attempts were also being made to achieve a definitive defence of poetry on other grounds—and I have already outlined in an earlier chapter those which sought to make use of Aristotle's theory of imitation.[5] The main difficulty for the sixteenth

---

[1] P. de Tyard, *Le Premier Curieux*, 75. For further examples of sixteenth-century aphorisms about the lying of poets, see Clements, *op. cit.* 10–11.

[2] C. G. Osgood, *Boccaccio on Poetry: being the Preface and the Fourteenth and Fifteenth Books of Boccaccio's Genealogia Deorum Gentilium* (1930), 63.

[3] J. Legrand, *Sophologium* (1477 edn.), II, iv.

[4] Ch. Estienne, preface to the translation of Terence's *Andria* (1542), in Weinberg, *op. cit.* 90.   [5] See pp. 54ff.

century was that as soon as poetry acknowledged that it did not represent facts, in the narrow sense of the word, as soon as it ceased to be mere history and could begin to call itself poetry at all, it at once became attached to the opposite pole of lying. Poetry was like a metal bar placed between two magnets which were so powerful that the bar had to cling to one or the other of them; there was no possible resting-place between them, for as soon as the bar was separated from one magnet it stuck fast to the other. The problem that faced the theorists of poetry was that of building for themselves a half-way house between the two extremes, a house which could stand up by itself and which could justify its existence to the world as a self-supporting structure. C. S. Lewis summed up this point very neatly when he wrote that 'sixteenth-century critics are really contributing to, or concluding, an age-old debate; and that debate, properly viewed, is simply the difficult process by which Europe became conscious of fiction as an activity distinct from history on the one hand and from lying on the other'.[1]

Let us examine more closely this term 'fiction', for it occurs quite frequently in sixteenth-century discussions of poetry. Indeed, the use of fiction was held to be one of the distinguishing marks of poetry. Du Bellay, for instance, differentiated between the historian and the poet on just this score:

> Cestuy-la sans user d'aucune fiction
> Represente le vray de chascune action...
> Cestuy-ci, plus hardy, d'un art non limité
> Sous mille fictions cache la verité.[2]

Quite clearly, Du Bellay was using the word in a positive, approving sense; the 'fictions' of the poet were the result of his *hardiesse*, they were the products of his 'art non limité'. But such connotations were far from usual in the sixteenth century. Cotgrave's list of synonyms has a very different colouring. To him *une fiction* was 'a fiction, inuention, lie, fib, cog [i.e. deception], a thing imagined, fained, or foisted in'. Huguet is even more condemnatory; he offers 'feinte, mensonge, hypocrisie' as equivalents of *fiction*, and provides ample evidence that in

---

[1] Lewis, *op. cit.* 319.   [2] Du Bellay, *Œuvres poétiques*, vi, 164.

sixteenth-century French the word often kept very bad company. From his examples we can see that it inhabited the same semantic area as the words *dissimulation* and *fard*, in which the ideas of disguise and deceit were predominant. Certainly this was Rabelais's view of fiction. Pantagruel promised the learned *conseillers* of the Parlement, for instance, that when he had heard what the litigants had to say, he would give his own frank opinion on the matter: 'je vous en diray mon opinion sans fiction ny dissimulation quelconques.'[1] And in the *Quart Livre* Rabelais tells how an Italian woman, who was alleged to speak from her stomach with the voice of 'l'esprit immonde', was carefully put to the test, 'pour houster tout doubte de fiction et fraude occulte'.[2] Calvin used the word in a similar vein to describe the purifying effect of the true faith: 'la vraye Foy chrestienne ...prend siege au cœur de l'homme, le nettoyant de fard, de fiction, et Hypocrisie.'[3]

Fiction, then, was a dangerous word for sixteenth-century theorists of poetry to use, for it was in a way to concede the point at issue from the beginning, and to admit that poetry does indeed consist of *mensonges*. It did seem possible, however, to use the cognate verb *feindre* to describe the activity of the poet, without necessarily condemning him out of hand as a liar. Feigning had not yet gone the way of fiction, and was apparently still regarded as a fairly reputable activity. *Feindre* still preserved its connection with the realm of material objects, which seems to have been the original home of its Latin parent, *fingere*.

Fingere had begun by meaning simply to touch, or to handle. Then it came to be used in a more general sense, to mean to form, shape, fashion, make—both material things and also thoughts or ideas. Quite early the word was associated especially with the plastic arts, meaning to model in wax or clay or stone.[4] This sense is still present in the sixteenth-century French *feindre*. Ronsard, for example, describes Jupiter's making of a man thus:

> Luy adonques print une masse
> De terre, & devant tous les Dieux,

[1] Rabelais, *Œuvres*, III, 131.   [2] Rabelais, *Le Quart Livre*, 236.
[3] J. Calvin, *Institution de la religion chrestienne*, ed. A. Lefranc (1911), 189.
[4] See Lewis & Short, *op. cit.* under *fingo*.

> Dedans il feignit une face,
> Un corps, deux jambes, & deux yeulx.[1]

Similarly, Du Bellay asserts that

> On peult feindre par le cizeau
> Ou par l'ouvraige du pinceau
> Toute visible chose,

or explains, at the beginning of the poem *De sa peine et des Beautez de sa Dame*, that

> Il me plaist icy de peindre
> Mieulx que ne la sçauroit feindre
> Un Apelle ingenieux,
> Ma peine contr'imitee
> Sur la belle Pasithee,
> Seule idole de mes yeux.[2]

In these cases, quite simply, *feindre* has the sense of 'to make a (material) copy of'. But, as Huguet points out, *feindre* was also applied to the literary arts, to signify representation 'par la parole ou les écrits'.[3] In the *Hymne de la Mort* Ronsard addresses Pierre Paschal with the following words:

> Tu me diras encor...
> ...que tu crains
> ...tout cela qu'ont feint les poëtes là-bas
> Nous attendre aux Enfers apres nostre trespas.[4]

And later, in the 1572 preface to the *Franciade*, he makes a very clear statement of the nature of poetry in terms of feigning. For him the poet's task is exactly that, to feign: 'le Poëte qui escrit les choses comme elles sont ne merite tant que celuy qui les feint & se recule le plus qu'il luy est possible de l'historien.'[5]

In the sixteenth century the connection of poetry with feigning was held to have an etymological justification. This argument depended on the fact that the Greek verb ποιεῖν (meaning 'to make', and also 'to do'), from which the Latin

---

[1] Ronsard, *Œuvres complètes*, III, 155.
[2] Du Bellay, *Œuvres poétiques*, IV, 220, and V, 56.
[3] Huguet, *L'Évolution du Sens des Mots*, 226.
[4] Ronsard, *Œuvres complètes*, VIII, 172.   [5] *Ibid.* XVI, 4.

noun *poeta* was taken, was usually translated into Latin as *fingere*. *Fingere* in turn was rendered into French as *feindre*. The poet, then, could be called a feigner. As long as feigning was practised only upon material objects, the word did not take on any pejorative connotations. The artifacts produced by the feigning of the plastic arts were, to be sure, mere copies or imitations of reality, but there was in fact no danger that they would be confused with reality, that they would be taken for their originals. In this field there was no difficulty in distinguishing 'truth' from 'falsehood'. When it was a question of representing in words, however, the problem was much more difficult. It was only too easy for the person dealing in words to deceive his audience as to the truth of the things which he was discussing, since there was no immediately obvious sign by which one could distinguish the one from the other. No one would normally mistake a statue for an actual human being; but there was no straightforward way of telling what was a true account of (say) a past event, and what was a false account. Even in classical Latin the verb *fingere*, over and above the unbiassed senses of forming mentally or in speech, representing in thought, imagining, and so on, had also acquired the accessory connotations of untruth and intention to deceive. Lewis & Short quote examples from Plautus and Terence where *fingere* has as its object such expressions as *fallacias* and *falsas causas ad discordiam*.

Something of these derogatory implications was certainly present in the sixteenth-century French word *feindre*, though to a far lesser degree than in *fiction*. We may see evidence for this in the recurrent attempts in the sixteenth century to point out that etymologically the poet was not a feigner, but a maker. Jules César Scaliger, for example, asserted in his *Poetices libri septem* that 'Poetae...nomen non a fingendo, vt putarunt, quia fictis vteretur: sed initio a faciendo versu ductum est'.[1] Montaigne was probably intending that the word *feindre* should have pejorative connotations when he wrote that 'les poëtes... feignent tout à leur poste [à leur guise]'.[2] Normally, however,

---

[1] J. C. Scaliger, *Poetices libri septem* (1561), 3.
[2] Montaigne, *op. cit.* II, 17.

feindre was quite simply the most appropriate verb to describe the activity of poets, and any implied condemnation was merely incidental. Montaigne himself gives an excellent instance of this in the essay 'De la Tristesse': 'Voyla pourquoy les poëtes feignent cette miserable mere Niobé...avoir esté en fin transmuée en rochier, *Diriguisse malis*, pour exprimer cette morne, muette et sourde stupidité qui nous transit, lors que les accidens nous accablent surpassans nostre portée.'[1] Feigning is the poet's specifically artistic activity, that by which he is able to represent (if we care to use Aristotle's terminology) the universals in and through the particulars. The same sort of thing is to be found in Rabelais, when Grandgousier asks Lasdaller whether he really believes that the plague is due to the agency of Saint Sebastian, and on receiving the answer 'Yes' replies: 'Ouy?...les faulx prophetes vous annoncent ilz telz abus? Blasphement ilz en ceste façon les justes et saincts de Dieu, qu'ilz les font semblables aux diables, qui ne font que mal entre les humains...comme les poëtes faignent un grand tas de Vejoves [anti-Joves] et dieux malfaisans?'[2] But Montaigne shows quite clearly where *feindre* stands when he refers to the historian Xenophon 'feignant ou recitant, mais, à mon advis recitant plustost que feignant, les rares perfections de ce grand Cyrus'.[3] Here he is making a definite distinction between feigning, i.e. fiction, untruth, on the one hand, and accurate reporting, or factual truth, on the other.

Such, then, was the status of feigning—an equivocal concept which was always in danger of being equated with lying and deceiving. The endeavour of sixteenth-century theorists of poetry was to stabilise the concept and firmly to set aside the disreputable aura of deceit, pretence, and untruth which surrounded it. In the passage which I quoted above from Ronsard's 1572 preface to the *Franciade* the poet was most careful to avoid being misunderstood on this question of feigning. The poet who feigns, he had written, is better than the poet 'qui escrit les choses comme elles sont'; but, he added in an immediate qualifi-

---

[1] Montaigne, *op. cit.* I, 8.
[2] Rabelais, *Œuvres*, II, 365.
[3] Montaigne, *op. cit.* III, 258.

cation of this statement, I do not mean that the poet should indulge in outlandish, 'untrue' feignings—far from it: 'non toutefois pour feindre une Poësie fantastique comme celle de l'Arioste, de laquelle les membres sont aucunement beaux mais le corps est tellement contrefaict et monstrueux qu'il ressemble mieux aux resveries d'un malade de fievre continue qu'aux inventions d'un homme bien sain'.[1]

Ronsard is here by implication aligning his kind of poetic feigning with healthiness. The 'Poëte qui feint' is equated with the 'homme bien sain'. It is instructive to examine the terms which Ronsard uses to reject the opposite point of view, that which associates feigning with untruth. *Fantastique, contrefaict, monstrueux, resveries, malade de fievre*—these are all strong words. Poetry is not the product of a sick, disordered mind. Its 'fictions' are not the hallucinations of fever, in which state the mind notoriously loses contact with reality and deludes itself in the most bizarre manner. Nor are they the products of the dreaming mind, where reason, being asleep, no longer exercises the necessary control over the errant senses, but allows them to form images at the behest of the passions; these images, too, have no foundation in things as they really are, but merely pander to the desires of the passions, which are by definition evil, since they participate in man's baser, material nature. Nor are poetic fictions *monstrueux*, they are not 'contre Nature', but are in fact part of the natural order of things, and, Ronsard implies, to be accepted and evaluated as such. They are not *contrefaits*, not counterfeit or spurious (there is the menacing word 'fraud' hovering in the background here). Ronsard is making a deliberate contrast, I think, between *feindre* and *contrefaire*; *contrefaire* is the deceitful kind of representing or imitating, whereas *feindre* is the legitimate kind, proper to poets and to artists in general.[2]

<hr/>

[1] Ronsard, *Œuvres complètes*, XVI, 4.
[2] We should note in passing that *contrefaire* did not invariably have a pejorative sense in the sixteenth century, for it could also mean simply 'to imitate', as in Ronsard's avowal of his debt to Horace: '[je] me rendi familier d'Horace, contre-faisant sa naive douceur' (Ronsard, *Œuvres complètes*, I, 44). The sixteenth-century examples cited by Littré in the historical section of his entry under *contrefaire* illustrate well the range of meaning covered by the word at that time.

Moreover, the result of feigning is not to be 'une Poësie fantastique'. We must remember that in the sixteenth century *fantastique* did not have the almost attractive connotations of the modern word; there had not yet taken place the revolution in taste which made fancifulness and whimsicality acceptable qualities in literary productions. The fantasy was a highly dangerous and suspect faculty, for if the reason did not keep careful watch over its activities it all too readily became the slave of the passions. *Fantastique* was thus a term of strong disapproval, of condemnation even. Huguet's synonyms run through a whole gamut of meaning, from *rêveur, pensif* at one end, through *bizarre* and *extravagant*, to *fou, insensé* at the other.[1] A good indication of the usual sixteenth-century connotations of the word is given by its presence in Ronsard's outburst of self-depreciation in the *Elegie à Jacques Grevin*:

> Je suis opiniastre, indiscret, fantastique,
> Farouche, soupçonneux, triste & melancolique.[2]

Finally, we should note the second of the two words which Ronsard sets in opposition to all this. The antithesis to the *fantastique–monstrueux–fièvre* group of ideas is summed up in the single adjective *sain*. But it is significant, I think, that Ronsard associates the feignings of the poet with the *inventions* of a healthy man. *Invention* was a key term in sixteenth-century poetic theorising, not only because of its place in the historical development of literary theory out of the systems of rhetoric (though that was certainly of major importance), but also because of the fact that, unlike *fiction*, it was a word which carried few pejorative associations. The semantic respectability of the word was later to be quite seriously compromised, but for the time being, at least, *inventer* was much nearer to *trouver* than it was to *controuver*. And for that reason it was a concept which could be very useful to the defenders of poetry. As long as *invention* remained unsullied by suggestions of untruth or deceit, then it might well be of some assistance in the task of refuting the wrong-headed charges under which poetry laboured. For

[1] Huguet, *Dictionnaire*, under *fantastique*.
[2] Ronsard, *Œuvres complètes*, XIV, 195.

there was nothing *fantastique*, or *monstrueux*, or *fiévreux* about invention, nothing irrational; it was a perfectly normal process of the mind, over which the reason and the judgement could ideally exercise full control. Some of the further consequences of this attitude towards invention I propose to examine in the following chapter.

[12]

INVENTION AND REASON

On the whole *invention* was a fairly safe concept for theorists of poetry to use in the sixteenth century. Although there were signs that the deterioration in the meaning of the word was already beginning, it was not yet fully under way. The word was perhaps just at the point where a shift of meaning was being slowly prepared, from that of finding something which is already in existence and merely requires discovery (in the sense of uncovering, or bringing into human awareness for the first time), to that of making something completely new, creating something which has never existed before. Littré does not hesitate to give as the first meaning of the verb *inventer*, 'créer quelque chose de nouveau par la force de son esprit'. It is interesting to notice, however, that the sense of creating something new took a long time to replace completely the earlier sense of discovering what was already in existence. One of the examples which Littré chooses to illustrate the meaning quoted provides a neat confirmation of this point. He takes a passage from Rousseau's *Emile*: 'Qu'il ["votre élève"] ne sache rien, non parce que vous le lui avez dit, mais parce qu'il l'a compris lui-même: qu'il n'apprenne pas la science, qu'il l'invente.' [1] Here the last clause must surely mean, 'let him come upon it, let him find it out, let him discover it in things', and not 'let him produce it out of his own head', or '...out of the void', which would tend to be the sense of 'créer quelque chose de nouveau' as applied to this context. Nowadays, of course, the meaning would be 'let him make it up', with the implication that this would result in pure fabrication.

In the sixteenth century, however, invention was still quite definitely a finding, a discovery, or a finding out, rather than a creating. Rabelais illustrates this point for us when at the end

---

[1] *Œuvres de J. J. Rousseau* (1793), IV, 277.

of the *Tiers Livre* he describes the beneficial action of the herb
pantagruelion and marvels that its uses were not discovered
long ago by the ancients: 'Et m'esbahys comment l'invention de
tel usaige a esté par tant de siecles celé aux antiques philosophes.'[1] Another good example is to be found in Bernard
Palissy's treatise *De la Marne*, where he discusses the use of
marl as a fertiliser: 'La premiere invention d'avoir trouvé la
marne peut avoir aussi esté trouvée en creusant les puits pour
chercher de l'eau...depuis, l'invention estant trouvée, l'on a
cherché apres...es pays où elle est usitée et conneue.'[2] A more
clearly 'intellectual' context is given by the following passage
from Guy de Brués's *Premier Dialogue contre les nouveaux
Academiciens*:

Les Peripaticiens, ont montré que cela [the squaring of the circle]
estoit impossible. Puis ilz ne se sont pas moins tourmentez, pour
trouver deux lignes moyennes proportionnelles entre deux autres
lignes droittes proposées. Platon a proposé ce probleme. Archite a
grandement travaillé à l'invention de ces deux lignes. Platon n'a pas
approuvé son invention, et s'est efforcé d'en trouver une autre,
laquelle Eudoxe a reprouvé.[3]

Thanks to its rhetorical background, however, invention was
regarded not only as more or less accidental discovery, but also
as an orderly and controlled, even systematised process, solidly
founded upon the faculty of reason. Nothing could be more
highly organised, more carefully classified, and more pains-
takingly elaborated than the so-called places of invention in the
classical rhetorics. Cicero gave a truly formidable list of these
places of invention in his treatise on the *Topica*. There he made
the division into 'intrinsic' topics (that is, topics which are
inherent in the subject) and 'extrinsic' topics (those which
depend upon outside authority). In the first division he included
definition, enumeration of parts, etymology, cognate words,
genus, species, similarity or analogy, difference, contraries,
adjuncts, antecedents, consequents, contradictions, efficient
causes, effects, and comparison with events of greater, or lesser,

[1] Rabelais, *Œuvres*, v, 367.
[2] Palissy, *Les Œuvres de maistre Bernard Palissy*, ed. B. Fillon and L. Audiat
(1888), II, 234–5. [3] Brués, *op. cit.* 148.

or equal importance. The 'authorities' comprising the second division were virtue, talent, wealth, age, good luck, skill, experience, necessity, and finally concurrence of fortuitous events.[1] Students of rhetoric were still being presented with this type of scheme in Renaissance schools. They used the list of topics as a sort of *aide-invention*, or rather as a basic guide to invention which indicated the proper method to follow in developing, or 'inventing', a theme.

Such was the full rhetorical setting for the concept of invention, and I would like to suggest that this highly ordered and reasoned approach to the method of rhetorical invention typified also the feeling of the sixteenth century for the concept of invention taken in a more general context. Invention was thought of as a normal and natural process of reasoning, whose rules had been elaborated by the ancient classical rhetoricians, and then absorbed into the medieval and Renaissance encyclopaedia. Invention was suspect only as far as reason itself was suspect; and providing always that it kept strictly to its own realm of secular knowledge and did not try to meddle too closely in matters of faith, reason was felt during a large part of the sixteenth century to be all-powerful and (potentially at least) all-knowing.

Very characteristic of the attitude towards invention which I have just outlined, and of the close connection between reason and invention in the sixteenth-century mind, is the treatment which Petrus Ramus gave to invention in his reformed scheme of dialectics.[2] What Ramus was aiming at was a complete re-organisation of the two disciplines of dialectics and rhetoric. In the sixteenth century rhetoric was still, as it had been throughout most of the Middle Ages, a sort of omnibus discipline, comprising not only grammar and all the rules of the art of speech, but also logic, philosophy, and ethics, for all these branches of learning, it was held, had an essential part to play in the formation of a good orator. Ramus considered this to be an

[1] Cicero, *Topica*, 386–442.

[2] Ramus, it is worth noting, had an interesting literary relationship with the Pléiade group. When he produced a French version of his *Dialecticae institutiones* in 1555 (the original had appeared twelve years before), several members of the Pléiade, and notably Ronsard himself, made translations of the 'snippets' from the Latin poets which Ramus had used to illustrate his various points.

unjustifiable mingling of content with outer form. He believed that rhetoric should be concerned solely with the principles and rules of the art of fine speaking. In other words, the rhetorician as rhetorician was to interest himself only in technical matters of expression, and not at all in the content which was to be expressed. Thus Ramus's art of rhetoric no longer had the fivefold division into invention, disposition, elocution, memory, and delivery in the classical manner, but consisted merely of Expression (the old elocution, or eloquence, whose purpose according to Ramus was the elegant adornment of speech) and Action, or proper delivery. Memory disappeared from the scheme in the interests of economy, since Ramus considered it to be a basic prerequisite for the orator, in the same way that he had to have a certain physical equipment in order to be able to speak at all. Invention and disposition Ramus removed altogether from the province of rhetoric, since they pertained rather to the matter of the composition, which rhetoric merely embellished. The main part of rhetoric was now Expression, dealing with the numerous tropes and figures of thought and speech. Invention and disposition were confined to Dialectics, which he held to be their rightful home.[1]

Just as rhetoric was for Ramus the art of speaking well, so dialectics was the art of reasoning well, 'l'art de bien raisonner'. Since the human reason operates in two ways, Ramus argued, by inventing and by judging, dialectics in turn has two parts, invention and judgement: 'Les parties de Dialectique sont deux, Inuention & Iugement: car...inuenter & iuger sont deux propres actions de la raison humaine, & ne s'y en trouue point de troisieme.' Not unexpectedly, Ramus proclaimed invention to be the first part of dialectics, the commencement of all right reasoning, just as formerly invention had been the first part of rhetoric, both in order of time and in order of importance: 'Inuention est la premiere partie de Dialectique, pour inuenter les raisons & arguments.'[2]

[1] For a fuller discussion of Ramus's scheme of rhetoric see F. P. Graves, *Peter Ramus and the Educational Reformation in the Sixteenth Century* (1912), 134–41.

[2] Ramus, *La Dialectique* (1576 edn.), fos. 1r⁰, 3r⁰. Cf. Cicero, *Topica*, 386: 'omnis ratio diligens disserendi duas hab[et] partis, unam inveniendi alteram iudicandi.'

Ramus's system of dialectics is based on a fully elaborated epistemology and metaphysics, which it is not my purpose to expound in detail here. Suffice it to say that Ramus believed that the method of dialectics could and indeed should be derived simultaneously from observation of the natural order of the universe and from observation of the natural processes of the human mind. These two elements, the natural order of the universe and the natural processes of the mind, infallibly correspond, so he believed, which means that the dialectical method of reasoning is able to give immediate and true access to things as they actually are:

Ita ars dialectica diligenter exposita [ad] naturalis dialecticae (cujus observatio est) similitudinem se referre et propriis germanisque coloribus exprimere, vim universam amplecti, membra partesque legitimis locis partiri, habitum denique totum imitari praedicabit. Hoc fundamentum est nostrae contentionis, hoc firmamentum quaestionis, haec summae et totam disputationem complectentis rationationis intentio est: *ars dialectica est imago naturalis dialecticae. . .vera ut dixi, legitimaque disserendi doctrina, est imago et pictura naturae.*[1]

An important term in Ramist dialectics is the word 'argument', which occurs in the sentence quoted previously from *La Dialectique.* It is worth examining for a moment the significance of this term in order to understand just what Ramus is claiming for the process of invention when he talks of inventing 'raisons & arguments'. An argument, writes Ramus, 'est ce qui est destiné & propre à declarer quelque chose, comme est vne chacune & simple raison considerée à par soy & separément, laquelle est comprinse & declarée par quelque mot exterieur, qui est le signe & note de la raison & argument'. The 'argument' is that which proclaims the true nature of a thing, that is to say it is the name of the thing or the mental conception of the thing. Since the order of the universe and the way in which the human mind operates correspond so exactly, there is no possibility that any epistemological slip might occur, no possibility

---

[1] P. Ramus, *Aristotelicae animadversiones* (1543), quoted by J.-O. Fleckenstein, 'Petrus Ramus et l'humanisme bâlois', in *La science au seizième siècle* (Colloque de Royaumont, 1957), 128; Ramus's italics. See also in the same volume R. Hooykaas, 'Pierre de la Ramée et l'empirisme scientifique au XVIe siècle'.

that there might be any gap or discrepancy between things as they are and things as they are perceived or thought by human minds. The *arguments* are thus the basic materials of dialectics, the bricks with which it builds: 'tel qu'est le mot en Grammaire, & le trope en Rhetorique, tel est l'argument en Dialectique.'[1] The dialectician perceives the arguments of things, and at once he is able to comprehend the order and arrangement into which they fall within the pattern of the whole universe. Things— that is, objects (defined as widely as possible) or the relationships between them—provide the arguments, as it were of their own accord; the arguments arise naturally from things, they are not foisted upon things by the human reason, but are already present in the things themselves.

The arguments, then, subsist in reality; the dialectician simply comes upon them. This is the key to Ramus's view of invention. Invention is carried out by following what, according to him, are the natural rules of thought, that is, by descending from universal *genera* to particular instances: '[l'homme] a en soy naturellement la puissance de cognoistre toutes choses'— this natural congruence of the cogniser with the cognised is, as I have already pointed out, the assumption which is fundamental to all Ramus's epistemological theory—

& quand il aura deuant ses yeux l'art d'inuenter par ces genres vniuersels comme quelque mirouer, luy representant les images vniuerselles & generalles de toutes choses, il luy sera beaucoup plus facile par icelles recognoistre les especes singulieres, & par consequence inuenter ce qu'il cherchera: mais il fault par plusieurs exemples, par grand exercice, par long vsage forbir & pollir ce mirouer, auant qu'il puisse reluire ny rendre ces images.[2]

And because this movement of thought from universals down to particulars corresponds to the actual order of external reality, it

---

[1] Ramus, *La Dialectique*, fo. 3r⁰.

[2] *Ibid.* fo. 37r⁰. We should perhaps remind ourselves that we have here the three requirements of the classical orator: *natura, ars, exercitatio* (see p. 42). These were in fact taken over as guiding principles by the humanist educational reformers; cf. Aeneas Sylvius Piccolomini, *Tractatus de Liberorum Educatione* (1450) (transl. W. H. Woodward, in *Vittorino da Feltre and other Humanist Educators*, 1905, 136): 'nature, training, practice—these seem to be the three factors of all education.'

9-2

is all the more easy to perform. All things are linked together
in the universal pattern, so that invention becomes to all
intents and purposes a process of memory, of recall:

puisque la nature de toutes choses s'entretient & s'entresuit, & que
l'esprit l'auroit cogneu totalement, il ne seroit pas hors de propos,
qu'apres qu'il se seroit souuenu de quelqu'vne de tant de choses, qu'il
ne puisse paruenir semblablement à la souuenance de toutes les autres
conioinctes & connexées, moyennant qu'il fut diligent à chercher &
qu'il ne se fascha du labeur & fatigue de l'inuention: Car telle inquisi-
tion ne seroit autre chose, que souuenance & recordation.[1]

Especially noteworthy, I think, both here and in the previous
quotation, is the association of *inventer* and *invention* with the
verb *chercher*.[2] Invention is being regarded as the result of a
seeking ('on invente ce qu'on cherche'); it is, as with the
classical Latin *invenire*, a coming into, a finding. To invent is
in rem venire, to discover, to lay open to view what Ramus calls
the arguments in a thing, to make manifest its true nature in the
proper, natural order. It is both a transcribing of the actual
order of reality and a natural operation of the mind. For this
reason the Ramist places of invention differ from the Ciceronian
topica not so much in the names by which they are called, as in
the system by which they are classified and arranged. This
system was based on a principle of binary fission, in which every
category was divided into two parts, each of which was divided
into two again, and so on and so on until all the necessary distinctions had been made. Thus in Ramus's scheme the major
division of dialectics was a twofold one into invention and judgement, or arrangement. The same method was carried over into
the classification of the places of invention. These were either
artificial, that is to say they had to be demonstrated, or inartificial, that is assumed without demonstration. Inartificial places

---

[1] Ramus, *La Dialectique*, fo. 36 r⁰–v⁰.

[2] This is, of course, not peculiar to Ramus. We have already noted an instance
from La Primaudaye, *op. cit.* 124: 'la fin de tout discours de l'entendement pretend
ou à l'invention, ou conclusion de la chose qu'on cerche.' And in a literary context,
we may take the well-known passage in which Sebillet attacks Du Bellay for his
so-called imitations: 'si je fay moins pour moy en traduisant anciens auteurs qu'en
cérchant inventions nouvelles, je ne suy toutefois tant a reprendre que celuy qui se
vante d'avoir trouvé ce qu'il ha mot a mot traduit dés autres' (preface to the translation of Euripides's *Iphigenia*, 1549, in Weinberg, *op. cit.* 143).

were either divine (oracular or prophetic) or human (legal or proverbial). Artificial places could be either primary or secondary. Primary artificial places were simple or compound, secondary artificial places were qualitative or quantitative, and each of these categories was split into two again and again, until there was formed a vast 'family tree' of invention, which together with its twin branch, judgement, made up the complete tree of dialectics.[1]

For Ramus, then, there was only one way to invent, and that was in accordance with the natural laws of dialectics. All invention was dialectical invention, for dialectics was merely the formalised or regularised version of the natural intelligence. The mind in following the natural processes of dialectics joined things together in thought in exactly the same way as they were joined together in reality. This operation constituted the process of invention, the coming upon the arguments which already existed in things. It is this view of invention which led Hardin Craig to see in Ramus's system of dialectics 'an emblem of the Renaissance mind', in as much as it posited a pre-existent body of true knowledge, already complete and perfect, which required only to be uncovered and revealed to the intellectual sight of men.[2]

There is an important difference between this attitude towards knowledge and the attitude of modern science. Science as we know it starts from a consideration of phenomena; it then forms hypotheses about the relations between certain selected phenomena or groups of phenomena, and finally checks these hypotheses against more phenomena, testing them for their reliability as predictions. If the hypotheses are found wanting in any way, they are modified and then rechecked, or if necessary rejected completely, and a fresh start is made. But this was not at all the Renaissance method of attaining knowledge. The Renaissance thinker believed that truth was to be known by

---

[1] For a complete exposition of this scheme see Graves, *op. cit.* 141–59.

[2] It is interesting to note that this is a thoroughly scholastic view of epistemology; cf. Aquinas's point that phenomena 'measure' (that is, they form or direct) the human mind: 'res naturales: ex quibus intellectus noster scientiam accipit, mensurant intellectum nostrum' (Aquinas, *Quaestiones disputatae*, 1586 edn., fo. 203r°).

consulting authorities and by correctly using the established methods of reasoned thought, that is, of dialectics or logic. As Hardin Craig has pointed out, 'The road to truth was ratiocination, not the free use of reason, but reason restricted to the discovery or rediscovery of a universe whose laws were the legacies of a wiser past or the fiats of an unimpeachable God.'[1] The function of reason, then, was not to form and to test hypotheses, not so much to make anything new, as to discover, to lay open a corpus of truth which was already complete in every detail, fully coherent and consistent, but which had not yet been completely appropriated by man. Given this epistemological standpoint, it is no paradox but an orthodox and direct statement of current views on the matter when Ambroise Paré writes of the power of 'cogitation', or reason, that 'icelle seule inuente le vray'.[2] It was a strong and widely held belief during the Renaissance that God had created a rational universe, and that the universe was therefore the legitimate object of man's rational knowledge. Through the proper use of his reason man could get to know the laws of Nature. And this 'proper use' consisted in conforming to the methods of logic, for what logic did was simply to fit the individual objects of thought into their set places in the pre-arranged scheme. This was the accepted epistemological method of the sixteenth century, and we shall find something which looks forward to the modern approach to the problem only in the later developments of Montaigne's thought. The first large-scale attack on the older method does not really take place until Bacon writes his *Novum Organum* in the early seventeenth century. Till then epistemological problems were usually glossed over with the assumptions first that the human intellect is so constituted that it can and does know the true nature of the things presented to it, and secondly that whatever is presented to the human intellect is a proper object of its knowledge. This was certainly Ramus's view, and in this particular at least he differed hardly at all from his enemies, the Aristotelians.

What I particularly wish to stress for the moment is the very

[1] H. Craig, *The Enchanted Glass: the Elizabethan Mind in Literature* (1950), 3.
[2] *Œuvres complètes d'Ambroise Paré*, ed. J. F. Malgaigne (1840–1), II, 660.

close connection between reason and invention. In Ramus's
system invention, since it is part of the method of dialectics,
cannot really go wrong. It is indeed the 'disciplina inveniendorum argumentorum, ut sine ullo errore ad ea ratione et via
perveniremus' of Cicero. This emphasis upon its rationality and
logicality was a very important element in the sixteenth-century
attitude towards the whole concept of invention. Invention
could be associated with whatever qualities of respectability
and reliability were attached to the concept of reason. And in
the sixteenth century these were considerable, for reason was
held to be above all else the distinguishing mark of man, the
power which raised him above animals in the cosmic scale of
being. As Erasmus aphoristically put it, 'Ratio facit hominem';[1]
or Louis Le Roy at greater length: 'Diev creant l'homme il luy
a donné par grande excellence raison & parole, & par ces deux
prerogatiues l'a separé des autres animaux.'[2]

For the early humanists especially, all the excellence of man
was epitomised in the faculty of reason. They believed man to be
essentially a rational being whose will was under the control of
his reason, so that he had within himself unlimited possibilities
for virtuous conduct. The ethical systems of Christianity,
Platonism, Aristotelianism, and Stoicism, which met and
merged in the early Renaissance, all agreed in their conviction
that right conduct for man consisted in using his gift of reason
to discipline the sensuous appetites that were in him, so that he
might ultimately attain to a knowledge of the highest truths of
the intellect and of the spirit. Man's innate right reason was
thus the key to piety and wisdom. Reason was a gift from God,
and therefore it was in some measure a reflection of the divine
nature: 'quo sapimus intus, & cogitamus, unde omnis est nobis
ratio atque consilium, hoc nos homines esse, factum ipsum
quidem ad imaginem effectoris sui Dei'.[3] Reason not only
raises men above the level of the animals, it is also the means
whereby men share in the higher forms of spiritual existence.
La Primaudaye, for instance, points out that since men are

[1] D. Erasmus, *Libellus...de Pueris statim ac liberaliter instituendis* (1529), 14.
[2] L. Le Roy, *De la Vicissitvde ov Varieté des Choses en l'Vnivers* (1579 edn.),
fo. 16 r⁰.   [3] Sadoleto, *De liberis recte instituendis* (1533), fo. 5v⁰–6r⁰.

beings 'participant de raison et d'intelligence', they have a certain 'convenance avec la vie des Anges'.[1] Reason is a 'guide divine', it is a light drawn from the divine light of God, 'comme vne lampe prouenante de la puissance de Dieu', by which man is enabled to perceive the truth of things: 'ratio perspicax ex sese est, & luminis particeps, mentis que habet oculum cernentem clarissime atque acutissime omnia.'[2]

Invention acquired considerable kudos from its association with the reason, and it may well have been this reflected glory which Ronsard was attempting to exploit, whether consciously or unconsciously, when he sought to bring the concepts of poetic feigning and poetic fictions within the sphere of influence of invention.[3] Yet to approximate feigning and fiction to invention was not to deal with the problem in its entirety, for poetry was heir to another set of associations which were probably even more damaging and damning than those which surrounded the concept of fiction. I am referring now to the concept, or concepts, of imagination. In modern times the concept of imagination, and more particularly of creative imagination, is almost a *sine qua non* of theories of poetry. For the sixteenth-century theorists, however, the question of imagination was a highly complex one, since at that time it was not regarded in the same unreservedly favourable light in which we view it today. Most people concerned with education, for instance, at some time or another deplore the widespread poverty of imagination among those in their charge, and do all they can to promote and encourage the development of that faculty. But the sixteenth century was not at all so enthusiastic; in fact on the whole it tended to be very wary of the imagination and all its doings. It will be the purpose of the next few chapters to show why this should have been so, and to consider in what ways (if any) the theorists of poetry were making use of the concept of imagination current in their age.

---

[1] La Primaudaye, *op. cit.* 90.
[2] *Ibid.* 10; Paré, *op. cit.* ii, 659; Sadoleto, *op. cit.* fo. 7v°.
[3] See pp. 123 ff.

[13]

IMAGINATION,
PLATONIC AND ARISTOTELIAN

The idea that poetry is a product of the faculty of imagination is one which has a very long history. Although there has usually been fairly general agreement that such a relationship does in fact obtain, a number of different theories have been put forward to explain its precise nature. In the Platonic scheme of thought, for instance, all artists, whether they were painters, poets, musicians, or sculptors, were regarded as 'image-makers', in as much as they produced artifacts which were images, or semblances, appearances, of things.[1] Clearly this activity of the artist has close connections with the activity of the imagination, since that faculty is by definition the maker and recorder of mental images, 'the painter,' as Socrates explains, 'who... draws images in the soul'.[2] If we follow the history of the various words which express these concepts of 'image' and 'imagination'—εἰκών, εἴδωλον, εἴκασμα, φάντασμα, εἰκασία, φαντασία—as they are used by Plato and the other Greek philosophers, we can see quite clearly how the relationship between the functioning of the imagination and the activity of the artist was established by semantic and verbal means. This particular piece of semantic history has been excellently set out by M. W. Bundy in the first three chapters of his book, *The Theory of Imagination in Classical and Medieval Thought* (1927).

The sixteenth century also accepted another line of reasoning as proof of the link between poetry and imagination. This was the physiological argument—based on the medical theory of qualities, elements, and humours—that the imagination was the part of the brain which was particularly characterised by the quality of hotness. A typical exposition of this point is to be

---

[1] See p. 52.   [2] Plato, *op. cit.* III, 595.

137

found in Juan Huarte's *Examen de ingenios para las scienzias* of
1575. Huarte adopted the customary classification of the mental
powers into three faculties—imagination, reason, and memory:

L'imagination prouient de la chaleur...les sciences qui appartiennent
à l'imagination, sont celles que disent ceux qui radottent & sont
transportez en la maladie, & non pas celles qui appartiennent à
l'entendement & memoire. Et veu que la frenesie, la manie & la
melancholie sont passions chaudes du cerveau, par cest argument on
peut prouuer que l'imagination consiste en la chaleur.

Further on Huarte specifies which these *sciences* are, 'que disent
ceux qui radottent & sont transportez en la maladie': 'De la
bonne imagination naissent & procedent tous les arts & sciences
qui consistent en figure, correspondance, harmonie, & proportion: qui sont la Poësie, l'Eloquence, la Musique, & sçavoir
prescher.' But the fact that Huarte talks here of 'la bonne
imagination' does not indicate that he has forgotten the associations he earlier alleged it to have with 'frenesie, manie', and
so on: 'Nous auons mis du commancement, la poësie au catalogue des sciences qui appartiennent à l'imagination, non point
d'auanture, ny par faute de consideration: mais pour donner à
entendre, combien sont eslongnez d'entendement ceux qui ont
bonne veine, pour faire des vers.' Further evidence, Huarte
feels, of the connection between poetry and imagination comes
from the fact that poetry and love invariably go together:
'quand vn homme commence à estre amoureux, il se met incontinent à la poësie.... Cela vient pource que telles œuures appartiennent à l'imagination: laquelle croist & monte d'vn degré, auec
la grande chaleur que la passion amoureuse a causé.'[1]

The imagination, then, is associated with *frénésie*, *manie*, and
with *passion*, all of which are by implication reprehensible conditions of the mind. They are all conditions which prevent the
mental pictures one has of things from corresponding to the true
state of things. This is why in the sixteenth century the products
of the imagination were so often said to be vain. According to
this theory of imagination they were indeed empty—empty of

[1] J. Huarte, *Anacrise, ov parfait ivgement et examen des esprits propres & naiz aux sciences, mis en François, au grand profit de la Republique, par Gabriel Chappuis Tourangeau* (1597 edn.), fos. 60r°–v°, 98v°, 103v°, 294r°.

truth, and unreal. The theme of 'vain imagination' in fact crops up quite frequently in medieval and Renaissance literature, nor does it disappear then, but persists until much later. Estienne Pasquier, for instance, writing to Ronsard in 1555, had observed that 'c'est un vice qui nous est propre, que soudain que voyons quelque chose succeder heureusement à quelqu'un, chacun veult estre de sa partie, sous une vaine promesse & imagination qu'il conçoit en soy, de mesme succes'.[1] And Montaigne too, discussing his own early and, as he now believes, mistaken views about money, described them as 'ces vaines et vitieuses imaginations', or poured scorn on 'la vanité de cette mesme imagination' which encourages man to think that he is the equal of God.[2]

In this last phrase Montaigne is attacking the imagination for being the all too willing servant of man's presumptuousness. There was a tradition of thought, however, which condemned the imagination on more general grounds than these. This was the neo-platonic and Stoic tradition, and its condemnation of imagination was based on the opposition (which is fundamental to the platonic view of man) between the material, physical senses and the non-material intellect. This opposition corresponds to that existing in the macrocosm between the world of material phenomena, or 'appearances', and the world of pure 'Ideas'. The 'stuff' with which the imagination was concerned consisted of the images (either immediate or remembered) which the five physical senses had formed in response to the stimulus of external objects. After a certain amount of processing the imagination passed these images on to the reason. Thus, in Plato's terms, the imagination dealt only with appearances, with the ever-moving, ever-changing flux of particulars. Such was the illusory, deceptive world of multiplicity and corporeality, the non-real world of 'becoming', which constituted the sole field of action of the non-rational part of the human mind, and which could by its very nature never be a source of truth. Imagination was bound (and this implied, bound down) by the laws of matter. Reason, on the other hand, was concerned with the immutable, stable Ideas, the universals,

---

[1] Pasquier, *op. cit.* 4.   [2] Montaigne, *op. cit.* I, 64, and II, 132.

which belonged to the realm of non-materiality and of pure 'being'. Here was the only true reality, and only in connection with this could one speak of knowledge and of truth. The objects of reason were intrinsically beautiful and good and desirable, whereas the things of matter, with which the imagination had to deal, were evil, ugly, and steadfastly to be rejected.

The Stoic gloss upon this tradition was to stress the necessity for the reason to exercise maximum control over the so-called passions, which were regarded simply as the appetites of the senses writ large. The Stoics' concern with problems of right conduct led them to emphasise the ethical aspects of the Platonic metaphysics above all others, and this had the effect of making the dichotomy between the reason and the senses more absolute than Plato himself may have intended it to be. As a result the Middle Ages were to take over from the Stoics a rather extravagant dualism which allowed nothing good to be in the senses and nothing bad to be in the reason. Christian philosophers were naturally sympathetic towards this emphasis upon the high excellence of the supra-sensible world and the disparagement of materiality, and they quickly utilised these Stoic attitudes and others in their propounding of the theology of St Paul.

In this scheme the position of imagination was an important one, since not only did imagination act as a sort of 'middle-man' between the senses and the reason, but it also enjoyed a certain measure of autonomy; and the autonomy of an inferior faculty which had to be strictly subordinate to a superior if its possessor was to be enabled to know the true, to will and (what is more) to do the good, could be extremely dangerous. For the imagination was indeed to some extent free to make its own syntheses of sense-experience, and it could not be guaranteed that these syntheses corresponded accurately to whatever had caused the individual, separate sense-impressions in the first place. Thus the imagination was doubly suspect. First, it could handle only the materials presented to it by the senses, which belonged to the inferior, base part of man. Secondly, it could exercise some measure of free-will in its handling of those sense-impressions. We must keep in mind the fact that man's freedom to choose his own course of action had been the cause of Adam's disobedience of God, of the Fall, and of the expulsion from Paradise. Freedom, in medieval Christian eyes, was a very dangerous possession.

All this constitutes the neo-platonic and Stoic aspect of the medieval tradition. But there was another important element in medieval thinking about the imagination, which had its origins rather in Aristotle's doctrines. Aristotle's account of man's mental processes was concerned not so much with prescription, not so much with indicating the proper way to raise oneself up to the contemplation of eternal truths, as with description, with determining the way in which man comes to have the knowledge which he does. This line of thought, as one might well expect, was based on an essentially different system of metaphysics and epistemology from the platonic. Aristotle made two basic assumptions which were directly opposed to Plato's doctrine. First, he accorded reality not to the supra-sensible world of Ideas, but to the here-and-now, to the world of material things. Secondly (and this is simply an extension of the metaphysical assumption into the field of epistemology), he placed the origin of whatever knowledge human beings possess not in the intellectual apprehension of the universal Ideas, but in sensation, in the apprehension of particulars through the senses. In the *De Anima* Aristotle had sought to rehabilitate the imagination, which Plato and his followers had as it were deprived of all rights, by redefining it in such a way that it became indispensable to the proper functioning of the mind. Aristotle claimed that the relation of the imagination to the reason was analogous with that of the senses to the imagination. Just as the senses presented their single sense-images to the imagination, so the imagination in turn presented its composite images to the reason. Thus the function of the imagination was to bridge the gulf between the two terms of the platonic duality. It was a power of the mind mid-way between, and linking together, the inferior sphere of sensation and the superior, purely intellectual sphere of ratiocination.

The medieval philosophers who followed the path of Aristotle in this matter—such men as Albertus Magnus, Aquinas, or Roger Bacon, for instance—were interested pre-eminently in describing what was to them the orderly progress of the mind from percept to concept, together with the physiological conditions underlying the act of cognition. Such a field of study readily lent itself to the methods of careful analysis, subtle distinctions, and precise subordination which were characteristic of so much of medieval philosophy. But another no less characteristic feature of medieval philosophy was the continual attempt to achieve a fusion between the neo-platonic and the neo-aristotelian traditions. As P. P. Morphos has written in the prefatory study to his edition of the dialogues of Guy de Brués, 'The view that Aristotle agreed with Plato and supplemented his theories rather than contradicted them has had a long tradition behind it since the times of late pagan Antiquity... it was given added authority in the Renaissance by Ficino, and after him by Pico della Mirandola.'[1]

In this way it comes about that even what we might call the empirical, Aristotelian tradition, which claimed for the imagination a legitimate and indispensable part in the process of cognition, was still strongly coloured by the Christian–neo-platonic disparagement of the senses. Thus in the sixteenth century we rarely find the Platonic or the Aristotelian views of imagination in their 'pure' forms. Rather is the sixteenth-century attitude towards imagination an amalgam of these two traditions emphasising according to circumstances now the prescriptive, now the descriptive point of view. What follows will be an attempt to disentangle the two strands, perhaps rather artificially, in order to obtain a more distinct view of the key components of the sixteenth-century concept of imagination.

---

[1] Brués, *op. cit.* 39. In corroboration of his remarks Morphos cites an interesting passage from one of Ficino's letters: 'Errant omnino qui Peripateticam disciplinam Platonicae contrariam arbitrantur. Via siquidem termino contraria esse non potest. Peripateticam vero doctrinam ad sapientiam Platonicam esse viam comperiet, quisquis recte consideraverit naturalia nos ad divina perducere, hinc igitur effectum est, ut nullus unquam ad secretiora Platonis mysteria sit admissus, nisi Peripateticis disciplinis prius initiatus.'

[14]

DESCRIPTIVE ACCOUNTS OF
IMAGINATION

We may characterise as Aristotelian in orientation, and therefore as descriptive rather than prescriptive, the psychologies which the Arab thinkers Avicenna and Averroes elaborated from the principles of Galen. Theirs were the so-called faculty psychologies, which came to form an important part of the medieval encyclopaedia.[1] The faculty psychologies distinguished five external powers of the mind, namely the five senses, and three internal powers, imagination, reason, and memory. These three internal powers were held to be located each in a separate region of the brain, and the relations between them constituted the sequence of cognitive processes from initial sensation to ultimate idea. According to this scheme the pair of ventricles situated at the front of the brain housed the imagination, the reason was contained in the middle ventricle, and the memory in the rearmost one. The ventricles of the imagination served as a meeting-place for the individual sensations of the five external senses; here the separate sense-images were joined together and formed into unified, purely mental images, from which the material dross of the external senses was removed, so that they were capable of being handled by the reason. This work of combining and refining was carried out by the mental power known as imagination. The mental images produced by the imagination entered the middle ventricle, where reason, the *vis cogitiva*, formed ideas about them, that is to say judged the images to be true or false, decided whether they represented things that were good and therefore desirable, or things that were evil and therefore to be rejected, and finally activated the will in the appropriate manner. The results of reason's deliberations, consisting

[1] See *Brett's History of Psychology*, abr. R. S. Peters (1953), 231–47, 256–78.

of the mental images together with the judgements and decisions connected with them, were sent down into the ventricle at the back of the head, where memory retained all this material until such time as the reason might wish to refer to it again.

The scheme outlined above, given sundry modifications in matters of detail, was still fully current in the sixteenth century. An excellent instance of this type of faculty psychology is provided by the surgeon Ambroise Paré. In 1575 Paré prefaced the collected edition of his medical works with an 'Introduction ou entrée pour parvenir à la vraye cognoissance de la chirurgie'; he included in this general outline of his subject a preliminary sketch of the mental functions as far as they concerned a sixteenth-century surgeon.

After dealing with the four elements, the four humours, and their corresponding temperaments (all these were the fundamentals of medical science right up to the end of the seventeenth century), Paré turns his attention next to the *facultés*. He distinguishes three main faculties, namely the animal, the vital, and the natural. The vital faculty, he states, is situated in the heart, which distributes warmth and life throughout the body. The animal faculty, or in other words the rational faculty (the adjective was taken from the Latin *anima*, in the sense of the rational soul, or mind, of man), is located in the brain. This organ, 'instrument de la premiere et principale faculté de l'ame, c'est à sçauoir animale et raisonnable',[1] distributes the animal faculty throughout our bodies by means of the nerves, which are the vehicles of feeling and movement. Having determined its location, Paré then subdivides 'la faculté animale' further into three *sortes*, namely *motive*, *sensitive*, and *principale*. The animal faculty in its motive aspects consists of the nerves and the muscles, as instruments of voluntary movement. The animal faculty considered as a sensitive power consists of the five external senses. And finally, the principal part is 'celle qui fait la ratiocination, la memoire, la fantasie ou imagination'.[2]

Later, in the main body of the work, Paré devotes a whole section to the anatomy of the brain. Here, after dealing with the general characteristics of the brain in terms of the tempera-

[1] Paré, *op. cit.* I, 212.   [2] *Ibid.* 53.

ments, Paré goes on to give a detailed account of the ventricles and their function. The two front ventricles, he notes, sweep back in a horn-like shape over the rest of the brain; they are large and capacious because the 'spirits' are still thick and unrefined when they enter the front ventricles. (The spirits which Paré refers to here acted both as the agents and as the medium for all sensation and thought. The origin of this theory is to be found in Aristotle's πνεῦμα.) The two ventricles at the front of the brain have a common outlet rather like the mouth of a pair of bellows, through which the spirits, 'informés des especes', pass into the middle ventricle. Following the tradition of the faculty psychologies, Paré regards the processes involved in cognition as forming a series of purifications in which the materiality is gradually drawn off from the images, or *espèces*, of the external senses, so that they become transformed into 'intellectual' images which are suitable for the reason to handle. Therefore the particular purpose of the ventricles at the front of the brain is to house 'la faculté imaginatiue et estimatiue, lors qu'il est question que l'ame par icelle examine toute et chacune piece illec rapportée par les sens exterieurs, les conferant ensemble et mettant par ordre, pour en auoir vray et iuste iugement de la faculté raisonnable'.[1] The imagination is thus the centre towards which all the external senses are directed. It joins their images together, linking the visual image with the image received through the sense of touch, for example, and submitting the composite image thus obtained to the faculty of reason. The imagination is the servant of the reason and acts, one might say, as an editor of the material brought in by its reporters, the senses.

Paré then goes on to discuss the middle ventricle of the brain, whose particular 'utilité et usage' it is to act as a 'tribunal et consistoire' for the rational faculty when the mind has to make judgements and decisions about the things presented to it by the imagination. From this ventricle a narrow passage equipped with a sort of valve leads down into the last ventricle of the brain, where the memory is lodged. Here is stored 'ce qui aura esté conclu et deliberé de l'esprit, à fin que toutes les fois que la

[1] *Ibid.* 215.

personne se voudra aider des conclusions prises auparauant, ou des choses notables qu'elle aura voulu retenir, elle puisse tirer de là, comme d'vn thresor, ce dont il sera besoin en temps et lieu'.[1]

It is noticeable that in this scheme of cognition, the imagination does not have anything to do with the ideas once they have been produced by the reason and handed down to the memory. The work of the imagination is really completed before the ideas are formed, since it mediates only between the senses and the reason. But there is also to be considered the question of the relations between the memory and the faculty of reason. When in order to guide its present deliberations the reason wishes to refer to its own past conceptions, ideas, judgements, etc., it is the task of the memory to present it with this material as required. The contents of memory, however, are in the form of greatly refined mental images, so that quite clearly some sort of imaginative power will be required vividly to picture forth material from the memory's storehouse at the behest of the higher faculties. If one adhered to the departmentalisation of the faculties in three separate regions of the brain, it was impossible that the imagination proper should fulfil this function, since there was no direct contact between the front pair of ventricles and the rearmost ventricle. And so in order to get over this difficulty the departmentalists often posited a special sort of imagination, attached to the memory as a subsidiary power and inhabiting the same ventricle as the memory.

Another solution which was adopted was to reject the rigid departmentalisation of the faculties in separate ventricles and to suppose that all three mental powers, imagination, reason, and memory, were to be found in each ventricle in more or less equal proportions. This had been the view of Galen and other Greek doctors, and perhaps the most notable of all its adherents in sixteenth-century France was the great Jean Fernel, physician to Henri II.[2] There is no need to follow the progress of this medical controversy in detail. We may simply note that the connection between memory and imagination is quite commonly made in the sixteenth century. Clear references to it can be

---

[1] Paré, *op. cit*, I, 217.   [2] See J. Fernel, *Physiologia* (1555), v, viii.

found, for instance, in Montaigne's *Essais*. In the introduction to his survey of 'coustumes anciennes' he declares, 'Je veux icy entasser aucunes façons anciennes que j'ay en memoire, les unes de mesme les nostres, les autres differentes, afin qu'ayant en l'imagination cette continuelle variation des choses humaines, nous en ayons le jugement plus esclaircy et plus ferme.'[1] Here imagination, in the service of judgement, is bodying forth memory-data in image form. Another instance of the alliance of memory with imagination occurs in the discussion of liars, where Montaigne distinguishes between those who make up everything and those who merely disguise the truth. The latter, he says, are less easily successful in their efforts at deception than the former, since the image of the thing as it really is is already imprinted upon their memories. From there it readily presents itself to the imagination and without the slightest difficulty it ousts 'la fauceté', which has not such a firm foothold. The wholesale liars have a much better chance of being believed, but even then, Montaigne comments, their figment easily slips out of their memories, for it is 'un corps vain et sans prise'.[2] We shall see later that the possibility of imagination handling material other than the plain images coming directly from the senses is of considerable importance in the sixteenth century's attitude towards that faculty.[3]

A more metaphysically coloured account of the imagination, though one still quite clearly based on the faculty psychology type of theory, is that of the philosopher, mathematician, and linguist Charles de Bouelles. Bouelles, or Bovillus as he was known in Latin, was particularly interested in matters of epistemology, and he published several treatises on this subject. His most extensive treatment of what we might call metaphysically conditioned psychology is to be found in the *Liber de Sensu*, which appeared in 1510.

The main purpose, perhaps, of this work is to demonstrate that the human mind is the centre of the universe in as much as it is the point at which non-material, divine intelligence comes into direct contact with the world of material things; it is the

---

[1] Montaigne, *op. cit.* I, 330.   [2] *Ibid.* 32.
[3] See pp. 156–66.

link, Bovillus argues, the *vinculum* between the *sensibilia* and the *intelligibilia*. Bovillus begins in the conventional way by distinguishing two kinds of senses in man: 'sensuum alius est exterior, alius interior.' The external sense is located on the surface of the body and is directed outwards towards the world at large, the 'maiorem mundum,' as Bovillus calls it, or macrocosm. The internal sense, on the other hand (and by this he means the imagination), is hidden within the body and is the sense concerned with the microcosm, with the lesser world of man himself. The interior sense is the common centre for all the external senses, 'ad quem (vt ad mare omnes aque) exteri omnes sensus, omnesque sensibiles species feruntur, rapiuntur, terminantur'. The external senses are the link which joins man with the universe ('sensus exterior est maioris & minoris mundi copula'), for it is the sense-impressions which bring down into man, into the microcosm, the outward forms or images of the macrocosm: 'per eadem sensoria rerum omnium species ab exteriore & maiore mundo: in minorem & interiorem mundum ad sensum usque interiorem & phantasiam deuoluunt.'[1] The external senses are the eye with which the body of man is able to look out beyond itself upon the world. And in exactly the same way the internal sense, the imagination, is the eye of the mind, by means of which the mind is enabled to look outside itself at the body. The imagination is the vehicle of communication between the body and the mind, and for that reason, just as the external senses are located on the outermost surface of the body in order that they may be continuously in contact with the world outside, so the internal sense is located on the outermost surface of the mind, so that it may be in continuous contact with the body:

sicut exterior sensus se habet ad mundum: ita & interior ad hominis corpus. Est enim exterior sensus aspectus hominis in mundum.... Interior vero sensus oculus est anime, quo illa despicit in corpus: aliquo pacto inter corpus, animamque medius & vt anime ora extremaue superficies....Sicut enim sensus exterior, est exterior ad totum hominem, velut totius hominis extremitas, mundique contingentia: ita

---

[1] C. Bovillus, *Liber de Sensu* (1510), fo. 22r⁰, v⁰.

et interior ora est extremaue superficies anime, corporisque contingentia & attactus.[1]

The interior sense is, as it were, the memory of the external
senses, retaining the images which are only fleetingly present to
the latter: 'sensibiles species sunt velut successiue, et ad
momentum euanide: in exteriore sensu. In interiore vero fixe et
permanentes.' Thus Bovillus maintains that the external senses
are practical powers, whereas the internal sense, the imagination, is a speculative power and is therefore of a higher order of
being, more perfect, than the external senses: 'Sensitiua virtus
in exteriore sensorio practica est: in interiore speculatiua ... is
est perfectus sensus: quam imaginationem & phantasiam
vocamus.' Bovillus makes a distinction between the susceptive
or presentative aspect of the activity of the imagination (that is,
its function as a receiver and passer-on of images from the
external senses) and the judging or judicative aspect; and he
insists that whilst the presentative imagination is part of the
material body and will therefore die with it, the judicative
imagination is part of man's immortal soul: 'Imaginationis vis
iudicatiua, pars est animi immortalis: presentatiua vero corporis
pars est, cum corpore interire nata.'[2] For Bovillus imagination
is the all-important link between mind and body, and he is
careful to keep it in balance between the two, participating in
both, and holding them together by virtue of its dual nature.

To grant the faculty of imagination such an important function is not, however, to give it also the status of a completely
independent mental power. Just as imagination presides over
the external senses, synthesising and refining the images which
they present to it, so, Bovillus points out, reason is set as a judge
and a critic over the imagination to refine its images still further
and to deliberate about them: 'Sicut exteriori sensui presidet
imaginatio, que est sensationum exteriorum resumptio & defecatio: ita & interne sensationi (quam imaginationem diximus)
preest ratio, illius arbitra & censoria, que est & defecatio &
repetitio, internarum omnium sensationum.' If the imagination
is freed from the control of reason, then the imagination will

---

[1] Bovillus, *op. cit.* fo. 24vᵒ.
[2] Bovillus, *op. cit.* fos. 23rᵒ, 24vᵒ, 27rᵒ.

become false and deceiving, for it will take what are merely the sensible forms of things (which it does in fact perceive truly) to be their real substance. Reason alone can distinguish what a thing really is from what it appears to be to the senses:

Tolle rationem presidem, ab imaginatione: continuo pellax erit falsa, & pseudola imaginatio . . . vera hactenus est imaginatio: qua spectrorum & phantasmatum vera apparitio. Nam veraciter ab ea videntur & conspiciuntur phantasmata. falsa autem est: cum rationis absentia, atque defectu: putat spectra, veras esse substantias. et que intus parent ita in re & mundo habere, atque esse. Ab sola quippe ratione: omne oritur discriminis, differitatisque rerum iudicium. a qua vnumquodque sub propria ratione, dinoscitur id esse quod est vt spectrum dinoscitur esse spectrum, non substantia: et substantia sese eidem rationis oculo substantiam.[1]

Imagination is fitted to handle only certain elements in the cognitive process, namely the *spectra*, the partly refined images of the senses. But if it is left to work without supervision, then confusion will arise, since the proper objects of reason, the real substances of things, are beyond its capacity. As long as the imagination is under the supervision of reason, however (and that is the normal situation), all will be well.

In this type of theory of the mind the imagination is fully integrated into the chain of cognitive processes. If the mind is to work efficiently, then all the subordinate powers, and not least the imagination, must play their several parts in attaining that end. A swift and lively imagination and a retentive, ready memory are therefore absolute necessities, and should be cherished as such. La Primaudaye, for instance, in discussing various excellences of the mind brings out well the importance of the imagination:

Les subtils et sages, par petites coniectures ou prinses de bien loin, apperçoivent ce qu'ils cerchent, et y parviennent. Il y en a des autres, qui sont de si grand esprit, qu'ils embrassent beauc   de choses à la fois, et si voyant comme en vn iect d'œil et en vn seul regard tout ce qui est à propos. En quoi il appert qu'ils ont l'imagination et la phantasie prompte, et vne memoire comme vn thresor tout ouvert, et la consideration prompte, et la souvenance entiere et vigoureuse. Car

[1] Bovillus, *op. cit.* fos. 40 v°, 41 r°.

si l'imagination et la phantasie est lente et tardive, ou la memoire enserrée, ou si la consideration cesse, ou la recordation est debile, le discours sera tardif et rencontrera bien mal.[1]

Just as *souvenance* or *recordation*, recalling, is the action of the memory, so *considération* is the action of the imagination. This would seem to be a sort of preliminary scanning operation, the surveying of a wide range of material and the selection of 'ce qui est à propos', so that the reasoning power, 'le discours', may proceed about its higher business with the maximum accuracy and speed. This is indeed a task of some responsibility.

In Montaigne's view also the imagination can be very closely connected with the powers of reasoning and cogitation and judgement, and can have the task of assisting those powers in some of their highest endeavours. Imagination is the means whereby some people have been able to raise themselves so far above the condition of man and above his worldly scale of values that even the highest positions of authority and power seem to them mean and base: 'D'autres, ayant leur imagination logée au dessus de la fortune et du monde, trouverent les sieges de la justice et les thrones mesmes des Roys, bas et viles.' In fact Montaigne seems to suggest that this scorn of earth-centred values is one of the benefits of possessing a sound imagination, for in another essay when he is discussing the merits and demerits of retirement from the world he writes that 'l'imagination de ceux qui, par devotion, recherchent la solitude, remplissant leur courage de la certitude des promesses divines en l'autre vie, est bien plus sainement assortie.'[2] Here imagination looks forward to the life to come, and from this looking-forward draws the strength to deny 'les appetits charnels'.

For Montaigne the high quality of the imagination is also a mark of the great man. All of us, he writes, are shut up inside our own little selves, able to see no further than the end of our noses. Socrates, on the other hand, when he was asked where he came from, did not reply, 'Athens', but 'the world': 'Luy, qui avoit son imagination plus plaine et plus estandue, embrassoit

[1] La Primaudaye, *op. cit.* 124.
[2] Montaigne, *op. cit.* I, 144, 276.

l'univers comme sa ville, jettoit ses connoissances, sa societé et ses affections à tout le genre humain, non pas comme nous qui ne regardons que sous nous.' Imagination has the power of bringing all things within reach of the mind. Montaigne further considers the imagination able to deal with matters of truth and usefulness, or at least things can present themselves to the imagination as true and/or useful: 'C'est la misere de nostre condition, que souvent ce qui se presente à nostre imagination pour le plus vray, ne s'y presente pas pour le plus utile à nostre vie.'[1] What we may note here is that imagination is held to have a close concern with the problem of conflicting value-judgements. Imagination is not simply presenting to the higher faculties a 'common image' compounded of separate sense-images, but it is collating different judgements about the same 'common image' and setting them impartially before the mind.

Huarte had allotted to the imagination much the same sort of function when he stressed the importance of 'la bonne imagination' to doctors in making diagnoses and treating patients. Huarte based his views on the theory that 'l'imagination est celle qui cause le iugement, & la cognoissance des choses particulieres, & non l'entendement, ny les sens exterieurs'. The senses do not know their objects, writes Huarte, they merely perceive them. The understanding, on the other hand, knows merely what steps are appropriate in any given case; but it does not know the individual case—that is the function of the imagination:

l'entendement...enseigne seulement à prendre l'indice de ce qui promet plus de danger: mais la seule imagination demonstre, lequel des indices est le plus grand, conferant le mal que fait la chaleur, auec celuy du symptome, la cause, le peu de force, ou grande vertu...c'est vne grace qui vient d'vne fecondité de l'imagination, qui s'appelle autrement *Solertia*, qui veut dire Industrie [i.e. skill, shrewdness, *adresse*], laquelle par signes communs, incertaines coniectures, & de peu de fermeté en moins d'vn rien, trouue mille differences de choses esquelles consiste la force de medeciner & pronostiquer certainement.[2]

[1] Montaigne, *op. cit.* I, 168–9, and II, 205.
[2] Huarte, *op. cit.* fos. 166v⁰, 167v⁰–168r⁰. We should remember, however, that Huarte's overall judgement of the imagination was a very harsh one (see p. 138).

Imagination is here a distinguishing, discriminatory power, judging particulars, whereas *l'entendement* is concerned only with universals.

Accounts of the activity of imagination such as those just quoted from Bovillus, La Primaudaye, Montaigne, and Huarte, indicate that in the sixteenth century the imagination was not condemned to consort exclusively with the senses, but was allowed to play a key role in even the highest processes of the mind. In this light imagination is seen to be a much more versatile and valuable power than that which the faculty psychologies confined to the front ventricles of the brain. It now appears as an indispensable assistant for the understanding, presenting it not only with the images of whatever sense-objects are relevant to the matter in hand, but also with more general and 'abstract' ideas, judgements, and so on, which have been stored up in the memory.

We should not make too much of this point, however. By and large for the sixteenth century the imagination was simply the image-making faculty, which pictures objects and events already experienced or perceived, but no longer present to the senses. But it could also picture things which had never actually formed part of one's experience. To take our examples once more from Montaigne: the imagination may picture a fabulous palace which one has only read about and never actually seen, or it may enable one to keep images of great men of antiquity constantly before the mind's eye, so that they become models for one's own conduct. And it is imagination which makes the sight of the outside of a prison so unpleasant to Montaigne, for he himself has never been inside one, 'non pas seulement pour m'y promener'. Imagination also and perhaps especially pictures things that belong properly to the future, things which have not yet been experienced. The bodily sufferings of old age and death, in fact any 'mal advenir', these are familiar objects of the imagination. In 1572 Montaigne's advice for dealing with the problem of death was the formula of the Stoics: 'A tous instans representons la à nostre imagination et en tous visages.' Later, however, death ceased to be such a terrifying prospect: 'Mon imagination m'en presente quelque visage facile, et, puisqu'il faut mourir, desirable.'[1]

Yet despite its undoubted powers in a picturing capacity the imagination was held to have serious limitations. It was limited by the fact that in the final analysis all its pictures had to be based on sensations already experienced. This was, of course, the Aristotelian position: that there is nothing in the mind which was not formerly in the senses. For instance, Montaigne points out that it is quite impossible, whatever process of reasoning or analogy one may use, to fix in the imagination of a blind man any apprehension of light, colour, or sight. He has never been able to perceive such things through his own senses, and this will prevent him from having any mental picture of them at all. Imagination can never pass beyond itself into the unknown; it can only relate things to itself, and deal with them in terms of itself. In this, so Montaigne claims, it is no different from anything else in the world: 'chacune [chose] raporte les qualitez de toutes autres choses à ses propres qualitez; lesquelles nous pouvons bien estendre et racourcir, mais c'est tout; car, hors de ce raport et de ce principe, nostre imagination ne peut aller, ne peut rien diviner autre, et est impossible qu'elle sorte de là, et qu'elle passe au delà.' In other words, if we have received in our imagination the image of a lion's body and the image of a lion's head, we can imagine a lion with three heads and only one body. By the same process we can imagine a cyclops. But we cannot imagine anything outside our sphere of earthly experience. Thus we can have no clear picture of the first cause and being, but merely a vague, undefined idea which each man fills out according to his own capacity: 'ce n'estoit autre chose que l'extreme effort de nostre imagination vers la perfection.' We can do no more.[2]

Imagining lions with three heads was not likely to have any very serious consequences. Although the Renaissance was deeply fascinated by every possible kind of 'monstre et prodige' (and it was a favourite pastime of savants to collect instances of such phenomena from the ancient writers with the help of Pliny

---

[1] Montaigne, *op. cit.* I, 87, 279, 340, and III, 222, 320.
[2] Montaigne, *op. cit.* II, 207, 229–30, 299.

and others, and then to add as many modern ones as they had heard of), it would not have mattered too much if three-headed lions did not exist after all. But in more everyday matters, and especially in matters of ethics, when one was faced with the problem of deciding upon the line of conduct appropriate to a particular set of circumstances, then it was vitally important to know whether the pictures presented to the mind by the imagination corresponded with things as they really were, or not. The sixteenth century, it is generally agreed, was an age in which men's minds were much exercised by problems of ethics. It was precisely in issues of this nature that the theories of imagination I have just been discussing, which treated the faculty primarily as an essential part of the cognitive process, were pushed into the background; all the emphasis was now placed upon what I have called the prescriptive type of theory, which took up a strongly admonitory, moral standpoint towards the imagination, regarding it as a dangerous ally to the regiments of sin.

PRESCRIPTIVE ACCOUNTS OF IMAGINATION

Philosophers who followed a Christian–Stoic line, that is to say those who concerned themselves above all with ethics or who treated all the material of philosophy in ethical terms, emphasised always the point that the imagination was free, to a certain extent, to do as it pleased with the sense-data which were presented to it, and that it was therefore likely to be a continual source of deception. For, as we have just seen, imagination was a faculty which not only pictured 'choses absentes', things once experienced and now summoned up from the memory to help the reasoning powers in making judgements, but also could produce images without their having any necessary correlation with things as they really were, or even on occasion without their being derived directly from reality at all. The distance between the images of the imagination and things as they really were could often be quite considerable, so that one could be led to make erroneous judgements and to make serious mistakes in deciding upon some course of action.

The great disadvantage of the imagination from the point of view of the moralists was precisely that it was so closely connected with the senses, and that it therefore participated in the base, material, non-rational part of man's nature. For thanks to its lowly position in the hierarchy of the mental powers there arose the possibility, and even the probability, that imagination would ally itself with desire, and that the combination of these two powers would overrule reason and thus disrupt the orderly functioning of the mental processes. The theoretical background to this fear is again Aristotelian psychology. Aristotle had divided the rational functions of the mind into two main classes —knowing and willing. Willing he took to be the dynamic aspect of behaviour, the impulse which exists in all living creatures to attain to a better, because more complete, more perfect state. Just as there were three different modes of knowing, according to whether they were carried out by the senses, by the imagination, or by the reason, so there were three different modes of willing, which were also correlated with these powers. The three modes of willing were first, desire (the willing of the senses, which included all activities that either bring pleasure or avoid pain; hence desire was also called appetite or passion), secondly, wish (the willing of the imagination, which differs from desire in that it is somewhat amenable to reason), and finally, will itself, which is the result of rational deliberation.[1]

Guillaume du Vair, in the *Traité de la Constance et Consolation es calamitez Publiques* published at the end of the sixteenth century, explained very carefully how the disruption of the proper workings of the mind came about, tracing the process through from the first perception by the senses to the final rousing of the passions:

Les sens, vraies sentinelles de l'ame, disposez en dehors pour observer tout ce qui se presente, sont comme une cire molle, sur laquelle s'imprime, non la vraie et interieure nature, mais seulement la face et forme exterieure des choses. Ils en rapportent les images en l'ame, avec un temoignage et recommandation de faveur et quasi avec un prejugé de leur qualité, selon qu'ils les trouvent plaisantes et agreables à leur particulier, et non utiles et necessaires au bien universel de l'homme....De tout cela se forme en nostre ame cette inconsiderée opinion que nous prenons des choses...aussi tost qu'elle est conceue, sans plus rien deferer au discours et à l'entendement, elle s'empare de nostre imagination et, comme dans une citadelle, elle y tient fort contre la droite raison...si elle nous veut faire fuir quelque chose, elle nous la peint hideuse et espouvantable; si elle nous la veut faire aimer, elle lui farde le visage, lui fait la bouche et les yeux rians. Puis elle descend en nostre cœur et remue nos affections avec des mouvemens violens d'esperance ou de crainte, de tristesse ou de plaisir; et, pour troubler nostre repos, sousleve en nous les passions qui sont les vrais seditieux de nostre ame.[2]

[1] Cf. Brett, *op. cit.* 90–129.
[2] G. du Vair, *Traité de la Constance et Consolation es calamitez Publiques*, ed. J. Flach and F. Funck-Brentano (1915), 66–7.

Du Vair is quite clearly using the extended military metaphor to bring out the reprehensibility of the actions of the senses and of the imagination. The senses are appointed as sentries to warn the mind of what is going on at the outside perimeter of the body. By their nature they are capable of perceiving only the outward appearances of things, not their true essence. Yet instead of merely reporting the presence of outside things they take it upon themselves to present to the mind (*l'ame*) their own biassed view of the nature of those things. They do this without referring the matter to their superior officer, the reason. The senses have in this respect usurped far more than their allotted share of responsibility. Making judgements about the nature of things is not their task, but the task of a superior, non-material mental power. The senses are not fitted to perform such a function, since they cannot attain to true knowledge, which is achieved only by the reason. By presenting to the imagination not the simple sense-data but sense-data distorted by their own private opinions about them, they upset the orderly sequence of psychological processes, which should proceed from sense-perception, through rational judgement, to willing and acting. But now the imagination becomes the stronghold of a full-scale insurrection. It is the revolt of a subordinate against those set in power over it, the crime of lese-majesty.

Montaigne, too, repeatedly refers to the partnership between imagination and desire. There is the passage in which he describes how in the passionate time of his youth his imagination made some things seem more attractive than they really were, simply because he wanted them: 'je voyais evidemment grossir et croistre les avantages du subjet que j'allois desirant, et agrandir et enfler par le vent de mon imagination.' Imagination serves desire by presenting it with the materials it wants, and by presenting them in a favourable light. In fact imagination stimulates desire, and it might almost be said that desire is formed, is given a definite shape, by the picturings of the imagination. Montaigne says that he cannot understand 'comment on vienne à allonger le plaisir de boire outre la soif, et se forger en l'imagination un appetit artificiel et contre nature'.[1] The

---

[1] Montaigne, *op. cit.* ii, 15, 275.

metaphor contained in the verb *se forger* casts an interesting light on the relations between imagination and appetite, or desire.

In fact for Montaigne the expression 'par imagination et par souhait', or 'par imagination et par desir', is almost a *phrase fixe*, so regularly do the two nouns appear together in the *Essais*. It is evidence of our utter stupidity that 'non par jouyssance, mais par imagination et par souhait, nous ne puissions estre d'accord de ce dequoy nous avons besoing pour nous contenter'. Desire and imagination bear witness to the diversity of man, to his instability and waywardness: 'N'est-ce pas un singulier tesmoignage d'imperfection, ne pouvoir r'assoir nostre contentement en aucune chose, et que, par desir mesme et imagination, il soit hors de nostre puissance de choisir ce qu'il nous faut?' Or on another occasion they are associated with Montaigne's awareness of the limitations imposed upon him by his own temperament: 'les productions de ces riches et grandes ames du temps passé sont bien loing au dela de l'extreme estendue de mon imagination et souhaict.'[1]

In the second book of the *Academie Françoise* La Primaudaye explains at some length the manner in which the *affections*, which he defines as 'les mouvemens & actes de la puissance qui est en la nature de l'ame à suivre le bien, & eviter le mal', should properly be controlled by the judgement of reason, and the great disturbance that results if they are allowed to become carried away by the tumultuous activity of the imagination:

entre les mouvemens de l'ame, il y en a qui vont devant le iugement, & les autres le suivent: combien qu'ils sont souventesfois si soudains & tant precipitez, qu'il semble bien qu'ils se soient desbridez sans avoir attendu aucun iugement...combien qu'il faille que les affections soient aiguillonnées par le iugement, il ne s'ensuit pas pourtant qu'elles ne puissent estre esmeues, que ce iugement rassis n'y soit tousiours qui ordonne des choses apres le discours de la raison. Car il leur suffit d'vn autre iugement qui ne suit pas vn examen tant diligent, mais seulement ce que la fantasie [i.e. the imagination] lui presente, sans en faire autre grand discours. Et ce iugement estant ainsi esmeu par la fantasie, est le plus frequent & le plus ordinaire, qui conduit &

---

[1] Montaigne, *op. cit.* II, 283, 354, and I, 342.

gouverne les actions humaines.... Et par ainsi la seule imagination & fantasie tirant à soy tumultuairement, comme elle est turbulente & legiere, quelque espece & apparence d'opinion & de iugement, par laquelle elle iuge ou bon ou mauvais ce qui lui est presenté, est cause que nous vivons entre de merveilleux troubles de toutes affections, de crainte, de desir, de tristesse, & de ioye... si la raison & le iugement sont gouvernez & vaincus par les affections, & la raison par la fantasie, l'estat de l'ame est du tout renversé & perverti, comme si le corps voulant cheminer, mettoit la teste en terre, & eslevoit les pieds en haut pour marcher.

Imagination is a great disturber of the peace, a great agitator; 'elle est turbulente & legiere'—the two epithets summarise well the charges laid against the faculty. That is why reason must be very careful not to get itself mixed up with imagination, but to keep a strict watch over it. Being 'prince & seigneur' ruling over all the other mental powers, reason must

[tenir] bien son rang sans se mesler et confondre, et s'embrouiller avec l'imagination et la phantasie, desquelles il faut qu'il soit le iuge, pour approuver ou condamner ce qui sera bon ou mauvais, et pour les corriger et arrester, et tenir en bride. Car si la raison se mesle et s'embrouille avec elles, elle en sera tellement troublée, qu'elle ne pourra point iuger comme elle doit, des choses qu'elles lui apporteront et presenteront, ains sera transportée, comme si elle estoit deposée de son siege, et comme si les chambrieres gouvernoient leur maistresse, et prenoient le lieu d'icelle.[1]

In order to appreciate the full horror that such a prospect held for the sixteenth-century mind (and also the prospect of sentries becoming insubordinate), we must remember the firm belief of the Renaissance that the universe was organised at all levels according to the same rigidly hierarchical and divinely ordained pattern. The relationship of God with His Creation was mirrored in the relationship of a king with his subjects, of a freeman with his household, of the reason with the bodily appetites. Any attempt to behave in a manner out of keeping with one's proper station was an act of the utmost blasphemy and impiety, a Satanic revolt as it were, an attempt to overthrow the divine order of things which could only end in cataclysmic disaster.[2]

---

[1] La Primaudaye, *op. cit.* 108, 159–60, 196.
[2] See E. M. Tillyard, *The Elizabethan World Picture* (1950).

La Primaudaye was particularly emphatic about the necessity of keeping the imagination in its proper place. In the chapter immediately preceding the one from which I have just quoted he had written: 'Car si elle [imagination] n'est gouvernée & refrenée par la raison, elle trouble & esmeut tout le sens & l'entendement, comme vne tempeste en la mer.' Imagination is a thoroughly bad lot, tending continually to degrade the mind, to drag it down to the level of the senses, whereas the reason strives to raise it up to the understanding and contemplation of higher things. This is the lifelong struggle that goes on in man's inner being between imagination and reason, the struggle of the *zwei Seelen* in Faust's breast: 'il s'esmeut vn combat entre la raison & l'imagination & phantasie. Car l'imagination & la phantasie, comme plus prochaines des sens corporels, tirent l'ame aux choses corporelles: mais la raison & l'esprit l'aiguil-lonnent, & la font eslever & adresser aux choses plus hautes & plus excellentes.' Man is torn between the false lure of the 'biens imaginez du corps' and the lasting value of the 'vrais biens de l'ame'. And most men, being weak, undisciplined creatures, prefer the 'biens imaginez'.[1]

For Montaigne imagination serves not only the baser, more or less straightforwardly physical desires, but also the more complex psychological desire for self-aggrandisement. The flights of man's imagination are a sure indication of his great 'presomption'. It is by the aid of the imagination, and entirely without other and more reliable justification, that man convinces himself of his pre-eminent position in the universe, and of the value of what he is pleased to call his knowledge:

l'homme... se sent et se void logé icy, parmy la bourbe et le fient du monde, attaché et cloué à la pire, plus morte et croupie partie de l'univers, au dernier estage du logis et le plus esloigné de la voute celeste, avec les animaux de la pire condition des trois; et se va plantant par l'imagination au dessus du cercle de la Lune et ramenant le ciel soubs ses pieds. C'est par la vanité de cette mesme imagination qu'il s'egale à Dieu, qu'il s'attribue les conditions divines, qu'il se trie soy mesme et separe de la presse des autres creatures.[2]

[1] La Primaudaye, *op. cit.* 105, 107–8, 117.
[2] Montaigne, *op. cit.* II, 132. This passage is a fine example of medieval-style cosmology.

This power of man's imagination to convince him that he holds a particularly exalted and privileged position in the universe, this independence of things as they really are, is what distinguishes man from the animals in Montaigne's eyes. The imagination of animals deals only with the immediately perceived sense-data, and cannot go beyond the present sensory experience.[1] But man alone of all the creatures possesses 'cette liberté de l'imagination et ce deresglement de pensées, luy representant ce qui est, ce qui n'est pas, et ce qu'il veut, le faux et le veritable'. This capacity of the human imagination for independent activity may seem a great boon, but in fact 'c'est un advantage qui lui est bien cher vendu et du quel il a bien peu à se glorifier, car de la naist la source principale des maux qui le pressent: peché, maladie, irresolution, trouble, desespoir'.[2] This is indeed a high price to pay for a mere 'deresglement de pensées'!

I have already touched on the connection of the imagination with *péché* (implicitly at least) by discussing the link between imagination and bodily desires, and between imagination and human presumptuousness—'nostre maladie naturelle et originelle', as Montaigne calls it.[3] But the association of imagination with *maladie* in a more strictly physical sense was also a commonplace of medieval and Renaissance thought. Just as the imagination could engage in picture-making activities without the prior stimulus of the bodily senses, so also could it reverse completely the normal direction of its relationship with the body and exert a direct and powerful influence upon physical states. This, of course, was an aspect of the imagination's activities which concerned medical men, and not unexpectedly we find Ambroise Paré devoting a few pages to the topic. 'Iceluy sens', he writes, referring to imagination, the internal sense, 'a grande seigneurie en nous, tellement que le corps naturellement luy obeit en plusieurs et diuerses choses, lorsqu'il est fort arresté en quelque imagination.'[4] Statements of this sort,

[1] Cf. La Primaudaye, *op. cit.* 119: 'combien qu'elles ["les betes"] ayent quelque imagination, phantasie et apprehension des choses qui sont presentées à leurs sens corporels: cela n'a lieu qu'à l'heure et sur le champ qu'elles leur sont presentées.'
[2] Montaigne, *op. cit.* ii, 141.   [3] *Ibid.* 132.   [4] Paré, *op. cit.* ii, 658.

followed by a selection of *exempla* culled from post-classical or contemporary anthologists, were *de rigueur* in sixteenth-century treatments of imagination. The Renaissance was greatly interested in what Spingarn called 'the pathology of the imagination: [for] they conceived of it primarily as a source of physical or mental aberration'.[1] We have seen something of the mental aberrations caused by the imagination; let us now turn to the physical side.

In keeping with the current fashion for making a display of largely second-hand erudition, Montaigne's earliest version of the essay 'De la force de l'imagination' consisted of a conventional string of *exempla* showing the sort of effect which imagination could have upon the body.[2] In this essay he quotes, for instance, the famous story of King Cyppus of Italy, who watched a bull-fight with such passionate interest that he dreamt about bulls throughout the whole of the following night and woke up to find a pair of splendid horns sprouting from his forehead. Then some people, says Montaigne, attribute both the scars of King Dagobert of the Franks and those of St Francis of Assisi to 'la force de l'imagination'. Dagobert's scars were supposed to have been caused by his dread of gangrene. St Francis received his in the course of an ecstatic meditation, and they appeared in the form of the stigmata. Perhaps Montaigne relished the half-blasphemous juxtaposition. At any rate, he thought that the psycho-physiological processes involved might be very similar in both cases, and might well account for all so-called miracles as well as for visions and hallucinations. Montaigne was also well acquainted with the sixteenth-century equivalent of modern 'psychological injections'; in fact he thought that this was probably the only way in which cures could be effected at all: 'Pourquoy praticquent les medecins avant main la creance de leur patient avec tant de fauces promesses de sa guerison, si ce n'est afin que l'effect de l'imagination supplisse l'imposture de leur aposeme? Ils sçavent qu'un des maistres de ce mestier leur a laissé par escrit, qu'il s'est

[1] J. E. Spingarn, *Critical Essays of the 17th Century* (1908), I, x–xi. Cf. the passage from Huarte which I quote in p. 138.
[2] After the 1588 edition he added a number of more personal instances.

trouvé des hommes à qui la seule veue de la medecine faisoit l'operation.' And he goes on to cite trick cures of this sort.[1]

But the occasion of imagination's most powerful effect upon the body is through the medium of fear. In one of the cases I have just quoted from Montaigne, that of King Dagobert, fear was involved. Ambroise Paré also mentions the interaction of fear and imagination. He quotes the instance of people who, when watching a tight-rope walker and 'le voyant en peril de se rompre le col, bras et iambes, trembloient de peur, ne l'osans bonnement regarder'. And the effect is not only upon the spectators, but also upon the performer of such feats: 'cette vertu imaginatiue fait cheoir la personne de dessus quelque planche, ou quelque lieu haut, pour la grande apprehension et timidité qu'elle a de tomber.'[2] Montaigne has a more spectacular case to offer: 'il y en a qui, de frayeur, anticipent la main du bourreau. Et celuy qu'on debandoit pour luy lire sa grace, se trouva roide mort sur l'eschafaut du seul coup de son imagination.'[3] Imagination pictures what might happen, or what has happened to others in the past, and the image is so vivid, has such a power of compulsion, that what is pictured does in fact happen. 'Fortis imaginatio generat casum', as Montaigne had written at the beginning of his chapter, quoting from 'les clercs'.

Another supposed effect of the imagination is to be found in the sixteenth-century belief that pregnant women transfer to their unborn children the form of any 'ardente et obstinée imagination' which they might have during their pregnancy: 'il advient souventesfois que les phantasies & imaginations des femmes enceintes sont si vehementes & si violentes, qu'elles impriment au corps des enfans qu'elles portent, les images & formes des choses, sur lesquelles elles ont arresté & fiché leur imagination & phantasie, & ausquelles suivant icelle elles se sont plus affectionnées.'[4] The danger was held to stem not only from 'visions nocturnes' and 'songe[s] fantastique[s]', which impressed their images upon the imagination when the body and the higher faculties were asleep, but also from the simple act of looking at things which might make a vivid and striking

---

[1] Montaigne, *op. cit.* i, 107.   [2] Paré, *op. cit.* ii, 659.
[3] Montaigne, *op. cit.* i, 100–1.   [4] La Primaudaye, *op. cit.* 106.

impression upon the senses. This belief has a long literary history which can be traced back at least as far as Empedocles in the fifth century B.C. Paré cites a number of ancient authorities for his instances of a white child born to an Ethiopian princess (the result of looking at a striking portrait of Andromeda), of a child 'velue comme un ours' (caused by the sight of an image of St John the Baptist clad in a cloak of skins), and of a dark child born to white parents. These, he claims, are examples of 'monstres qui se font par l'imagination'. Paré points out that the mother-to-be must avoid picturing or looking at 'choses monstrueuses' only before the child is fully formed in the womb. Once this has happened 'l'imagination n'aura aucun lieu'. Finally, as confirmation of the testimony of the ancients, Paré cites a couple of recent cases in Europe of children born as 'monstres' thanks to the power of the imagination. As Malgaigne, Paré's nineteenth-century editor, remarks, the *monstres* in question were probably what we call anencephalics.[1]

The case of pregnant women is a particular instance of the general principle that the imagination can have an effect not only upon one's own body, making one tremble, sweat, blush, fall off planks, drop down dead, and so on, but also upon the body of someone else. Just as by looking at diseased eyes one's own eyes become diseased, so 'l'imagination esbranlée avecques vehemence, eslance des traits qui puissent offencer l'object estrangier'. That is the method witches use to cast spells upon their victims. Similarly, the ancients record that certain women of Scythia could kill a person they were angry with simply by looking at him. Tortoises and ostriches hatch their eggs in this way. For in this respect at least animals can command and are subject to the same effects of the imagination as human beings. Montaigne tells of a cat which he watched staring at a bird in a tree until the bird fell as if dead at the cat's feet, 'ou ennyvré par sa propre imagination, ou attiré par quelque force attractive du chat'. There are so many instances of this sort of thing, Montaigne comments airily, that everyone can think of his own examples.[2]

The imagination is also the cause of the delusions of madmen

---

[1] Paré, *op. cit.* III, 23–5.   [2] Montaigne, *op. cit.* I, 109.

and of the not so mad. Montaigne had pointed to man's delusions about his place in the universe. Paré discusses the more
certifiable delusions. The imagination is situated in an extremely
dangerous position, for, being in the front of the head, it is the
first part of the brain to receive the bad and excessive humours,
or 'vapours', which may rise up at intervals from the organs of
the lower part of the body, from the liver, for instance, the
spleen, or the heart. These vapours are quite likely to spread
throughout the brain and to infect the memory and the reasoning
faculty as well as the imagination. Paré instances the 'resveries'
(here with the sixteenth-century connotations of madness,
folies) caused by 'les vapeurs des mois retenus, [qui] esleuées
iusqu'au cerueau par les veines et arteres, quelquesfois infectent
tellement le cerueau de leur puanteur et malignité, que sa substance en est estourdie et abrutie, et ses fonctions abolies et
deprauées ou corrompues, non seulement en imagination, mais
aussi en memoire et ratiocination'. Women suffering from this
disorder laugh or cry without reason, or even try to strangle
themselves or to throw themselves out of windows.[1]

In the 'Introduction' Paré had already devoted a whole
chapter to other examples of 'maladies faites par imaginations
fantastiques'. There is the case of the man who believed that he
was an earthenware vessel, and took great care not to bump into
anything for fear of being shattered into a thousand fragments;
this example Paré takes from Galen. Then there are the instances
quoted by Avicenna of men who thought they were kings, or
wolves, or devils, or birds. Finally, Paré adds a few cases from
his own experience, such as that of 'une dame de nostre Cour'
who claimed to have been poisoned with mercury and to be able
to feel it running through her limbs. She was cured by being
given a bath of herbs, which she was told would draw out the
mercury; a few ounces of mercury were secretly introduced into
the bath and then shown to her afterwards: 'Alors fut bien
ioyeuse et creut estre guarie.'[2] This would have appealed to
Montaigne.

As a summary of the sixteenth-century view of imagination,
we may say that thanks to the position of that faculty in the

---

[1] Paré, *op. cit.* II, 782.   [2] Paré, *op. cit.* I, 98–9.

hierarchy of the mental powers its images and 'opinions' were acknowledged to have if not absolute, then at least relative value by comparison with those of the senses, which represented the basest and most material functions of the mind. Thus La Primaudaye was expressing a standard sixteenth-century point of view when he wrote that the things which imagination set up as being desirable were 'encore plus stables & plus fermes que celles de tous les sens corporels'. As soon as this had been said, however, it was necessary to climb on to the next rung of the ladder and to emphasise that although what was desirable to the imagination was indeed superior to that which the senses sought, it was nevertheless greatly inferior to the pleasures of the understanding. And so La Primaudaye continued, almost at once: 'Mais les voluptez de la raison & de l'entendement & de l'esprit, sont encore de beaucoup plus longue durée. Car elles sont pures.'[1] The others are impure in that they are still contaminated by gross materiality. Only the pleasures of the understanding reach into the sphere of pure intellectuality. And these, of course, are the true end of man; he should not let himself be tricked into remaining at a lower level. If he does not go beyond the pleasures of the senses, he is not a man but merely an animal. His true fulfilment lies only in reason and understanding, which form the essence of his nature as a man. Imagination, then, is simply an intermediate stage on the way to rationality. Well used, it can be a help along that path. All too often, however, it is a hindrance and a source of deception and illusion.

[1] La Primaudaye, *op. cit.* 190.

[16]

IMAGINATION LINKED WITH
INVENTION

After this rather lengthy excursion into psychology and ethics
(which has been necessary in order to obtain a clear picture of
the connotations of the sixteenth-century concept of imagination)
we must now return to the field of poetic theory, and consider
how this ambivalent concept was used in Pléiade theorising.
A point which is worthy of attention, I think, is that there is a
striking approximation of the two terms 'imagination' and
'invention'. As in the case of invention, imagination was commonly used in the sixteenth century to denote both the faculty
itself and also the product of the faculty's operations. *Une
imagination* at its simplest is an image or mental picture.
Montaigne uses the word, for instance, for the picture of
Tamburlaine which one paints for oneself on the basis of what
one has heard about him. Or again he uses it quite frequently to
refer to the image one has in one's mind of what death will be
like.[1] We can find many more examples in Montaigne and other
sixteenth-century writers of *imagination* used in this straightforward sense of pictorial representation in the mind.

There are other contexts, however, in which the word has a
rather more general sense than this and where it seems to be
more or less the equivalent of 'idea', or 'opinion'. Let us limit
ourselves for the moment to examples from Montaigne's *Essais*.
We see the author marvelling at the results produced by the
tutors of the young Cato: 'C'est grand cas d'avoir peu donner
tel ordre aux pures imaginations d'un enfant.' Or in the
description of his own character as a young man Montaigne
comments, 'je...nourrissois des imaginations hardies et des
opinions au dessus de mon aage'. *Une imagination* can even be

---

[1] Montaigne, *op. cit.* III, 24, and (e.g.) I, 54.

a philosopher's theory, that of Zeno, for instance, concerning the mind: 'Zenon peignoit de geste son imagination sur cette partition des facultez de l'ame.' And Socrates' mind, according to Montaigne, was normally full of 'grandes et si reglées imaginations'. Even innate ideas come under the rubric of *imaginations*: 'Les communes imaginations, que nous trouvons en credit autour de nous et infuses en nostre ame par la semence de nos peres, il semble que ce soyent les generalles et naturelles.' This use of the word is repeated later: 'Les plus fermes imaginations que j'aye, et generalles, sont celles qui, par maniere de dire, nasquirent avec moy.'[1]

What is especially interesting for our present purposes, however, is that *imagination* is often used with the meaning of idea, or conception, when the writer is thinking of its expression in words. Pontus de Tyard was using the word in this way when he claimed that 'chacun exprime en sa langue naturelle plus naifvement les imaginations de son esprit, qu'en un langage aprins tant prompt & familier le puisse-il avoir'.[2] Guillaume Des Autelz, listing the excellences of the work of a certain poet (probably Maurice Scève), mentions especially the 'imaginations & apprehensions ingenieuses, inuentions diuines, propres & poetiques descriptions', etc., etc.[3] Similarly, Montaigne in the *Apologie de Raimond Sebond* acknowledged that 'en mes escris mesmes je ne retrouve pas tousjours l'air de ma premiere imagination'. The idea and the expression of the idea do not always tally. Elsewhere, however, he was more optimistic, and proclaimed confidently that 'qui a en l'esprit une vive imagination et claire, il la produira'.[4]

In this last sentence of Montaigne we can perhaps hear an echo of a tradition, represented by Cicero and Quintilian, which reserved a special place in rhetorical technique for the powers of the imagination. The function of an orator's images, Quintilian asserted, was to make the matter of his speech so vivid that the hearer had the impression of being actually present at the scene described: 'Quas φαντασίας Graeci vocant, nos sane visiones

---

[1] Montaigne, *op. cit.* III, 282, I, 189, 121, and II, 194, 251, 379.
[2] P. de Tyard, *Le Second Curieux*, 128.
[3] Des Autelz, *op. cit.* 72.   [4] Montaigne, *op. cit.* II, 271, and I, 183.

appellemus, per quas imagines rerum absentium ita repraesentantur animo ut eas cernere oculis ac praesentes habere videamur.... Insequitur ἐνάργεια, quae a Cicerone illustratio et evidentia nominatur, quae non tam dicere videtur quam ostendere; et adfectus non aliter, quam si rebus ipsis intersimus, sequentur.'[1] Montaigne may well have had this tradition of rhetorical theory more directly in mind when in his discussion of style he wrote: 'Je veux que les choses surmontent et qu'elles remplissent de façon l'imagination de celuy qui escoute, qu'il n'aye aucune souvenance des mots.'[2] Montaigne is anxious that the style should not obscure the subject-matter, but should allow it to be presented directly to the mind of the hearer. And this is very much the same point that Quintilian had made.

'Les imaginations d'un écrivain', in fact, are quite simply the ideas which he is trying to put into words. Indeed they might well be regarded as his *inventions* under another name. Within a certain range of meaning the two terms seem to be more or less interchangeable.[3] Let us take, for example, the passage in which Montaigne discusses the part played by his reading of other men's books in the composition of his own. As I read, he says, I am not continually on the look-out for likely material: 'Je feuillette les livres, je ne les estudie pas: ce qui m'en demeure, c'est chose que je ne reconnois plus estre d'autruy: c'est cela seulement dequoy mon jugement a faict son profict, les discours et les imaginations dequoy il s'est imbu.' A few years later, in an addition to one of the essays, he returned to the same topic and acknowledged blandly, 'es raisons et inventions que je transplante en mon solage et confons aux miennes, j'ay à escient ommis parfois d'en marquer l'autheur'.[4] The phrase 'raisons et inventions' seems to me to be exactly parallel in

---

[1] Quintilian, *op. cit.* II, 432–6. The Aristotelian source for this point is to be found in the *Rhetorica*: 'liveliness is got...by being graphic (i.e. by making your hearers *see* things)' (Aristotle, *op. cit.* XI, 1411*b*).

[2] Montaigne, *op. cit.* I, 185.

[3] The limits of this range of meaning are nicely indicated by the following quotation from Le Caron, *op. cit.* fo. 135r⁰: 'laisson l'antiquité en sa gloire, car nostre France plus heureuse laquelle iadis s'espouantoit des fieres & vanteresses imaginations d'elle, consacre maintenant à la memoire les plus haultes & excellentes inuentions, desquelles la poësie deuoit estre perfaite.'

[4] Montaigne, *op. cit.* II, 84, 371.

meaning to the earlier 'discours et imaginations'. Both *raison* and *discours* have here their sixteenth-century sense of *réflexion,* or *raisonnement,* which tends to suggest that *invention* and *imagination* have much the same meaning also. Again, we have just seen Montaigne proclaim his conviction that 'qui a en l'esprit une vive imagination et claire, il la produira'. Similarly, in the same edition of the same essay, he talks of 'producing', or bringing forth, inventions: '[je] laisse...courir mes inventions ainsi foibles et basses, comme je les ay produites.' Aristotle's view of the human soul he refers to as an *invention*; Zeno's is an *imagination.* The atoms of Epicurus, Plato's Ideas, Pythagoras's numbers, these are *inventions*; Aquinas's ideas about God and the universe are *imaginations.* In all these cases it seems difficult to make any distinction between the two terms.[1]

In none of these examples, however, is Montaigne specifically discussing the way in which the human mind works. These one can perhaps classify as 'casual' uses of the words in question. Even if there were a valid distinction to be made between imagination and invention, Montaigne did not need to make it, for that was not the point at issue on these occasions. But in contexts where we might expect an author to take some care in selecting the most exact terms one still has the impression that the sixteenth century made no absolute distinction between the process of imagining and that of inventing. There is, for instance, the passage in which La Primaudaye points out that in one way or another all the active, productive aspects of human behaviour have 'quelque commencement & quelque fondement en nature & es œuvres de Dieu'.[2] That active, productive behaviour comprises thinking, imagining, and 'doing' in general ('penser, imaginer, faire'), and the end-products of all three activities are denoted by the same word *inventions.* For La Primaudaye to think is to invent, to imagine is to invent, and to do or to make is to invent. We have seen Ramus maintain that invention according to the laws of logic is the one natural way of thinking, the way in fact in which men actually do think,[3] and the association of invention with producing something in a

---

[1] *Ibid.* I, 156, 183, and II, 117, 194, 204, 242.
[2] See p. 107.   [3] See pp. 128 ff.

material sense is familiar enough to us nowadays. Less familiar, perhaps, is the semi-equation of inventing with imagining, and I emphasise this point because it links up with two pages of Pléiade poetic theory, one from Peletier and one from Ronsard, in which the authors bring together imagination and invention in a very direct way.

'Inuancion', wrote Peletier in his *Art Poëtique*, 'ęt un dessein prouuenant dę l'imaginacion dę l'antandęmant, pour paruęnir à notrę fin.'[1] The old rhetorical background to the concept of invention is still very much in evidence; the task of invention is held to be the production of a piece of writing which will serve some particular end, to persuade or to dissuade, in the phraseology of the rhetoricians. Invention is the finding-out of appropriate material, and for that purpose the collaboration of the 'imaginacion dę l'antandęmant' is required, to picture forth the mental material that comes under survey. The invention comes upon the material and the imagination gives it shape. The two powers must presumably work together in a close partnership, for the invention can hardly come upon things without the imagination at once giving them shape, nor can the imagination give them shape unless the invention comes upon them. They are the two powers which together form the single productive and presentative faculty; or rather, they are the single faculty considered from two different points of view.

Ten years later in the *Abbregé de l'Art poëtique françois* Ronsard made the same point when he stated that 'l'invention n'est autre chose que le bon naturel d'une imagination concevant les Idées & formes de toutes choses qui se peuvent imaginer tant cellestes que terrestres, animées ou inanimées, pour apres les representer, descrire & imiter'.[2] It is important, I think, to note the way in which this assertion is phrased. Invention, Ronsard claims, is the true, natural activity of the imagination as it conceives the ideas and forms of all things. Ronsard seems almost to be using the concept of invention as a guarantee for the imagination. And just as later, in the 1572 preface to the *Franciade*, Ronsard was careful to forestall any possible misinterpretation of his use

---

[1] Peletier, *op. cit.* 88.
[2] Ronsard, *Œuvres complètes*, XIV, 12–13.

of the term 'feigning' to denote the proper activity of the poet,[1] so here too he at once explains exactly what he means by invention and imagination in this sense: 'Quand je te dy que tu inventes choses belles & grandes, je n'entends toutesfois ces inventions fantasticques & melancoliques, qui ne se rapportent non plus l'une à l'autre que les songes entrecoupez d'un frenetique, ou de quelque patient extremement tourmenté de la fievre, à l'imagination duquel, pour estre blessée, se representent mille formes monstrueuses sans ordre ny liayson.'[2] And these are the very terms, *songes/rêveries, fièvre, monstrueux*, that he will use again in 1572 to describe 'une Poësie fantastique'. Ronsard is most anxious to dissociate himself from all this and from all the disreputable companions that were traditionally foisted upon poetry. On the contrary, he emphasises the healthiness of the imagination when considered from the point of view of poetic invention. Invention is 'le bon naturel' of imagination, its true and rightful nature, expressing itself in true and rightful action which is coherent and valuable, by contrast with the 'songes entrecoupez' of those suffering from fever or madness and with the 'monstres' which are perversions of Nature.

Imagination brings forth mental constructs of things, it conceives and produces them, gives them shape, embodies them, and makes them vividly present in the mind's eye of the hearer by means of description and imitation. Its function is to make likenesses of things, likenesses in the double sense both of images, or pictures, and at the same time of imitations, or copies, of the original. And this, Ronsard is saying, is exactly the same process as invention, as coming upon material. It seems to me that the *rapprochement* of these two concepts is not at all accidental and that, as I will show in the next chapter, it has a definite significance when considered in terms of the Pléiade's attempted defence, or justification, of poetry.

[1] See p. 123.
[2] Ronsard, *Œuvres complètes*, XIV, 13.

[17]

IMAGINATION, INVENTION,
AND POETRY

Given the terminology of sixteenth-century theories of the
mind's working, Ronsard's definition of invention as '[l']
imagination concevant les Idées & formes de toutes choses...
pour apres les representer, descrire & imiter' is a fairly accurate
description of what happens when we engage in active and productive thought, that is when we try to form an idea about
something and the idea gradually comes into being in our minds.
Language hardly permits us to express this mental event, or
complex of events, by one single image. We commonly say that
we have found the solution to some problem which we have been
thinking about, or that we have formed an idea about something.
These turns of phrase, I would suggest, correspond fairly
closely to the concepts of invention and imagination which I have
been examining in the previous chapter. We do quite often use
just these metaphors of finding and of forming to describe the
mental activities which are involved in having ideas or attaining
concepts. Yet we seem to separate the two processes from one
another only for our own greater convenience in thinking about
thought. At the moment when the mental seeking or scanning
is coming to an end—because we are somehow aware that
'we've got it', that we have found what we are looking for—
then the idea, the concept, whatever we may call it, is making
itself apparent to us in a clear form. We have a certain feeling
about the rightness or appropriateness of the thought even
before it is fully formed in our minds, so that to some extent we
have indeed already found it. But we have not yet fully come
into the thought, not yet fully taken possession of it, until its
shape is complete in the mind. This is the moment when the
thought is coming into being, and we use two separate metaphors to describe the process. In the actual thought-process

itself, however, the two actions presumably co-exist and are mutually inclusive and contemporaneous, neither of them beginning or ending before the other. As Ronsard was pointing out, invention is imagination, and imagination is invention.

In my treatment of the sixteenth-century concept of imagination I have made perhaps too clear-cut a distinction between what I. A. Richards has called ' a *projective* outlook, which treats imagination's products as figment' (which I have labelled the prescriptive aspects of imagination), and ' a *realist* outlook, which takes the imagination to be a means of apprehending reality' (which I have termed its descriptive aspects).[1] Certainly it is a useful distinction to make, for it sets out clearly the two main historical approaches to a theory of the imagination. But in dealing with sixteenth-century attitudes towards the faculty we must remember that the two methods of approach, projective and realist, prescriptive and descriptive, were hardly ever completely separated from one another. Paré wrote his account of the imagination mainly from the physiological point of view; for him 'l'imagination est une apprehension et recognoissance des choses et obiects qui nous sont representées par les cinq actions sensitives'. The imagination is here playing the role of a necessary link in the chain of cognitive processes. But Paré also recognised that the imagination produces fantastic visions which, except in their component parts, do not correspond to any reality outside the mind: 'd'icelle viennent les idées et visions qu'on appelle fantasies, laquelle...le plus souvent est occupée en songeant et resvant plusieurs choses qui n'ont esté et iamais ne seront.' Since the imagination is so unreliable a source of information, and since in addition ' iceluy sens a grande seigneurie en nous...nous avons encore besoin d'une plus haulte faculté pour savoir discerner si les choses imaginées, veues, ouyes et senties par dehors, sont bonnes ou mauvaises'. And this 'plus haulte faculté' is, of course, reason: ' icelle seule invente le vray, iuge le faux, et distingue ce que de l'un ou de l'autre s'ensuit ou repugne...et ainsi discerne la chose se devoir faire ou non.'[2] In Paré's account of the imagination the descriptive and the pre-

---

[1] I. A. Richards, *Coleridge on Imagination* (1934), 26.
[2] Paré, *op. cit.* I, 58, and II, 658–60.

scriptive elements are never very far apart, so that he alternates between condemning the faculty and demonstrating how essential is its contribution to cognition. Similarly, for Montaigne the products of our imagination are *vaines, vitieuses, sotes, fauces, fantastiques, irresoluës, contraires*, but they can also be *solides et de toute verité, grandes et reglées, fermes et generalles, vives et claires*.[1] The imagination may move in either of these directions.

Prescriptive and descriptive elements were both present in the sixteenth-century attitude towards imagination, but I think there is little doubt as to which of them predominated. The sixteenth-century world-picture was still based on a fusion of the Platonic cosmology (strongly tinged with Aristotelianism) with that of the Old Testament. The universe it portrayed was a beautifully ordered universe arranged in a fixed system of multiple hierarchies which reached from God, down through the Angels, Man, animals, and plants, to inanimate matter, and then returned again to God. The preservation of this orderliness, the ensuring that all things were included in it and fitted exactly into the established pattern, had been one of the main philosophical concerns of the Middle Ages. The breaking-up of the neat system (which, when it came, took place on all levels— social, political, philosophical, and psychological) was a long and painful process which was only just beginning in the sixteenth century. The Renaissance revival of learning marks no sudden emancipation of thought. The categories and classifications and orientations of the medieval world-picture still persisted in the sixteenth century. They were becoming a little unsteady perhaps, but they represented the last refuge of minds horrified by the cosmic anarchy and chaos which seemed to be impending on all sides. Imagination was still therefore part of the lowly world of the senses and could only intermittently rise above its proper station there. The senses, and the imagination with them, belonged to the irrational and deceiving part of man's nature, by which he participated in blind matter and in the sins of the flesh. The cosmological aspect of this doctrine was reinforced by the extremely powerful ethical tradition compounded of neo-

[1] Montaigne, *op. cit.* I, 64, 161, 183, 310, 353, 361, II, 251, 373, 379, and III, 18. Cf. Huarte's ambivalent attitude towards the imagination (see pp. 152–3 and 138).

platonism, Stoicism, and Christianity to which the Middle Ages adhered. The value of imagination as an essential element in the cognitive process could not but be smothered beneath the blanket of such strong moral opprobrium.

Invention, on the other hand, was regarded in a predominantly favourable light in the sixteenth century. Even Montaigne, who did not have a very high opinion of the powers of the human mind, had something to say for invention. Like our imaginations, our inventions could be *fauces* and *fantastiques*, but he also granted them a word or two of real praise; they were on occasion *subtiles*, or *delicates*, and Montaigne regretted that as a young man his own invention was *lasche*.[1] Invention could be a very valuable part of one's mental equipment in as much as it was associated with the reason, and was therefore on the right side of the division between body and mind. Its methods of operation had been systematised and formularised by the classical rhetoricians in a coherent body of rules. And in the view of Ramus and his followers invention achieved the further dignity of corresponding exactly with the order of the universe. Not only was its function to discover already existent reality (which was recommendation enough in itself, for this meant that invention was concerned with the truth, with things as they really were), but it could also be certain of performing that function with complete infallibility. The way in which the mind naturally worked (i.e. by a logically conducted process of invention) mirrored the way in which the universe was ordered (i.e. in accordance with the rules of logic). There was thus no gap between human logic and divine logic. Invention was an expression of the rationality of the human mind, just as the universe was an expression of the rationality of God's will. The disagreeable implications of the theory that the orator was often concerned with mere probabilities and verisimilitudes were played down in the assumptions of this epistemology. The truth of things already existed whole in potentiality; the mind had merely to be brought into contact with that truth in the appropriate manner for it to be translated into actuality. And this was precisely what invention was, a coming into the truth of things.

---

[1] Montaigne, *op. cit.* i, 185, 189, 233, ii, 204, 205.

Despite their tendency to lie on different sides of the body–mind frontier, imagination and invention had one very important quality in common. Both terms designated the active functions of the mind *vis-à-vis* the world outside the mind. Invention was the entering of the human mind into the raw material of thought, the sallying forth beyond the walls of the citadel. Imagination was the shaping and representing of that same raw material, the fashioning of it, the assimilation of it to the substance of the mind. In each case the mind was active; it was no longer passively receiving the sense-impressions through the medium of the five external senses, it was no longer in a passive relationship of potentiality with things. It had now begun to initiate activity on its own account and to function as a free agent.

This freedom, however, was (or ideally ought to be) confined within close limits, for the reason had not yet been brought into full play. This was most obviously so, of course, in the case of the imagination. Yet strictly speaking the process of invention could also be regarded as a pre-rational activity. For invention was the seeking-out of particulars appropriate to some general topic, and not until it was a question of the disposition of these particulars and their proper arrangement did judgement, the rational power *par excellence*, become totally engaged. And the function of imagination, of course, was precisely to assemble and to organise sensory images and memory images in order to present them to the reason. Only when the imagination had performed these tasks was there any material which the reason could handle at all. Imagination and invention were thus the servants of reason; but this was a rather ambiguous relationship, for the reason was to a very large extent dependent upon them in its dealings with things outside itself. They were the powers which the reason employed in order to move outwards, beyond itself, the means whereby it was able to act upon external things, and to enter into a relationship of knowledge with them.

This relationship of the individual human mind with things outside itself was closely paralleled by that between the poet and 'Nature' (taken in the widest possible sense), which was normally designated by the term imitation.[1] Ronsard seems to have

[1] See pp. 51 ff.

been conscious that this was so, for in one passage of the *Abbregé* he quite clearly draws together the concepts of imitation and invention-and-imagination. He is comparing the orator with the poet, and states, 'le but. . .du Poëte est d'imiter, inventer, & representer les choses qui sont ou qui peuvent estre vraisemblables'.[1] Commentators have drawn attention to this sentence for the light which it throws upon Ronsard's acquaintance with the Aristotelian principles of verisimilitude and probability.[2] This, however, is to concentrate only upon the final part of it; the first part is also worth studying in some detail. For the three verbs, *imiter, inventer, représenter*, denote what the poet does, the nature of his activity, as opposed to the nature of the objects upon which he exercises that activity. In my view these verbs should not be read as indicating that the poet has three distinct aims which he pursues successively or separately, now one, now another, now another; rather should the three words be taken together to form a composite statement about the nature of poetic activity in which the last two (*inventer* and *représenter*) explain and elaborate upon the first (*imiter*).

Aristotle had maintained that poetry, like the other arts, is a form of imitation, and that the object upon which such imitation should be exercised is the not-yet-actual, the *vraisemblable*; Ronsard followed him in this. But of what does the process of imitation consist, what *is* imitation? In order to imitate something, to copy it, one had first to seek it out, or come into it, and then to give it material form as a work of art; in sixteenth-century terms one invents the thing, and one represents it. As we have just seen, when the things in question are mental rather than physical entities, then inventing and representing (which I would read as a near-synonym of imagining, in the sense of 'imaging', making images of) can well be regarded as the two different aspects of a single process. Even when it is a question of purely physical entities, it is perhaps true to say that one fully comes into the nature of a thing only in the effort to represent it in a work of art; similarly, one is truly able to represent something only when one fully comes into its nature. The imitation

---

[1] Ronsard, *Œuvres complètes*, XIV, 13.
[2] See, for example, Franchet, *op. cit.* 191 ff.

which is art is thus a double process of inventing-and-representing. And as in the case of imitation, so here too I would suggest that the theorists were making some attempt to exploit these concepts in the interests of a defence of poetry.

Poetry had started under the severe handicap of being equated with untruth and with lies. In this connection invention was a concept worth concentrating on for two reasons. First, invention was already generally acknowledged to be the principal part of poetry, so that there was the advantage of employing well-established terminology; and secondly, despite the possibility of some pejorative implications, it did have close affiliations with certain concepts of orderliness and reason. But invention as it stood lacked one element which was of the highest importance for poetry, namely the capacity for picture-making and image-forming. During the sixteenth century the Horatian tag 'ut pictura poesis' was very commonly taken to mean that poetry should be a speaking picture. This fitted in with another Renaissance requirement for poetry, that it should be a vivid representation which made the readers (or the audience) feel that they were actually present at the scene described. Such was the task of the poetic images produced by the imagination. Thus imagination had an essential part to play in the making of poetry, and it was necessary that a place should be found for it in the theory. But to bring in imagination was to be back in the realm of lies and untruths, under the sway of the deceiving passions and the senses, and to be faced with the same dilemma as in the case of fiction.[1] Favourable connotations of imagination did indeed exist, but it was difficult for them effectively to make their presence felt. The problem was to find a way of rehabilitating the imagination which would enable it to achieve a certain measure of stability while occupying the middle ground between truth and lies. To ignore imagination completely in the theory of poetry would have been to omit a key component; yet to include it was to brand poetry 'liar'.

One possible way of working towards a resolution of this difficulty consisted in bringing together the concepts of invention and imagination, and attempting to amalgamate them. The

[1] See pp. 118 ff.

relationships between the two concepts as they were formulated in the sixteenth century can perhaps be shown schematically by means of the following diagram:

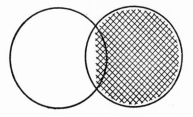

The left-hand circle represents the concept of invention, while the right-hand circle represents the concept of imagination. The unshaded portions of the circles stand for the favourable connotations of the concepts, and the shaded portions stand for their unfavourable connotations. (By favourable and unfavourable I mean 'associated with truth' and 'associated with lying' respectively, together with the whole series of analogous oppositions—rationality and irrationality, mind and body, reason and senses, intellect and passions, spirit and matter, light and dark, fire and earth, etc., etc.—which so fascinated the Renaissance mind.) The connotations of invention were thus mainly favourable, whereas those of imagination were mainly unfavourable. Poetry may be thought of as being situated somewhere within the area which the two circles have in common. I have also tried to suggest that at the actual moment when a thought is being produced in our minds something is going on which can very well be described by the dual concept of invention-and-imagination. This also is mirrored in the overlapping of the two circles.

Because of the connections between them a complete amalgamation of the concepts of imagination and invention would probably have been well suited to further the efforts of Ronsard and the others to investigate and to formulate a theory of the nature of poetic activity. There was the possibility that the favourable connotations surrounding the concept of invention might have been utilised in order to obviate the condemnation and mistrust under which the imagination had laboured for so many centuries. If it could have been successfully argued that in the poetic process the power of imagination was exercised upon the same kind of already-existent (though, in Aristotelian terms, not-yet-actual) entities which were come into, or found, by invention, then more weight might have been added to the view that in so far as poetry was concerned imagination was by no means the treacherous purveyor of untruth and sinfulness which its detractors claimed it to be. A change of attitude of this sort, coupled with the full appreciation and exploitation of the Aristotelian theories of imitation and verisimilitude, might well have laid the way open for the development of a rather more 'autonomous' view of poetry, which would not require it to be an exact representation of some factual reality, and which would enable it to encourage the activities of the imagination without misgiving. The conviction that what is potential, what is *vraisemblable*, is of a higher order of truth than the actuality of any purely material reality would enable the imagination freely to come into new images made from its own experience, images which existed in potentiality in that experience and were awaiting discovery by some process of invention; and these would be the images which made apparent the universals through the particulars.

For poetry had somehow to make room for itself exactly where it seemed that there was no room. Either there is the truth of actuality, said the sixteenth century, or there are lies. But poetry was fiction, neither entirely the one nor entirely the other, and different in essence from both. The poet, in fact, was something of an uncomfortable anomaly in his capacity as the inhabitant of a limbo which his contemporaries claimed did not exist. That limbo might have been fashioned out of the materials of such concepts as imitation, invention, imagination, *vraisemblance*, etc., and I would suggest that in the two passages from the *Abbregé de l'Art poëtique françois* which I have quoted in this chapter Ronsard was reaching—rather tentatively perhaps —in just that direction.[1] He seems to have considered imitation, invention, and imagination all to be terms which referred to the same activity (poetic creation, as we would call it nowadays), but none of which alone could give a completely adequate

[1] See pp. 174 and 179.

account of it; each had an essential contribution to make. He also made the important point that the poet had dealings with an order of reality beyond the here-and-now, namely with the 'Ideas and forms' of things, or with the *vraisemblable*, thus differentiating poetry from the ordinary run of human discourse. Out of this conjunction of terms a theory of poetry might have been evolved which would stress its uniqueness among the human activities, and which would also free it from the demands of any extra-poetic criteria, so that it could be justified in terms of itself alone. Yet neither Ronsard nor any member of his group took full advantage of these opportunities (if such we may call them) which seem to have been already within reach. There is in their writings no formal elaboration of these points along the lines which I have indicated. There is simply a series of tantalisingly rich hints about whose development we can speculate in terms of what might have been, but which we cannot confirm by citing this or that text. We have finally to consider the reasons for the Pléiade's apparent inhibitions in these matters.

[18]

CONCLUSION

To a modern reader it may well appear that the poets of the Pléiade have rather arbitrarily stopped short in developing their ideas about the nature of poetry and of poetic activity, or even that they have not yet begun to ask the right sort of questions. But this is not to be explained by alleging lack of wit on their part or inability to pursue a train of thought sufficiently far. It is rather that the modern reader is misled by viewing sixteenth-century matters from a twentieth-century vantage-point. For in a certain sense the modern reader can be said to know some of the answers already to the problems which the Pléiade theorists were facing. He knows, for instance, what use was made of the concept of imagination in later ages, and this knowledge encourages him to hunt for indications of the later developments in the writings of the Pléiade and to feel more than a little disappointed when he does not find them there. He is also better informed about the significance and implications of Aristotle's theory of imitation than the sixteenth century could be, simply because the intervening years have given scholars time to make thorough and critical studies both of Aristotle's own texts and of the character of Greek thought as a whole and the scholastic elaborations upon it. We cannot legitimately expect of Ronsard that he should have been three or four hundred years in advance of the thought of his time. He was after all first and foremost a practising poet; he did not set out to be an expert on Aristotle, nor did he devote his whole life to philosophical speculation. In his theorising he simply took up the conceptual materials which were to hand and made whatever use of them he thought appropriate to his purposes. The answers which we know, as a matter of historical fact, were given to certain problems were not necessarily the answers which were available in the sixteenth century.

What this really means is that the problems were not yet susceptible of being posed in such a way that the answers which we expect could have been given. The same words might well have been available both then and later ('imagination' is a clear instance), but the meanings and connotations of those words are likely to differ quite considerably from one age to the other. That is why it has been necessary in this study to consider in some detail the wider contexts, outside the restricted field of poetic theory, in which such terms as imitation, invention, imagination, and so on operated during the sixteenth century. All the words I have been dealing with here were necessarily embedded in an intellectual system which, unlike our modern fragmented view of the universe, maintained a high degree of self-integration and inner coherence. The sixteenth-century cosmos was a hierarchically ordered whole, complex indeed, but unified by the fact that each item within it had an established place and an established end. It was axiomatic that anything which man might discover about the universe would merely provide additional confirmation of this divinely ordained pattern. In this system, however, the poet was something of an odd man out—or so the Pléiade felt him to be. The traditional didactic view of the poet's function (that he offered his audience moral instruction in a pleasing form) seemed inadequate; the poet was not simply a skilful lay preacher. Yet the concepts which the Pléiade had to use in presenting their case were still part of the system in which, to their way of thinking, the poet's true situation was in doubt. And this is a most important factor which must always be taken into account in any consideration of the significance of the Pléiade's theoretical pronouncements. I will now endeavour to draw together the threads of my argument by reviewing the main concepts I have discussed in terms of the effect which their extra-poetic connotations had upon the theorising of the Pléiade.

In dealing with the concept of imagination in the sixteenth century I divided my discussion into two parts, outlining first what I called the descriptive accounts of the faculty, and then the prescriptive accounts. Each of these two aspects presented to the contemporary theorist difficulties which prevented imagination from being used as the leading concept in any effective justification of poetry.

If the theorist accepted the descriptive psychologist's view of imagination, he was dealing with a faculty whose activity consisted of carrying out one rather restricted type of operation within the sequence of cognitional processes. The function of the imagination was twofold. On the one hand it formed composite images out of the individual images presented to it by the senses, purged them of their material dross, and passed them on to the reason for its consideration and judgement. The other half of its task was to body forth in image-form impressions, ideas, judgements, etc., which had been stored up in the memory, and again to transmit these images to the reason, so that it could use them in making judgements appropriate to present circumstances. This was indeed a necessary and valuable activity, but one which was carefully supervised and controlled. Ronsard, we may note, stressed the freedom of the imagination as much as he could. For him imagination conceived the Ideas and forms 'de toutes choses qui se peuvent imaginer';[1] its limitations, he is saying, are merely those of its own capacity. But he was not able to make very much of this point, for it was considered by the sixteenth century to be a highly dangerous state of affairs if any subservient agent (such as the imagination, for instance, which owed allegiance at all times to the faculty of reason) were allowed to usurp more than its due measure of freedom. To be free from the properly constituted forms of control was almost necessarily to err and to wander from the path of truth. The freedom of a subordinate to act as he pleased could not but threaten the stability of the established order of things, and strict precautions had to be taken to ensure that the threat did not materialise. Thus, by comparison with our modern views of the imagination, the faculty had in the sixteenth century only a limited role to perform. It was a presenter of images, or at best a juxtaposer of them. It could never have been entrusted with the task of digesting and transforming the elements of the visible universe, as Baudelaire was to demand of it.[2] In the sixteenth century it would have been impossible to hail imagina-

[1] Cf. p. 172. [2] See p. 92.

186

tion as 'la reine des facultés'; at that time royalty belonged to reason alone.

There was also, however, the difficulty of the imagination's associations with the world of the senses and the base passions. Because it was so closely connected with the physical body imagination was always likely to be seduced by the appeal of sensual desire, which sought its own pleasure instead of assisting reason in its pursuit of truth and right action. The relationship between desire and imagination was such that each one stimulated the other, until reason was completely overwhelmed in the great tumult and disturbance of the passions which the two inferior powers had produced. And the only possible outcome of such a situation was sin and error. Given this possibility, the poet had always to be on his guard against the excesses of the imagination. He had not only to watch carefully over the productions of his own mind, but also to be wary of arousing the imagination of his audience in such a way that the passions would subvert the authority of the rational powers. This was the basis of a common charge brought against poets by moralists; poetry, they said, stirred up the base passions, and therefore there could be no good in it. In this respect love poetry was a particularly obvious target, although the charge was often laid against poetry in general. The poet, for instance, would be compared unfavourably with the historian; the latter, it was held, maintained a proper balance between 'profit' and 'plaisir' whereas, in the case of the poet, 'son but principal est de delecter'.[1] Little material for an acceptable justification of poetry was to be found in this quarter.

Thus in sixteenth-century poetics imagination tended to be thought of as simply the picture-making faculty, which produced vivid representations of the things it conceived, but without attaining to any higher function. Hemmed in on all sides by controls and by feelings of mistrust, it was a servant, sometimes rebellious, but always lacking the visionary power which would have enabled it to handle images freely and to form them into significant wholes. We have to wait until the far-reaching developments in philosophical thought of the seventeenth and

[1] J. Amyot, Preface to the translation of Plutarch's *Lives*, in Weinberg, *op. cit.* 167.

PLÉIADE POETICS

eighteenth centuries are complete before imagination can begin to be conceived in the Coleridgean manner as an 'esemplastic power'.[1]

The case of invention is in a way the opposite of that of imagination, for here we have a term which has almost disappeared from the vocabulary of poetic theory. In the sixteenth century, however, the word was widely used by theorists, largely because of the close connection which obtained at that time on the theoretical level between poetry and rhetoric. Just as for Cicero invention had been the first and principal part of rhetoric, so it was the first and principal part of poetry for Ronsard. But in order to appreciate the full implications of the use of that term by the Pléiade we must also understand its significance in the field of contemporary epistemology and logic.

Despite the well-known contact of Ramus with the poets of the Pléiade, it is doubtful whether they took over his theory of invention into the literary sphere in any very detailed or specific manner. Yet his idea that invention dealt with 'arguments' which declare and make manifest the true natures of things and which also designate the interrelationships between them might well have had promising possibilities for the theory of poetry, had it been linked with a faculty of imagination which was allowed some measure of freedom in its picture-making activities. However, not only was the liberty of the imagination severely curtailed, but invention in the Ramist scheme was also close-set with important restrictions. It too acted as the servant of reason for the purposes of cognition. Furthermore, Ramus was very much of a systematiser in logic; he was concerned above all with expounding a method which demonstrated the exact congruence existing between rational thought and the divinely established order of reality. He was thus more interested in the systematic ordering of the cosmos and its mirroring in human logic than in considering invention more or less as an end in itself—which would be the attitude required for any independent theory of poetry.

Yet the Pléiade did derive certain undoubted benefits from the Ramist view of invention. Ramus had laid great stress upon

[1] S. T. Coleridge, *Biographia Literaria*, ed. J. Shawcross (1907), i, 107, 195 ff.

188

the fact that invention was a process of finding, and of finding something which was already in existence. Invention did not make things up, it simply came into and revealed the true nature of things. This conception of the process was obviously likely to be of inestimable value in countering the charge that poets are liars and that their fictions deceive because they have no basis in reality. The poet's fictions, as Ronsard was to claim, were not 'resveries d'un malade de fievre continue', but inventions, possessing such qualities of trustworthiness as that term could imply.

There was another point in which the poets of the Pléiade were probably much influenced by Ramus's emphasis on the orderliness of the inventive process, and that is in the structure of their works. It is significant, I think, that Ronsard cites as one of the characteristics of '[une] imagination...blessée' the fact that it produces 'mille formes monstrueuses *sans ordre ny liayson*'.[1] One of Ronsard's most notable achievements as a poet is his ability to render the constant flux and variety of things whilst at the same time preserving, at a deeper level within a poem, an impression of developing harmony and order. This is particularly noticeable in the cosmological 'Hymnes', but it is in fact a marked feature of all Ronsard's work. In this respect we can perhaps draw a direct line between Ronsard and Malherbe, the poet of *raison*, balance, and harmony.[2]

Apart from its specifically Ramist connotations invention was mainly exploited as a term which indicated the quality which we nowadays would call originality. The *inventions* of a poet were the thoughts or conceptions, call them what one will, which he produced on his own account, by contrast with those which he took over from other writers. Excellence of invention was held to be the most important factor in the achievement of those qualities of uniqueness, spontaneousness, and directness in a poem which the sixteenth century prized under the name of *naïveté*. Invention was thus the very antithesis of literary imitation, for it was the process of doing something which had not been done before, of treading *un sentier* hitherto *inconnu*. We

[1] See p. 173; my italics.
[2] A model analysis—in that it brings out just those aspects of Ronsard's work which I am referring to here—is Marcel Raymond's treatment of the ode *A sa Maistresse* in his *Baroque & renaissance poétique* (1955), 128–30.

must always remember, however, that for the sixteenth century an invention was not a figment, not something which had its existence only in the mind of the inventor. To invent was simply to come into something which already existed and to make it manifest for the first time. This strong link with existent (but unknown) reality is an essential element in the Pléiade's view of invention which it is easy for the modern reader to ignore.

In more general terms, of course, invention persisted for another two centuries as a standard component of the terminology of literary theory, denoting simply the seeking out and finding of material. Then, as the theories of literary production which stemmed from the classical theories of rhetoric were replaced by those based on a newly evolved concept of the poetic imagination, the meaning of invention came to be mere inventiveness, that is, facility in producing and developing varied material, whether of incident and character (as in the case of the novelist and the dramatist) or of image and form (as in the case of the poet). And this is the condition of the word in literary contexts today.

With the third concept used by sixteenth-century theorists to describe the activity of the poet, namely that of imitation, we enter upon rather complex metaphysical considerations. I have earlier attempted to indicate how closely Aristotle's view of the artist as an imitator of reality depended for its cogency, and indeed for its validity, upon an appreciation of the rather difficult relationships between particulars and universals, and between actuality and potentiality. The result of the poet's imitation is to improve upon material reality by representing the particulars of Nature in such a fashion that the universals inhering in them are clearly revealed. This revelation of the potentiality embodied in things (which we normally apprehend only in their actuality) brings us into contact with a higher order of reality than that of the things which are being imitated. The imitation gives a clearer indication of the interrelationship and inter-penetration of the two levels of existence than does Nature itself. Thus *le vraisemblable* is in fact of greater value than *le vrai*, in the sense of mere actuality. In the sixteenth century, however, Aristotle's theory of poetry as a kind of imitation was

190

propounded without the necessary support of the Aristotelian metaphysical and epistemological framework. The concept of potentiality had already been weakened to the point where it was replaced by the concept of mere possibility, 'ce qui peut estre'. Because it was divorced from its proper setting the concept of imitation itself also tended to be trivialised into the vivid, or lively, representation of the details of Nature more or less for the sake of their own picturesqueness. We have seen this tendency at work in the theorising of Ronsard.[1]

There was, however, a more serious danger still. The metaphysical and epistemological vacuum surrounding the Aristotelian theory of imitation could all too easily be filled by the Platonic view of that process, which was quite familiar to sixteenth-century minds. In the Platonic scheme of metaphysics with its clear-cut scale of values the imitation was always, and necessarily, inferior to that which was imitated. Objects in the material world were themselves merely imitations of the eternal Ideas emanating from the divine mind, and their inferiority consisted above all in the fact of their gross materiality, which was infinitely lower in the hierarchy of being than the pure intellectuality of the godhead. Any imitation, or copy, of the material appearance in the form of an artifact must therefore be even further removed from the ideal original. When this view of imitation is substituted for the Aristotelian attitude, it is impossible to consider *le vraisemblable* as something supremely valuable in its own right. To aver that the poet is concerned with a seeming truth is at once to invite unfavourable comparison with the one ideal Truth, which resides only in the divinity. *Le vraisemblable* is merely an appearance, remote from and of inferior substance to its original, and necessarily a falling-away from that original. It is therefore fundamentally untruth. Needless to say, this evaluation of the poet's imitations is precisely the one which the theorists of the Pléiade were striving to refute.

On the other hand, the second sense in which the word 'imitation' was used—that of taking the great authors of the immediate or distant past as literary models—was of inestimable value to the sixteenth-century defenders of poetry. The

[1] See pp. 60 ff.

Pléiade poets were aiming to produce, in the words of Du Bellay, 'quasi comme une nouvelle poësie'; this was the element of originality in their work, the element of *invention*. But they were also very much concerned to assert their links with the past by laying great emphasis on the part played in their work by imitation. A clear statement of this position occurs in the preface which Du Bellay wrote for the second edition of *L'Olive*: 'Voulant donques enrichir nostre vulgaire d'une nouvelle, ou plustost ancienne renouvelée poësie, je m'adonnay à l'immitation des anciens Latins & des poëtes Italiens.'[1] 'Une nouvelle, ou plustost ancienne renouvelée poësie'—this phrase sums up exactly the Pléiade poets' view of their own work; they felt themselves to be the true continuators of a line of tradition which reached right back to the very first origins of poetry. Ronsard develops this point at some length in the famous 'feux follets' passage of the *Elegie à Jacques Grevin*:

> Le don de Poësie est semblable à ce feu,
> Lequel aux nuicts d'hyver comme un presage est veu
> Ores dessus un fleuve, ores sur une prée,
> Ores dessus le chef d'une forest sacrée,
> Sautant & jaillissant, jettant de toutes pars
> Par l'obscur de la nuict de grans rayons espars:
> En un mesme pays jamais il ne sejourne,
> Et au lieu dont il part jamais il ne retourne:
> Il saute sans arrest de cartier en cartier,
> Et jamais un pais de luy n'est heritier,
> Ains il se communique, & sa flame est montrée
> (Ou moins on l'esperoit) en une autre contrée.
> Ainsi ny les Hebreux, les Grecs, ny les Romains
> N'ont eu la Poësie entiere entre leurs mains:
> Elle a veu l'Allemagne, & a pris accroissance
> Aux rives d'Angleterre, en Escosse, et en France,
> Sautant deçà delà, & prenant grand plaisir
> En estrange pais divers hommes choisir,
> Rendant de ses rayons la province allumée,
> Mais bien tost sa lumiere en l'air est consumée.
> La louange n'est pas tant seulement à un,
> De tous elle est hostesse, & visite un chacun,

[1] Du Bellay, *Œuvres poétiques*, I, 12.

CONCLUSION

Et sans avoir egard aux biens ny à la race,
Favorisant chacun, un chacun elle embrasse.[1]

Ronsard is here seeking to justify himself not in his own personal right as an individual, but as the humble recipient of the divine gift of poetry. Poetry is not something which can be perfected by any one poet, or even by the poets of any one country. It is a continuous process in which the individual poets each make their own greater or lesser contributions to the whole. What is important in this process is not the individual contributions as such, but the total entity, Poetry, of which they form part. In myself, Ronsard is saying, I am nothing; whatever honour or glory I may achieve is gained only in virtue of my participation in the world-wide tradition of poetry. His claim is simply that at the moment France is the fortunate country which plays host to 'la Poësie'.

Nowadays, to call an artist 'imitative' is to criticise him, for in the arts we tend to regard originality more highly than any other quality. We may therefore feel that the poets of the Pléiade were making a grave error when they attached so much importance to the imitation of literary models. But if we talk of imitation rather in terms of 'tradition' (as I have just attempted to do), we may be able to take a kinder view of it and to see what lies behind the Pléiade's concern with their own relationship to the poetry of the past. Forty years ago T. S. Eliot drew attention to

our tendency to insist, when we praise a poet, upon those aspects of his work in which he least resembles anyone else. In these aspects or parts of his work we pretend to find what is individual, what is the peculiar essence of the man. We dwell with satisfaction upon the poet's difference from his predecessors.... Whereas if we approach a poet without this prejudice we shall often find that not only the best, but the most individual parts of his work may be those in which the dead poets, his ancestors, assert their immortality most vigorously.

And he went on to discuss the necessary relationship between a new poet's work and the poetry of the past: 'No poet, no artist of any art, has his complete meaning alone. His signifi-

[1] Ronsard, *Œuvres complètes*, XIV, 193–4.

cance, his appreciation is the appreciation of his relation to the dead poets and artists. You cannot value him alone; you must set him, for contrast and comparison, among the dead. I mean this as a principle of aesthetic, not merely historical criticism.'[1]

Since the time of the Romantics there has indeed been a marked tendency among critics to place the highest premium upon the production of new poetic images. Thus the poetic ideal has quite often been considered to be embodied in the work of Victor Hugo, many of whose images are striking above all for their sheer originality. Yet no less excellent a poet is he who takes a traditional, thoroughly conventionalised image (such as that of the rose, for instance, symbol of beauty) and gives it renewed currency by highlighting forgotten facets, by revealing those which have hitherto been ignored or unrealised, by handling it in wonderment as if for the first time, or indeed by exploiting its use by other poets in analogous contexts for his own purposes.[2] The members of the Pléiade were certainly men who were fully alive to the value of the tradition contained in the poetry of the ancient Greeks and Romans and the modern Italians, and fully aware too that here was a body of poetic material from which they could profit, and with which they must come to terms if they were to help bear the torch of poetry through the ages. By setting themselves to follow the ancients they were providing a guarantee, so to speak, of their own worth. The poets of the Pléiade, so they themselves claimed, were true heirs of the old masters, and they and their work acquired dignity, value, and glory from this association.

Concern with the imitation of poets in 'the great tradition' was thus one major tactic employed by the Pléiade in its attempt to achieve a justification of poetry. The other tactic, which also

---

[1] T. S. Eliot, *Selected Essays* (1951), 14–15.

[2] Cf. Weber, *op. cit.* I, 430, on Du Bellay's use of 'traditional' images in the *Regrets*: 'Souvent l'image dans *Les Regrets* n'a rien d'original ni de pittoresque. Empruntée à la tradition antique ou pétrarquiste, elle a pour fonction d'élargir l'émotion en l'associant ou en l'opposant successivement à des êtres ou à des objets qui lui confèrent une résonance universelle.' The same critic provides an excellent illustration of this point in his discussion of the dying swan image as it appears in *Regrets* xvi, and he goes on to suggest what advantages traditional images may have over 'original' ones: 'l'image dépouillée des arêtes trop vives de la vision pittoresque, idéalisée par le rêve, devient l'expression directe d'un état d'âme' (*ibid.* 440, 443).

provided a link with the great literature of the past and ultimately with the first poetry of all, was to lay heavy emphasis
upon the divine inspiration which true poets received. I have
already drawn attention to the enthusiasm with which poets of
the sixteenth century proclaimed the divine origin of poetry and
to the repeated assertions by the Pléiade that the poet is one
possessed by a divine fury, 'cete fureur divine,' wrote Du
Bellay, 'sans la quele ne fault point que nul espere faire chose
qui dure'.[1] This, in fact, was held to be what marked the difference between mere versifiers and those who genuinely deserved
the name of poets:

> Deux sortes il y a de mestier sur le mont
> Où les neuf belles Seurs leurs demeurances font:
> L'un favorise à ceux qui riment & composent,
> Qui les vers par leurs nombres arrangent & disposent
> Et sont du nom de vers dicts versificateurs:
> Ils ne sont que de vers seulement inventeurs,
> Froids, gelez & glacez, qui en naissant n'apportent
> Sinon un peu de vie, en laquelle ils avortent...
> Et ne sont jamais leus, car Phebus Apollon
> Ne les a point touchez de son aspre eguillon...
>   L'autre preside à ceux qui ont la fantasie
> Esprise ardentement du feu de la Poësie,
> Qui n'abusent du nom, mais à la verité
> Sont remplis de frayeur & de divinité.[2]

But the theory of divine inspiration had a wider significance than
merely that of being a touchstone by which good poets might be
distinguished from bad.

The full neo-platonic account of divine fury (as it was given,
for instance, by Pontus de Tyard in the *Solitaire Premier*) was
able to furnish a complete metaphysical justification of poetry.
Poetry, 'la fureur Poëtique procedant du don des Muses', was
held to be the first of the 'quatre degrez' by which the human
soul was enabled to rise up out of the world of materiality and
multiplicity and to rejoin 'le souverain *un*, commencement
eternel de toute chose...la source de son souverain bien, et

---

[1] Du Bellay, *Deffence*, 169–70.
[2] Ronsard, *Œuvres complètes*, xiv, 195–6.

felicité derniere'.[1] Yet this was in fact a justification of poetry bought at a fairly heavy price. In this scheme poetry had a definite part to play in the re-ascent of the human soul into the realm of spirit, but it could never be anything other than a subordinate part. Poetry was merely one stage on the journey upwards; it was not something which would take the soul the whole way. Poetry merely brought about a preliminary harmony within the soul, which had then to be perfected by means of an understanding of the 'mysteres et secrets des religions' before it could come into communion with the divine, eternal beauty. The whole orientation of this scheme was towards the salvation of the soul, and each part in it—including poetry—was of value only in so far as it contributed to that ultimate purpose. Poetry was something which one discarded, or grew out of and left behind in the progress of one's soul towards reunion with the source of all being. It was not something which could be regarded as supremely valuable in its own right. As it stood, therefore, Pontus's very carefully elaborated version of the theory of divine fury could not provide exactly the justification of poetry which Ronsard and his fellow-theorists were seeking. Some adaptation would have to be made, and just how this was done we can see most clearly in the works of Ronsard.

That Ronsard could not be satisfied with the subordinate position which Pontus's scheme forced upon poetry is shown, I think, by the rather cavalier fashion in which he treats the strict neo-platonic sequence of the four divine furies. Pontus had imagined the soul as returning to 'la source de son souverain bien' by means of a ladder in which 'la fureur poëtique' formed the bottom-most rung, with 'l'intelligence des mysteres et secrets des religions' above it, 'ravissement de prophetie, vaticination, ou divination' above that again, and 'l'amoureuse affection' as the highest rung of all. Ronsard not only failed to observe this order, altering it now to prophecy, poetry, religious mysteries, and love (in the *Ode à Michel de l'Hospital*), now to religious mysteries, love, poetry, and prophecy (in the poem to M. de Belot);[2] he also, by having the Muses preside over all four kinds of fury, generalised poetic fury in such a way that it

[1] See p. 30.   [2] Ronsard, *Œuvres complètes*, iii, 143, and xv, 18.

came to include the others.[1] He thus exalted poetry above all else, making it sufficient unto itself, and not simply a stage through which the soul passed on its way to a final reunion with the godhead. Such a remodelling of the neo-platonic theory of divine inspiration exalted not only poetry, but also the poet himself. The poet was first of all a man apart, and it is interesting in this respect to find Ronsard seeking to mark this difference from other men by calling attention to the suffering which the gift of divine inspiration brings to its recipient. Thus in the *Elegie à Jacques Grevin* he bewails his own situation in a very 'Romantic' manner:

> ...je sçay que mon art grevement me tourmente...
> Car pour avoir gousté les ondes de Permesse
> Je suis tout aggravé de somne & de paresse,
> Inhabile, inutile: & qui pis, je ne puis
> Arracher cest humeur dont esclave je suis.
> Je suis opiniastre, indiscret, fantastique,
> Farouche, soupçonneux, triste & melancolique,
> Content & non content, mal propre, & mal courtois.[2]

He could bear all this had he achieved any perfection in his art:

> De tant de passions je seroy satisfait:
> Mais me voyant sans plus icy demy Poëte,
> Un mestier moins divin que le mien je souhaitte.[3]

But, as he writes elsewhere, because Apollo has endowed him with 'fureur d'esprit' and with 'art', because

> Il me haussa le cœur, haussa la fantasie,
> M'inspirant dedans l'ame un don de Poësie,
> Que Dieu n'a concedé qu'à l'esprit agité
> Des poignans aiguillons de sa divinité,[4]

the poet is also a man far above the ordinary run of human beings; he is a man particularly beloved of God. Divine inspiration comes only to 'celui lequel Dieu a voulu plus cherir &

---

[1] On this point cf. R. V. Merrill & R. J. Clements, *Platonism in French Renaissance Poetry* (1957), 123 ff.

[2] For a discussion of the relationship between this self-portrait by Ronsard and the *topos* of the poet as *studieux* and *mélancholique*, see D. B. Wilson, *op. cit.* 91 ff.

[3] Ronsard, *Œuvres complètes*, xiv, 195.   [4] *Ibid.* xii, 46.

decorer'.[1] In fact the poet seems to become almost a god himself. In the *Hymne de l'Automne* Ronsard described in some detail the effect of being endowed with this 'don de Poësie':

> Quand l'homme en est touché il devient un prophete,
> Il predit toute chose avant qu'elle soit faite,
> Il cognoist la nature, & les secrets des cieux,
> Et d'un esprit bouillant s'esleve entre les Dieux.[2]

This is to grant the poet powers which no other men can possibly possess. We may see, perhaps, in the emphasis which Ronsard placed upon the divine source of the poet's inspiration a parallel with our modern doctrine of the creativity of poets, who are thought of as performing (to quote once more the words of A. R. Chisholm) 'a series of creative acts, corresponding to the incessant Creation which furnishes the starting-point of poetic activity, namely the external phenomena'. Both theories divinify the poet, as it were, the one by asserting that in poetic activity the divine being enters into and takes possession of the poet's mind, the other by claiming close kinship between the poet's activity and that of God in creating *ex nihilo* the phenomenal world. It was not open to the sixteenth century to adopt the second position; at that time creation was held to be the prerogative of God alone, and man could have no hand in it. But the poet was able to receive emanations from the divine mind—always provided, of course, that his own soul was in a condition which fitted it to receive them. In this way Ronsard and the Pléiade could assert the uniqueness and self-sufficiency of poetry and also its freedom from the demands of any extra-poetic criteria. For after all, what surer guarantee could there be for the true worth of poetry than the fact that it came down to men from God? Through inspiration the poet was directly linked with the source of all truth and all goodness and all beauty.

A final word should be said, perhaps, about the question of whether the poets of the Pléiade believed in the theory of divine inspiration as being literally true. I am not, of course, discussing whether they really believed in Apollo and the nine

---

[1] Le Caron, *op. cit.* fo. 149r⁰.   [2] Ronsard *.Œuvres complètes*, XII, 46.

Muses and the other apparatus of the classical myth, for that was a highly conventionalised form of expression, but whether they believed poets to be driven by some sort of supra-human *daimon* which took complete possession of their minds. Quite obviously it is impossible for us to decide this matter with any degree of certainty, but it is possible, I think, to appreciate why the Pléiade should have made so much of this point, and stressed so often the divinity of the poet's immediate inspiration and the divine origin of his art as a whole. Because of the serious disabilities of a number of the concepts which were available to the poetic theorist in the sixteenth century it was difficult, as we have seen, for the Pléiade to achieve any completely satisfactory justification of poetry in purely theoretical terms. What the group could do, however, was justify poetry in terms of status. In the reiteration of the statement that their works were the result of this communion with divinity the Pléiade were aiming to exalt poetry as high as possible among all the various forms of human activity. Literal belief in the details of the theory was from this point of view unimportant. The important thing was the high status which was given to the poet by the whole theory. As Brunetière once wrote, 'la Pléiade a prétendu relever la dignité du poète en même temps que celle de la poésie; — et elle y a réussi'.[1]

[1] F. Brunetière, *Manuel de l'Histoire de la Littérature française* (1898), 78.

BIBLIOGRAPHY

ABRAMS, MEYER HOWARD. *The Mirror and the Lamp: Romantic Theory and the Critical Tradition.* New York, 1953.

Ad C. Herennium de Ratione Dicendi (Rhetorica ad Herennium). Loeb Classical Library, London, 1954.

AMYOT, JACQUES. *Les Vies des Hommes Illustres Grecs & Romains, Comparées l'vne auec l'autre par Plutarque de Chaeronée, Translatées de Grec en François.* Paris, 1559.

AQUINAS, THOMAS. *Quaestiones disputatae.* Paris, 1586.

ARISTOTLE. *The Works of Aristotle,* ed. W. D. Ross. Oxford, 1908–52.

BACON, FRANCIS. *Novum Organum,* ed. T. Fowler. Oxford, 1878.

BARFIELD, OWEN. *History in English Words.* 2nd edn., London, 1956.

—— *Saving the Appearances: A Study in Idolatry.* London, 1957.

BAUDELAIRE, CHARLES. *Œuvres complètes,* ed. Y.-G. Le Dantec. Paris, 1956.

BOCCACCIO, GIOVANNI. *Boccaccio on Poetry: being the Preface and the Fourteenth and Fifteenth Books of Boccaccio's Genealogia Deorum Gentilium,* ed. C. G. Osgood. Princeton, 1930.

BOUHOURS, DOMINIQUE. *Remarques nouvelles sur la langue françoise.* 3rd edn., Paris, 1682.

BOVILLUS, CAROLUS. *Liber de Sensu.* Paris, 1510.

BRETT, GEORGE SIDNEY. *Brett's History of Psychology,* ed. and abr. R. S. Peters. London, 1953.

BRUÉS, GUY DE. *The Dialogues of Guy de Brués: a Critical Edition with a Study in Renaissance Scepticism and Relativism,* ed. P. P. Morphos. Baltimore, 1953.

BRUNETIÈRE, FERDINAND. *Manuel de l'Histoire de la Littérature française.* Paris, 1898.

BUNDY, MURRAY WRIGHT. *The Theory of Imagination in Classical and Medieval Thought.* Urbana, 1927.

CAESAR, CAIUS JULIUS. *De Bello Gallico.* Loeb Classical Library, London, 1946.

CALVIN, JEAN. *Institution de la religion chrestienne,* ed. A. Lefranc. Paris, 1911.

CASTIGLIONE, BALTHAZAR. *The Book of the Courtier.* Everyman's Library, London, 1948.

CHAMARD, HENRI. *Les Origines de la Poésie française de la Renaissance.* Paris, 1920.

—— *Histoire de la Pléiade.* Paris, 1939–40.

Chambers's Twentieth Century Dictionary, ed. W. Geddie. 3rd edn., Edinburgh and London, 1959.

CHASTELLAIN, GEORGES. *Œuvres de Georges Chastellain,* ed. M. le Baron Kervyn de Lettenhove. Brussels, 1863–6.

CHÉNIER, ANDRÉ. *Œuvres complètes*, ed. G. Walter. Paris, 1950.

CHISHOLM, ALAN ROWLAND. 'Mallarmé: "Victorieusement fui le suicide beau..."', in *French Studies*, XIV, 2. 1960.

CICERO, MARCUS TULLIUS. *De Inventione*. Loeb Classical Library, London, 1949.

—— *De Oratore*. Loeb Classical Library, London, 1942.

—— *Orator*. Loeb Classical Library, London, 1952.

—— *Topica*. Loeb Classical Library, London, 1949.

—— *Tusculan Disputations*. Loeb Classical Library, London, 1950.

CLARK, DONALD LEMEN. 'The Requirements of a Poet', in *Modern Philology*, XVI, 8. 1918.

CLEMENTS, ROBERT JOHN. *Critical Theory and Practice of the Pléiade*. Cambridge, Mass., 1942.

COLERIDGE, SAMUEL TAYLOR. *Biographia Literaria*, ed. J. Shawcross. Oxford, 1907.

CONDILLAC, ÉTIENNE BONNOT DE. *Œuvres philosophiques*, ed. G. Le Roy. Paris, 1947–51.

COTGRAVE, RANDLE. *A Dictionarie of the French and English Tongves*. London, 1611.

CRAIG, HARDIN. *The Enchanted Glass: the Elizabethan Mind in Literature*. Oxford, 1950.

DES AUTELZ, GUILLAUME. *Replique aux furieuses defenses de Louis Meigret*. Lyon, 1551.

DU BELLAY, JOACHIM. *Œuvres poétiques*, ed. H. Chamard. Paris, 1908–31.

—— *La Deffence et Illustration de la langue françoyse*, ed. H. Chamard. Paris, 1948.

DU VAIR, GUILLAUME. *Traité de la Constance et Consolation es calamitez Publiques*, ed. J. Flach and F. Funck-Brentano. Paris, 1915.

ELIOT, THOMAS STEARNS. *Selected Essays*. London, 1951.

ERASMUS, DESIDERIUS. *Libellus...De Pueris statim ac liberaliter institu-endis*. Basle, 1529.

FABRI, PIERRE. *Le grant et vray art de pleine Rhetorique*, ed. A. Héron. Rouen, 1889.

FAGUET, ÉMILE. *Seizième Siècle: Études Littéraires*. Paris, undated.

FARAL, EDMOND. *Les Arts poétiques du XIIe et du XIIIe Siècle: Recherches et Documents sur la Technique Littéraire du Moyen Âge*. Paris, 1924.

FERNEL, JEAN. *Physiologia*. Venice, 1555.

FLECKENSTEIN, J.-O. 'Petrus Ramus et l'humanisme bâlois', in *La Science au seizième siècle* (Colloque de Royaumont, 1957). Paris, 1960.

FONTENELLE, BERNARD LE BOVIER DE. *Éloge de M. le Chevalier Neuton*. Paris, 1728.

FRANCHET, HENRI. *Le Poète et son Œuvre d'après Ronsard*. Paris, 1923.

FRAUNCE, ABRAHAM. *The Lawiers Logike*. London, 1588.

GADOFFRE, GILBERT. *Ronsard par lui-même*. Paris, 1960.

GILMAN, MARGARET. *Baudelaire the Critic*. New York, 1943.

—— 'From Imagination to Immediacy in French Poetry', in *Romanic Review*, XXXIX, i. 1948.

BIBLIOGRAPHY

GODEFROY, FRÉDÉRIC-EUGÈNE. *Dictionnaire de l'ancienne Langue française et de tous ses Dialectes du IXe au XVe Siècle*. Paris, 1937–8.

GRAVES, FRANK PIERREPONT. *Peter Ramus and the Educational Reformation in the Sixteenth Century*. New York, 1912.

HOOYKAAS, R. 'Pierre de la Ramée et l'Empirisme scientifique au XVIe Siècle', in *La Science au seizième siècle* (Colloque de Royaumont, 1957). Paris, 1960.

QUINTUS HORATIUS FLACCUS. *The Epistles of Horace*, ed. A. S. Wilkins. London, 1950.

HUARTE, JUAN. *Anacrise, ov parfait ivgement et examen des esprits propres & naiz aux sciences...mis en François, au grand profit de la Republique, par Gabriel Chappuis Tourangeau.* Lyon, 1597. (1st edn., Lyon, 1580.)

HUGUET, EDMOND. *Dictionnaire de la Langue française du seizième Siècle.* Paris, 1925 in progress.

—— *L'Évolution du Sens des Mots depuis le XVIe siècle.* Paris, 1934.

Le Jardin de plaisance Et fleur de Rethoricque, ed. E. Droz and A. Piaget. Paris, 1910.

LANGLOIS, ERNEST. *Recueil d'Arts de Seconde Rhétorique.* Paris, 1902.

LA PRIMAUDAYE, PIERRE DE. *L'Academie Françoise...de la Philosophie Hvmaine et Morale, & de la Naturelle & Diuine.* 4th edn., Lyon, 1615.

LE CARON, LOUIS. *Les Dialogues de Loys Le Caron.* Paris, 1556.

LEGRAND, JACQUES. *Sophologium.* Paris, 1477.

LEMAIRE DE BELGES, JEAN. *La Concorde des deux Langages*, ed. J. Frappier. Paris, 1947.

LE ROY, LOUIS. *De la Vicissitvde ov Varieté des Choses en l'Vniuers.* 3rd edn., Paris, 1579.

LEWIS, CHARLTON THOMAS & SHORT, CHARLES. *A Latin Dictionary.* Oxford, 1933.

LEWIS, CLIVE STAPLES. *English Literature in the 16th century, excluding drama.* Oxford, 1954.

LITTRÉ, ÉMILE. *Dictionnaire de la Langue Française.* Paris, 1878.

MAROT, CLÉMENT. *Les Œuvres de Clément Marot*, ed. G. Guiffrey. Paris, 1875–1931.

MERRILL, ROBERT VALENTINE & CLEMENTS, ROBERT JOHN. *Platonism in French Renaissance Poetry.* New York, 1957.

MILLER, PERRY. *The New England Mind: the Seventeenth Century.* New York, 1939.

MONTAIGNE, MICHEL DE. *Essais*, ed. M. Rat. Paris, 1952.

MORÇAY, RAOUL & MÜLLER, ARMAND. *La Renaissance.* Paris, 1960.

MURARASU, D. *La Poésie néo-latine et la Renaissance des Lettres antiques en France (1500–1549).* Paris, 1928.

NOLHAC, PIERRE DE. *Ronsard et l'humanisme.* Paris, 1921.

Nouveau Petit Larousse Illustré, Dictionnaire Encyclopédique, ed. C. Augé and P. Augé. Paris, 1949.

The Oxford English Dictionary, ed. J. A. H. Murray and others. Oxford, 1933.

BIBLIOGRAPHY

PALISSY, BERNARD. *Les Œuvres de maistre Bernard Palissy*, ed. B. Fillon and L. Audiat. Paris, 1888.

PARÉ, AMBROISE. *Œuvres complètes d'Ambroise Paré*, ed. J. F. Malgaigne. Paris, 1840–1.

PASQUIER, ESTIENNE. *Choix de Lettres sur la Littérature la Langue et la Traduction*, ed. D. Thickett. Geneva, 1956.

PATTERSON, WARNER FORREST. *Three Centuries of French Poetic Theory.* Ann Arbor, 1935.

PELETIER DU MANS, JACQUES. *L'Art Poëtique*, ed. A. Boulanger. Paris, 1930.

Petit Larousse, Dictionnaire Encyclopédique pour tous. Paris, 1959.

PICARD, RAYMOND. 'Les grands rhétoriqueurs', in *Tableau de la Littérature française de Rutebeuf à Descartes.* Editions Gallimard, Paris, 1962.

PLATO. *Platonis opera...Additis Marsilii Ficini Argumentis & Commentariis.* Basle, 1561.

—— *The Dialogues of Plato*, transl. B. Jowett. 4th edn., Oxford, 1953.

QUINTILIAN. *Institutio Oratoria.* Loeb Classical Library, London, 1953.

RABELAIS, FRANÇOIS. *Œuvres de François Rabelais*, ed. A. Lefranc. Paris, 1912 in progress.

—— *Le Quart Livre*, ed. R. Marichal. Lille and Geneva, 1947.

RAMUS, PETRUS. *La Dialectique.* 3rd edn., Paris, 1576.

RAYMOND, MARCEL. *Baroque & renaissance poétique.* Paris, 1955.

RICHARDS, IVOR ARMSTRONG. *Coleridge on Imagination.* London, 1934.

RIVAROL, ANTOINE DE. *Œuvres complètes.* Paris, 1808.

RONSARD, PIERRE DE. *Œuvres de P. de Ronsard*, ed. C. Marty-Laveaux. Paris, 1887–93.

—— *Œuvres complètes*, ed. P. Laumonier. Paris, 1914 in progress.

ROSENBAUER, A. *Die poetischen Theorien der Plejade nach Ronsard und Du Bellay. Ein Beitrag zur Geschichte der Renaissancepoetik in Frankreich.* Erlangen and Leipzig, 1895.

ROUSSEAU, JEAN JACQUES. *Œuvres de J. J. Rousseau.* Paris, 1793.

SADOLETO, JACOPO. *De Liberis recte instituendis.* Venice, 1533.

SAINTSBURY, GEORGE EDWARD BATEMAN. *A History of Criticism and Literary Taste in Europe from the earliest texts to the present day.* Edinburgh and London, 1949.

SCALIGER, JULIUS CAESAR. *Poetices libri septem.* Lyon, 1561.

SEBILLET, THOMAS. *Art Poetique Françoys*, ed. F. Gaiffe. Paris, 1932.

SMITH, LOGAN PEARSALL. *Words and Idioms.* London, 1933.

SPINGARN, JOEL ELLAS. *Critical Essays of the 17th Century.* Oxford, 1908.

TILLYARD, EUSTACE MANDEVILLE WETENHALL. *The Elizabethan World Picture.* London, 1950.

TORY, GEOFROY. *Champ Fleury: ou l'art et science de la proportion des lettres*, ed. G. Cohen. Paris, 1931.

TYARD, PONTUS DE. *Solitaire Premier*, ed. S. F. Baridon. Geneva and Lille, 1950.

—— *The Universe of Pontus de Tyard, a Critical Edition of 'L'Univers'*, ed. J. C. Lapp. New York, 1950.

BIBLIOGRAPHY

VALÉRY, PAUL. 'Au Sujet du Cimetière Marin', in COHEN, GUSTAVE, *Essai d'Explication du Cimetière Marin*. Paris, 1933.

VAN TIEGHEM, PAUL. 'La littérature latine de la Renaissance', in *Bibliothèque d'Humanisme et Renaissance*, IV. 1944.

VIDA, MARCUS HIERONYMUS. *M. Hieronymi Vidae Cremonensis Poetae, opera*. Basle, 1537.

VOLTAIRE, FRANÇOIS-MARIE AROUET. *Œuvres complètes de Voltaire*. Paris, 1818.

WEBER, HENRI. *La Création poétique au XVIe siècle en France de Maurice Scève à Agrippa d'Aubigné*. Paris, 1956.

WEINBERG, BERNARD. *Critical Prefaces of the French Renaissance*. Evanston, Illinois, 1950.

WELLEK, RENÉ. *A History of Modern Criticism: 1750–1950*. London, 1955.

WILSON, DUDLEY B. *Ronsard, Poet of Nature*. Manchester, 1961.

WILSON, HAROLD S. 'Some Meanings of *Nature* in Renaissance Literary Theory', in *Journal of the History of Ideas*, II, 4. 1941.

WOODWARD, WILLIAM HARRISON. *Vittorino da Feltre and other Humanist Educators: Essays and Versions*. Cambridge, 1905.

YATES, FRANCES AMELIA. *The French Academies of the Sixteenth Century*. London, 1947.

INDEX

Abrams, M. H., 73 n., 86 n.
ACTUAL, the, 54, 60–2, 177, 182, 190
Albertus Magnus, 141
ALLUSIVENESS IN LITERATURE, 69–70, 74–6, 194 n.
Amyot, J., 78 n., 187 n.
Aneau, B., 80, 110, 111
APPEARANCES, the, 52, 56, 60, 137, 139, 191
Aquinas, 59, 133 n., 141
Aristotle, 11, 18, 43 n., 58, 98, 99, 122, 142, 170 n.
  on cognition, 141, 145, 154, 156
  on imitation, 53–5, 59–62, 70, 73, 117, 179, 182, 184, 190–1
'ART', 2, 13, 14 n., 20, 47–8, 70, 77, 101, 110, 114
  and inspiration, 37–8, 41, 43, 47, 49–50, 67, 82, 88, 197
  and nature, 2, 41–6, 49–50, 69, 82, 131 n.
Averroes, 143
Avicenna, 143, 166

Bacon, F., 134
Bacon, R., 141
Barfield, O., 59, 91
Baudelaire, C., 92–3, 186
Binet, C., 21 n.
Boccaccio, G., 117
Bouhours, D., 78 n.
Bovillus, C., 147–50, 153
Brués, G. de, 43 n., 127, 142
Brunetière, F., 199
Bundy, M. W., 137

Caesar, 96
Calvin, J., 119
Castiglione, B., 51
Chamard, H., 2, 6, 69 n.
Chambers's Twentieth Century Dictionary, 95
Charles d'Orléans, 7 n.
Chastellain, G., 6, 19
Chénier, A., 87
Chisholm, A. R., 90, 198

Cicero, 42, 43 n., 89, 169
  on invention, 86, 97–100, 105, 127, 129 n., 132, 135, 188
Clark, D. L., 42
Clements, R. J., 2, 69 n., 117 n., 197 n.
Coleridge, S. T., 86 n., 93, 188
Condillac, E. B. de, 89–90
Cotgrave, R., 48 n., 79, 88 n., 118
Craig, H., 133, 134
CREATIVITY, 4, 5, 78 n., 96 n., 126, 182, 198
  creative imagination,12,86, 90–3, 136

DEFENCE OF POETRY, 3, 10–11, 94, 117–18, 124, 173, 180, 194, 199
DEGENERATION OF POETRY, 37–40
Des Autelz, G., 68, 83–4, 111–12, 115, 169
DIVINE FURY, 1 n., 2, 13, 29–36, 44, 47, 53 n., 82, 195–7; *see also*
  INSPIRATION
DIVINE POETS, 37–8, 40
Dolet, E., 20, 79, 110
Dorat, J., 26
Du Bellay, J., 8, 20, 22–3, 24 n., 26 n., 28, 73 n., 75, 194 n.
  on 'art', 37–8, 44–6, 48 n.
  on divine fury, 195
  on feigning, 118, 120
  on imitation, 55, 65–70, 74, 84, 115, 132 n., 192
  on invention,101–2,104,109,112,115
  on *naïveté*, 80, 82
Du Pont, G., 19
Du Vair, G., 157

Eliot, T. S., 193–4
Erasmus, D., 135
Estienne, C., 117 n.

Fabri, P., 99
Faguet, E., 67
Faral, E., 100
FEIGNING, 3, 10, 117–25, 136, 173, 180, 182, 189
Fernel, J., 146

205

INDEX

Morçay, R., 2 n., 69 n.
Morphos, P. P., 142
Müller, A., 2 n., 69 n.
Murarasu, D., 9 n.
Muret, M.-A., 26, 75

'NAÏVETÉ', 13, 40–1, 65, 71, **77–82**, 84, 189
NATURE, 13, 30, 81, 107, 134, 173, 178
'art' and nature, 2, 37–8, **42–7**, 49–50, 77
imitation of nature, **51–62**, 72–4, 79, 82, 89, 190–1
inspiration and nature, 41, 77
Neo-Latin Poets, 9 n., 80
Nolhac, P. de, 9 n.

ORIGINALITY, 5, 11, 78, 86–7, 189, 192, 193–4
Orpheus, 26–7, 37, 38, 39 n., 75
Ovid, 8, 64, 69, 110, 115
Oxford English Dictionary, 12 n., 14 n., 104 n.

Palissy, B., 78 n., 127
Paré, A., 134, 136 n., **144–6**, 162, 164–6 *passim*, 175
PARTICULARS, 53 n., 54–5, 59, 61, 73, 122, 131, 139, 141, 153, 178, 182, 190
Pasquier, E., 64 n., 109, 139
Patterson, W. F., 1, 5, 16 n., 19 n.
Peletier du Mans, J., 20–1, 22 n., 64–5
on 'art', 46
on divine fury, 33–4
on imitation, 55–6, 70–1
on invention, 101, 172
on *naïveté*, 80, 81 n.
Petrarch, 8, 58, 68, 69, 84, 115
Picard, R., 7 n.
Piccolomini, Aeneas Sylvius, 131 n.
Pindar, 7, 71, 83
Plato, 99, 137, 139–42 *passim*
on poetry, 10, 29, 33, 34 n., 43 n., **52–3**, 59 n., 117
Plutarch, 73 n., 78 n.
POETS AS LIARS, 10–11, 59, 117–18, 119, 180, 189, 191
POETS AS MAKERS, 12, 90, 114, 116
POETS AS MEN OF LEARNING, 8, 25–6
POETS AS MEN OF VIRTUE, 8, 26

POTENTIAL, the, 54, 60–2, 177, 182, 190–1

Quintilian, 42–3, 89, 97, 99, 169–70

Rabelais, F., 79, 104–6 *passim*, 119, 122, 126–7
Ramus, P., **128–35**, 171, 177, 188–9
Raymond, M., 189 n.
REASON, 131, 181
and imagination, 139–41, 143–6, 149–51, 156–7, 159–61, 167, 175, 178, 186–8
and invention, 125, 127–8, 134–6, 177–8, 180
RHETORIC, 42–3, 131, 169, 190
invention in rhetoric, **96–102**, 106, 113, 124, 127–9, 172, 177, 188
poetry as rhetoric, **17–23**, 99–101, 188
Rhetorica ad Herennium, 97, 100
Richards, I. A., 175
Rivarol, A., 87, 92
Roman de la Rose, 7 n.
Ronsard, P. de, 22, 24–5, 26, 40, 75, 184, 189, 192–3
on 'art', 28–9, 38–9, 46–9
on divine fury, 28–9, 34–6, 38–9, 196–8
on feigning, 119–20, 122–4, 136
on imagination, 85, **172–5**, 178–9, 182–3, 186
on imitation, 55, **57–62**, 71–2, 74, 178–9, 182–3, 191
on invention, 21, 84–5, 88–9, 100, 103, 110, 136, **172–5**, 178–9, 182–3, 188
on *naïveté*, 77, 79, 81–3
Rosenbauer, A., 2
Rousseau, J. J., 126

Sadoleto, J., 43 n., 135 n., 136 n.
Saintsbury, G., 72–3
Scaliger, J. C., 58, 121
Scève, M., 8, 111, 169
Sebillet, T., 16–17, 19–20, 41, 55, 65
on 'art', 43–4, 88
on divine fury, 26–8, 88
on invention, 88, 100–1, 111, 114, 115, 132 n.
Smith, L. P., 93
Spingarn, J. E., 163

207

INDEX